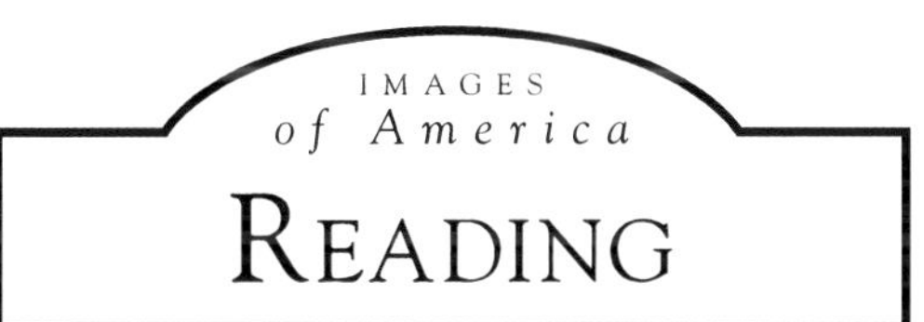
IMAGES
of America
READING

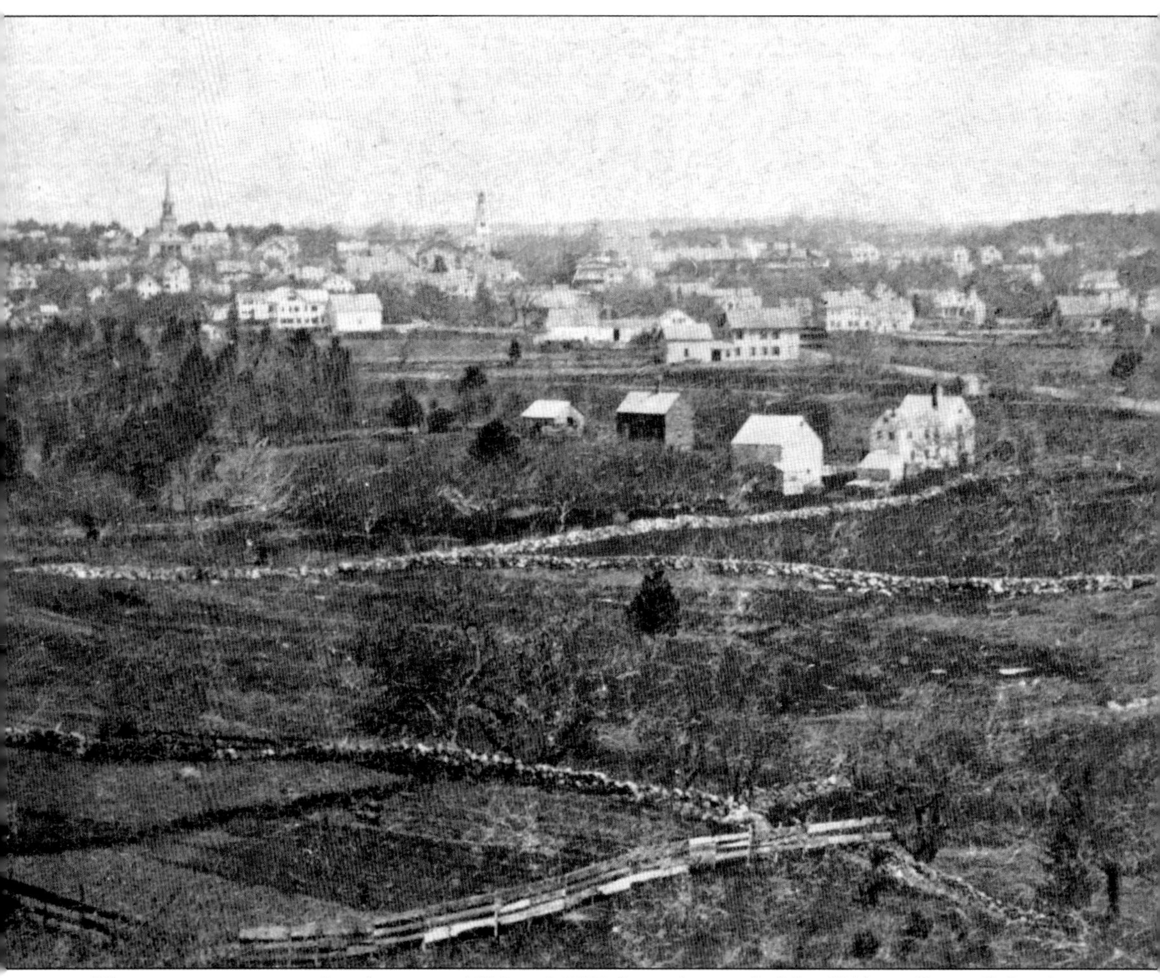

This stereoview was taken between 1854 and 1871 from the roof of the Walnut Street School at Leach Park (see page 102), the triangular intersection ("heater piece") of Summer Avenue, Walnut Street, and Hopkins Street. The two steeples on the horizon are the Bethesda (Congregational) Church built in 1850 on the left, and the Old South Church built in 1818 on the right. The Lyceum Building, erected in 1854, is visible, but the steeple of the Christian Union Church, built in 1871, cannot be seen. Looking across the fields toward Washington Park and Mudville are four buildings at the present-day Percy Avenue. (Authors' collection.)

On the Cover: This early 1900s photograph of the Reading Common shows the bandstand, designed by architect Horace Wadlin (see page 30), dedicated in July 1900 and moved to Memorial Park in 1930. The sepia postcard (No. 6360) is from a series published by Underwood & Underwood of New York and London. Seen in the photograph are the Old South Church with its lighted dial, the old high school to the left of the church, the elm trees with their hanging limbs, and 23 children on the bandstand and around the common. (Authors' collection.)

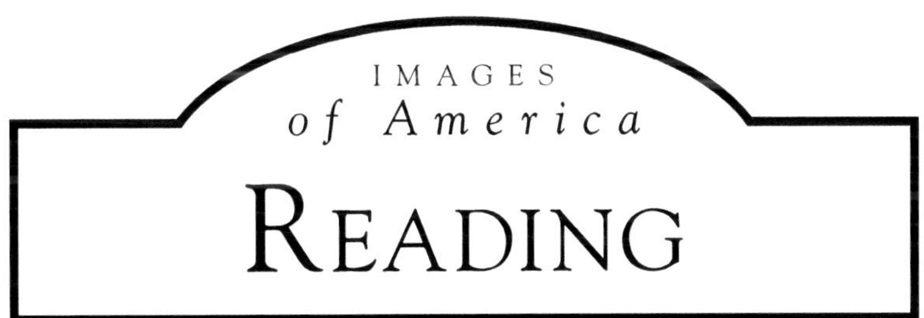

Everett A. and Virginia D. Blodgett

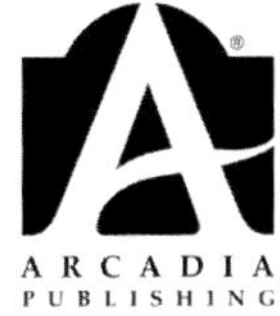

ISBN 978-1-4671-0308-4

Published by Arcadia Publishing
Charleston, South Carolina

Printed in the United States of America

Library of Congress Control Number: 2018959587

For all general information, please contact Arcadia Publishing:
Telephone 843-853-2070
Fax 843-853-0044
E-mail sales@arcadiapublishing.com
For customer service and orders:
Toll-Free 1-888-313-2665

Visit us on the Internet at www.arcadiapublishing.com

To all those who will keep their family genealogy and local history alive for future generations.

Contents

Acknowledgments

We would like to express our gratitude to those historians who have come before us and who have researched and recorded much of Reading's early history, including Lilley Eaton, Horace Wadlin, Loea Parker Howard, Clinton L. Bancroft, and many others. In more recent times, Eleanor and Nelson Bishop researched and wrote about Reading's early homes and worked to preserve early town records. Miriam Barclay, through the Reading Antiquarian Society, helped educate Reading's residents including its elementary schoolchildren at their schools, through its programs, and during their visits to Parker Tavern. They have all been responsible for sharing their love of history with us and for igniting our passion to pass it on to others. Thank you to Virginia Adams for her constant support of Reading history, Jean Underhill and Sally Stembridge for keeping and sharing their family stories, Carl Soule for his enthusiasm for collecting, the writers of *At Wood End*, Philip Rushworth, Nancy and Edward Smethurst, and many others for their help and encouragement. We would also like to thank Angel Hisnanick, Jim Kempert, and the Arcadia staff for their care and understanding during this process.

Images in this volume are from the authors' collection, except as noted.

Introduction

A series of land grants and land divisions over the course of more than three centuries determined the boundaries of the town of Reading. On March 13, 1639, the General Court of the colony granted Lynn residents a tract of land "whose bounds were six miles from the meetinghouse" so that they could expand Lynn's borders. On September 9 of the same year, the court further decreed that a group of inhabitants of Lynn would be granted four square miles beyond the bounds of the first six-mile grant for a new inland plantation called Linn Village. Seven families settled at the south end of the Great Pond (Lake Quannapowitt), and in 1644, Linn Village was incorporated as Redding. Seven years later, an additional two-mile grant extended the town from the Ipswich River north to Andover. Because King James threatened to remove the Charter of 1606, which allowed settlers to own land here, many towns sought to protect their future. On May 31, 1687, the Towns of Lynn and Reading purchased their lands from the Native Americans. (see *History of Reading, Mass.* by Eaton, Appendix A, page 687). In 1713, the area north of the Ipswich River was set off as Reading's North Precinct (second parish), and in 1769, Wood End, present-day Reading, became the West Parish (third parish). Although town meetings rotated among the three, the North and West Parishes shared political views that differed from those in the South Parish. That meant that by the early 1800s, the South Parish was frequently out-voted on many issues. Their request to be separated from the North and West Parishes was accepted by the legislature in 1812, and they became South Reading. It remained so until 1868, when they changed the name to Wakefield. The North Parish became North Reading in 1853, with the West Parish retaining the name Reading.

We have included a bibliography on page 126. There have been many publications about Reading's history, and they vary in their approach and information. Many can be found in the History Room at the Reading Public Library. The text also includes several references to the 1854, 1875, and 1889 maps. Those maps are printed in *At Wood End* and are available at the library. We encourage readers to seek out these sources and others for more in-depth information about Reading through its more than 375 years of history. *At Wood End*, published for Reading's 350th celebration, is still in print and available at town hall. In this new volume, we have attempted to add to what has been previously published. We have included items, photographs, and stories of some of the families who made Reading their home. Often, these stories are independent of each other, some are the result of discoveries from a family's genealogy, and still others are the result of the chronology of a business or property.

The authors' proceeds from this book will be donated to the Reading Antiquarian Society, which owns and maintains Parker Tavern; to Reading 375, to help support the events scheduled to celebrate this anniversary; and to help conserve some of the artifacts of Reading's history.

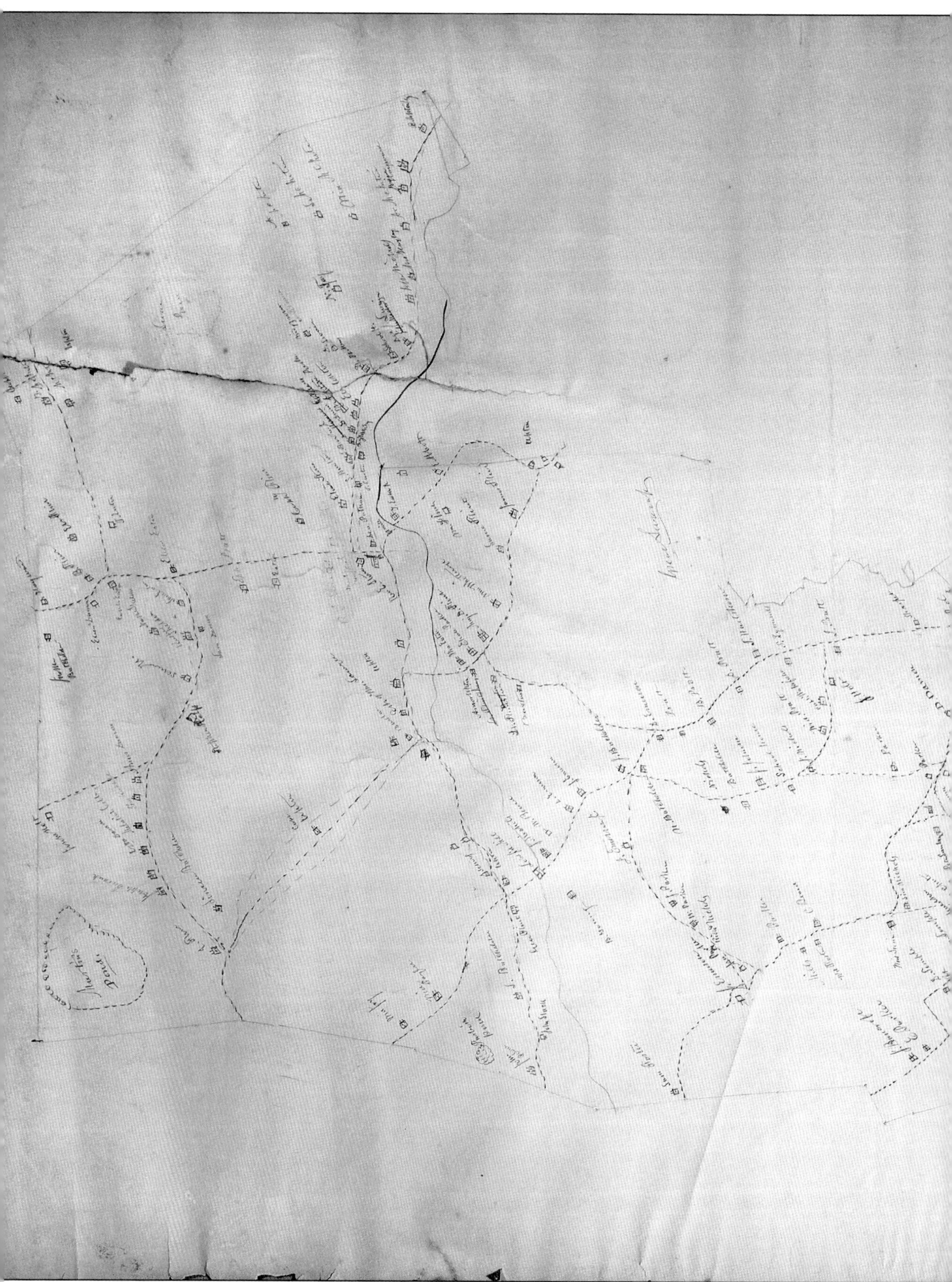

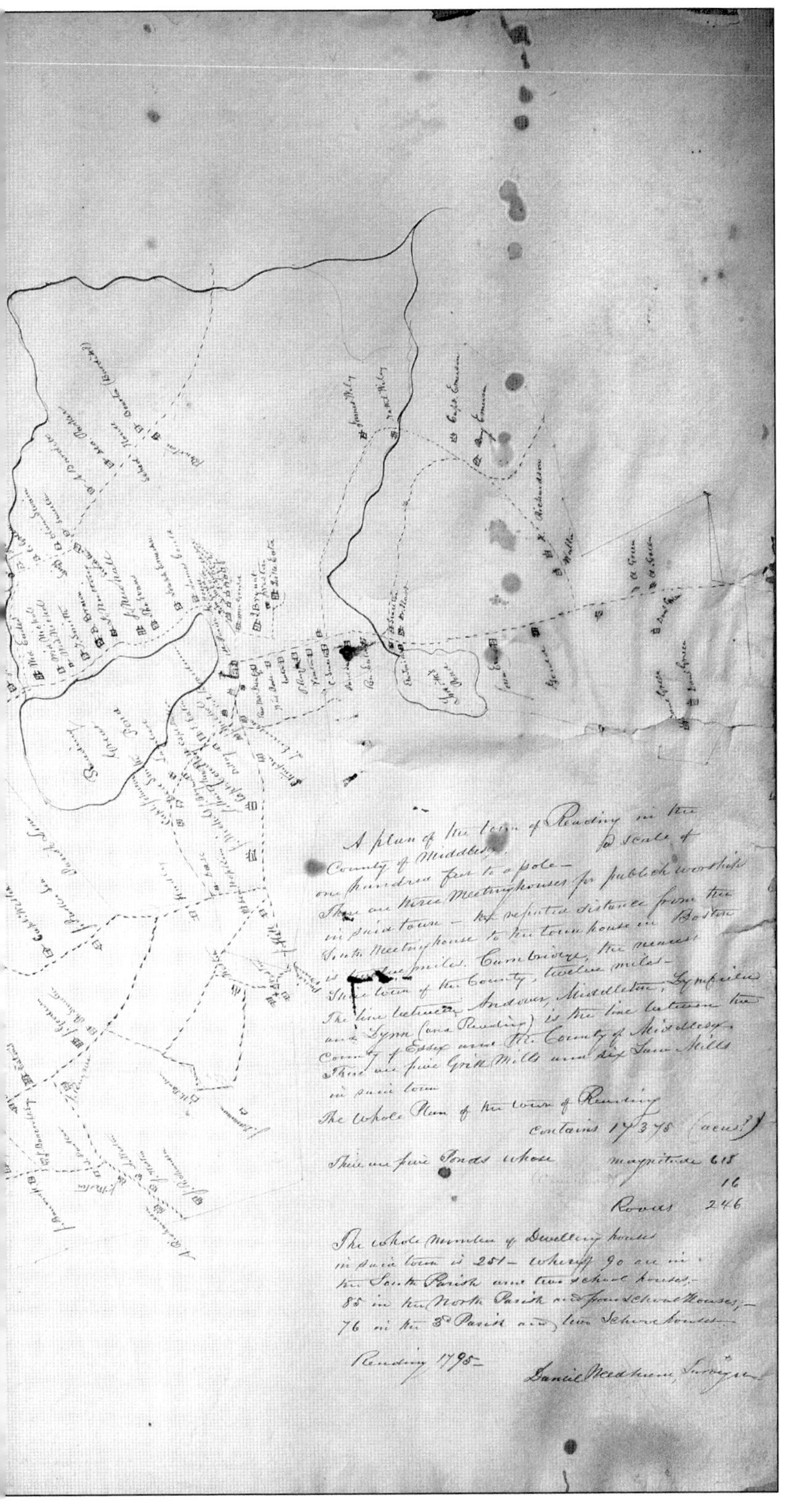

In 1794, the Massachusetts General Court required that each town provide a map showing rivers, county roads, bridges, places of worship, and the distance to the "Town House" in Boston. The Town of Reading paid Daniel Needham of Lynnfield $4 to draw the 1794 map, which is currently at the Massachusetts State Archives. That map, which includes the Town of Lynnfield, does not show individual houses. The map shown here is dated 1795, is larger than the 1794 map, shows only Reading (which at the time included Reading, Wakefield, and North Reading), and shows individual houses with their owner's names. A newly discovered watermark, shown on the next page, raises some intriguing questions.

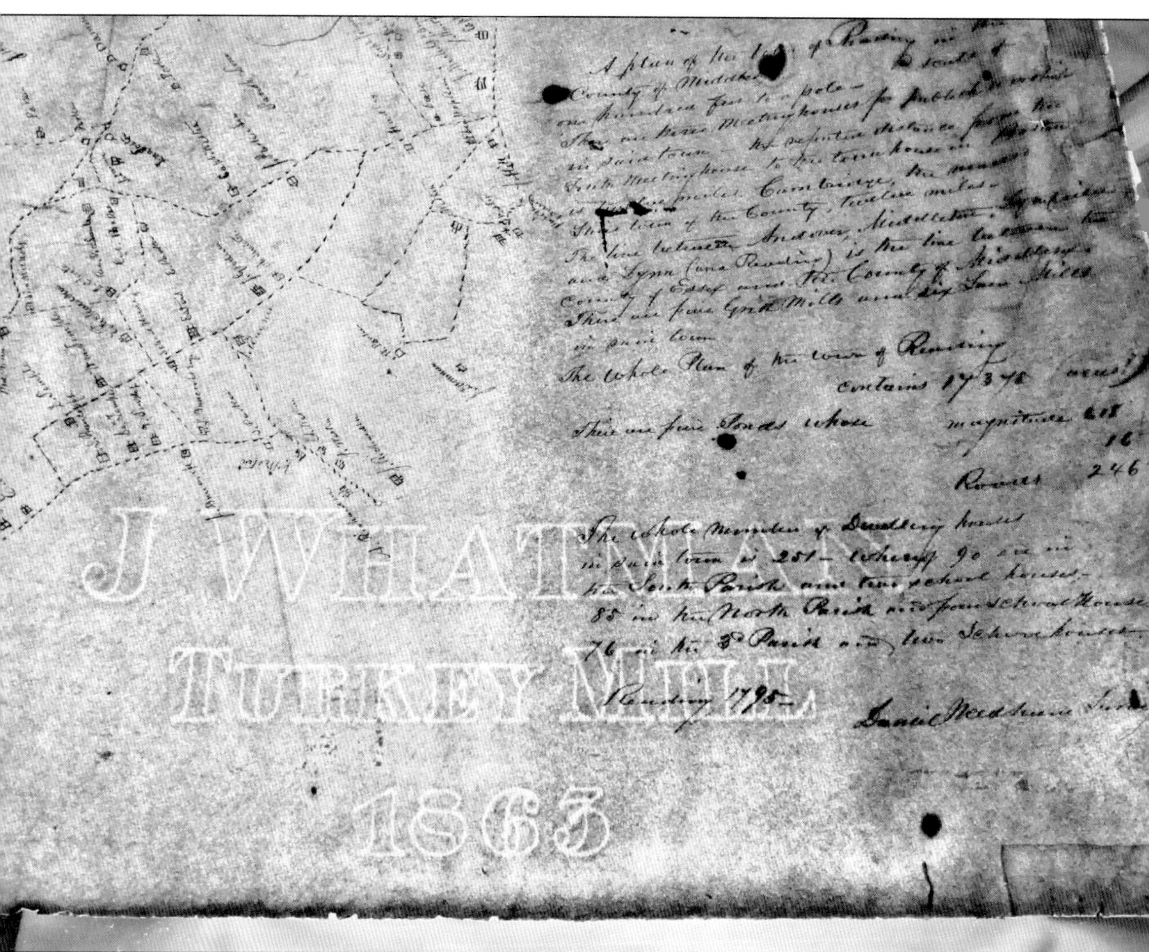

In preparation for this book, the map on the previous page was scanned. As the scanner light moved under the map, there were two surprises. First was the watermark shown here: "J. Whatman Turkey Mill 1863." The Whatman mill was founded in 1740 near Maidstone, Kent, England, and produced the finest quality paper for more than two centuries. Second, dozens of tiny pinholes could be seen along the major roads and town boundary lines. One conclusion is that the map on the previous page is a copy of Daniel Needham's 1795 map. It could not have been drawn by Needham, who died in 1844, before the paper was produced. An early photocopy of this map is at the Massachusetts State Archives, and a photograph of this map is in *Historical Sketches of Ancient Reading* (1935) and *Wakefield, 350 Years by the Lake* (1994). In each case, the location of tears and foxing marks are identical to this map. This map has been used by historians for their research for over a century. Does the original still exist?

One

Farms and Families

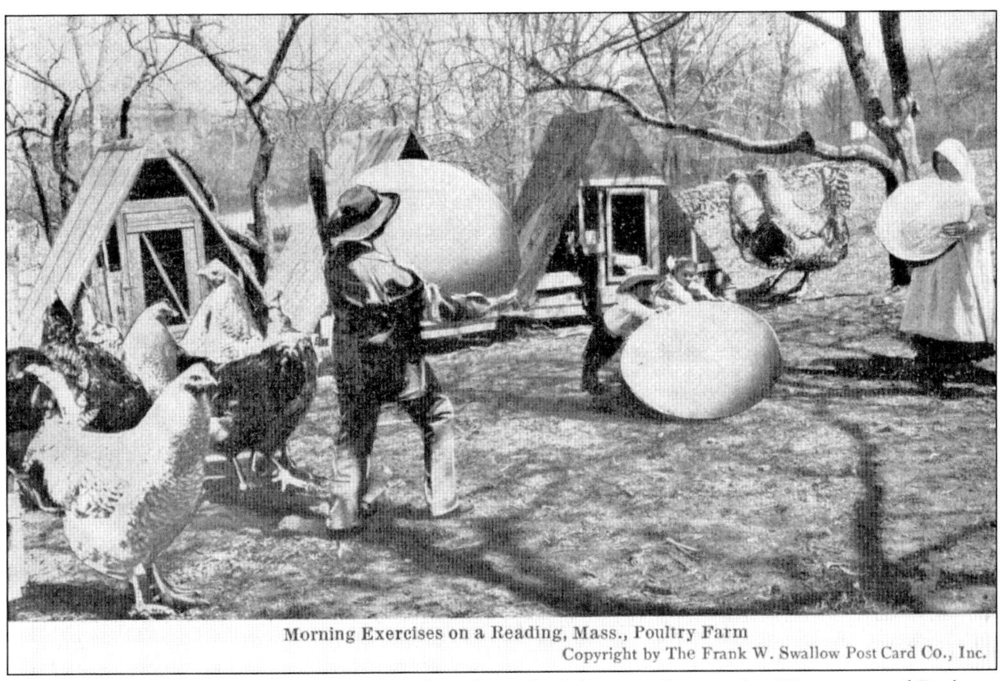

Some of the earliest settlers in Wood End, such as the Merrows, Bancrofts, Westons, and Parkers, established their farms near the west part of town in the mid-to-late 1600s. Over the next 300-plus years, Reading transitioned from farming to predominately residential with pockets of industry and business. This light-hearted postcard calls attention to the poultry business here in Reading.

KNOW all Men by these Presents, That

I Jonas Parker of Reading in the County of Middlesex and Commonwealth of Massachusetts Gentleman

in Consideration of ninety Pounds, lawful Money, paid by my son William Parker jun'r of the Town and County afore said Cordwainer

the Receipt whereof I do hereby acknowledge, do hereby give, grant, sell and convey unto the said William Parker his Heirs and Assigns a Tract of Land lying in said Reading west Parish it being the Easterly Part of my farme Containing Seventeen acres and a half more or less bounded as followeth beginning at the Rode at the Southwest Corner of the Land I bought of Charls Eaton from thence the line runs Northwardly by the wall to stake and stones then westwardly to a stake and stones by the Wall on the East side of the medow then Northwardly by said wall to Land of the Heirs of Capt Thomas Eaton bounded Northwardly on the Widow Mary Eatons third, Eastwardly and Southwardly on the Rode also one other peace of Land Containing by Estamation twenty two Acres more or Less Devided from the other by the Rode and is Bounded Northwardly on said Rode Eastwardly on the Rode til it Comes to Land of Ebenezer Hopkins then the line turns Southeastwardly then Southwardly by said Hopkinses Land and Land of James Weston to the Corner bounded Southwardly on said Westons Land and the Rode Westwardly on Land of Capt John Goodwin and the Rode also the Easterly half of the Dwelling House and the Easterly half of Barne on my said farme and half the yard before the House and one half the Barn yard and liberty to use the well for water also one half the Pew in the meeting house that my Honoured Father John Parker also my swamp lot at timber neck Containing ... acres more or less which was formerly Kindel Briants

TO HAVE AND TO HOLD the afore-described Premises to the said William Parker his Heirs and Assigns, to his and their Use and Behoof forever.

AND I do covenant with the said William Parker his Heirs and Assigns, That I am lawfully seized in Fee of the afore-described Premises, That they are free of all Incumbrances, That I have good Right to sell and convey the same to the said William Parker as above

AND that I will warrant and defend the same Premises to the said William Parker his Heirs and Assigns, forever, against the lawful Claims and Demands of all Persons.

In Witness whereof, I the said Jonas Parker and Mary my now married Wife in testimony of her Consent to this my act and Deed have hereunto set our Hands and Seals this tenth Day of march in the Year of our Lord *One thousand seven hundred and ninety* one

Signed, sealed and delivered in Presence of us,

James Bancroft

Jonas Parker

Jonas Parker

Mary her + mark Parker

Middlesex ss. March 18: 1791 THEN *the above-named* Jonas Parker *acknowledged the above Instrument to be* his *free Deed, before me,* James Bancroft *Just. Pacis.*

This deed, dated March 18, 1791, is for the sale of half of Jonas Parker's property on Walnut Street to his son William. The original house was built in the late 1600s and was one of the earliest in the West Parish, present-day Reading. The property then passed down through the family until half was deeded by Jonas to William. The house burned down in 1813, and shortly thereafter, a "new" house was built at what is currently 15 Strawberry Hill Lane. Of particular interest is the description, which entitles William to "the Easterly half of the Dwelling House and the Easterly half of Barne on my said farme and half the yard before the House and one half the Barn yard and liberty to use the well for water also one half the Pew in the meeting house." At that time, families owned their pew at the meetinghouse (church). (See *Reading's Colonial Rooftrees*, page 102.)

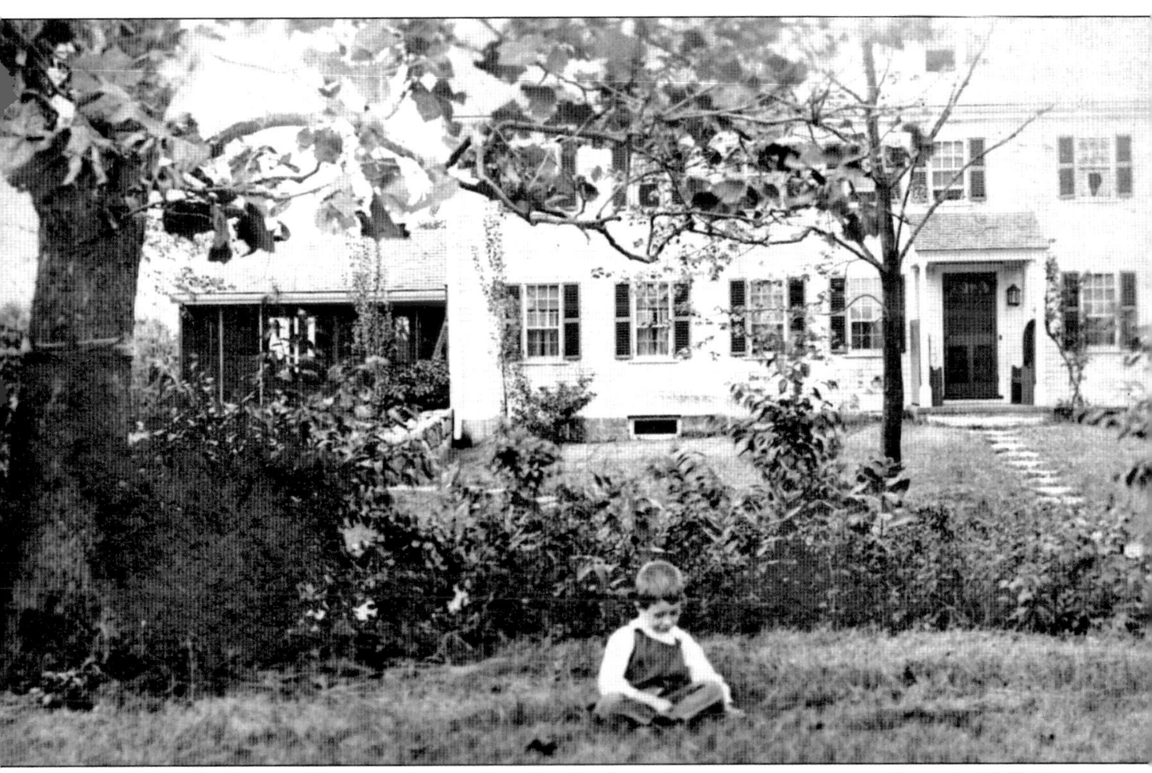

William Parker, son of Jonas, referenced in the deed on the previous page, was born in 1760. He built the home pictured here, at what is today 55 Walnut Street, probably a few years after marrying Sally Damon, of the John Street Damons, in 1783. Between 1911 and 1914, the Hopkins family lived here before moving to 348 Summer Avenue (new No. 472). They retained 10 acres when they sold the house. Their son Walter S. Hopkins Jr. had a vegetable stand, known as Hill End Farm, and later, Hopkins Farm, first near the 55 Walnut Street property and later at the southwest corner of Hopkins and Main Streets, where the Shell station is located today. By 1949, he owned property on both sides of Walnut Street totaling more than 26 acres, as well as almost 2 acres on Main Street. In 1953, he built the house at 56 Walnut Street. Pictured here is Blair Corkran, nephew of Walter, who worked at the farm during the summers in his teenage years.

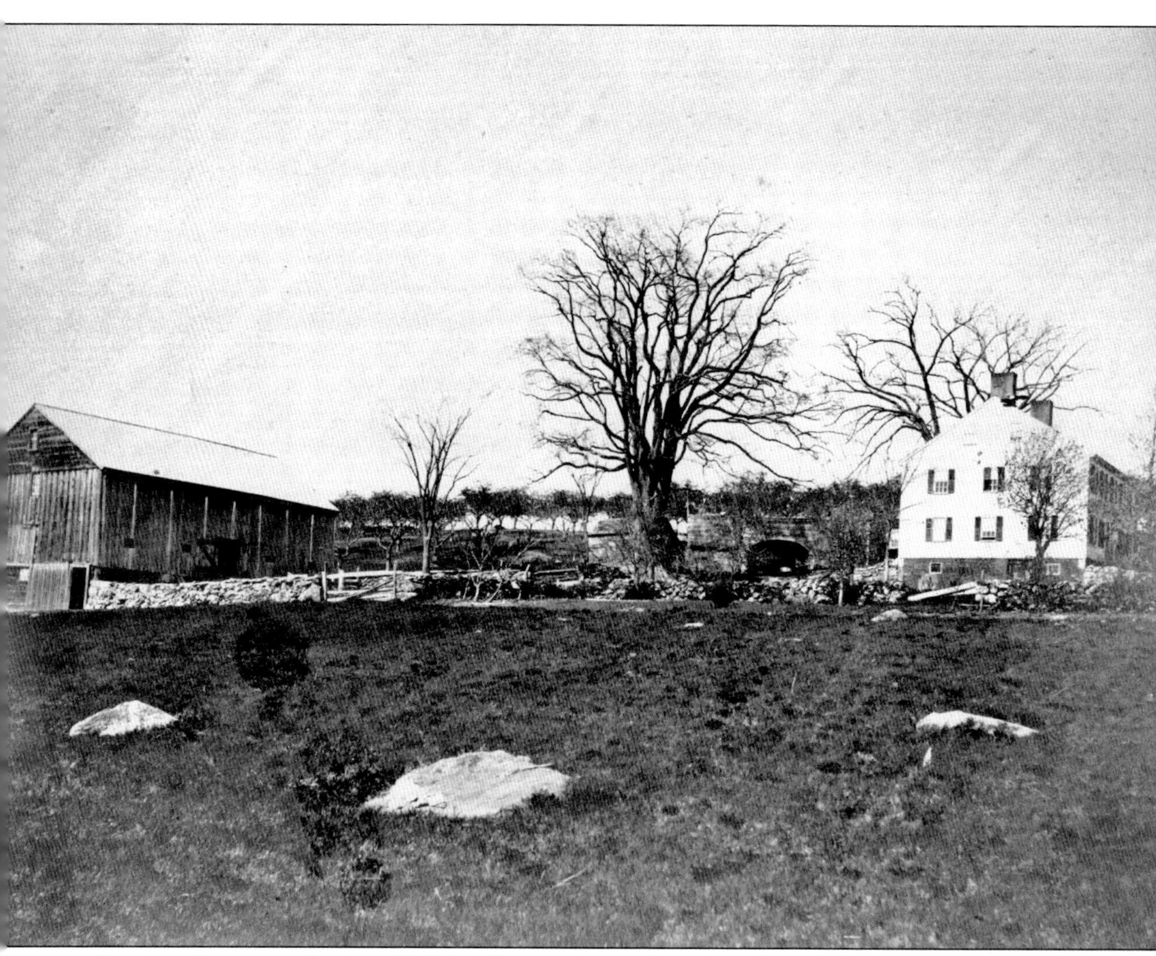

This farmhouse was built in 1742 by Thomas Bancroft at 343 West Street. It remained in the Bancroft family until 1880. The large barn on the left and the house were on opposite sides of West Street. A second barn, near the house, has an interesting arch and an unusual footprint, which can be seen on the 1854 map. In 1860, Thomas E. Bancroft was living here with his parents, George and Mary, and his sister Phila. He enlisted in the Civil War and was killed in 1864 near Laurel Hill in Spotsylvania, Virginia. In 1891, the Board of Cemetery Trustees in Reading sponsored a contest to name the cemetery and Phila's suggestion was chosen—"Laurel Hill." She wrote, "This name came to my mind while thinking of the brave soldiers who fell in defense of our country, some of whom gave up their lives at Laurel Hill." In 1913, the farm became a settlement for Chinese farm laborers, and the house was torn down in 1956.

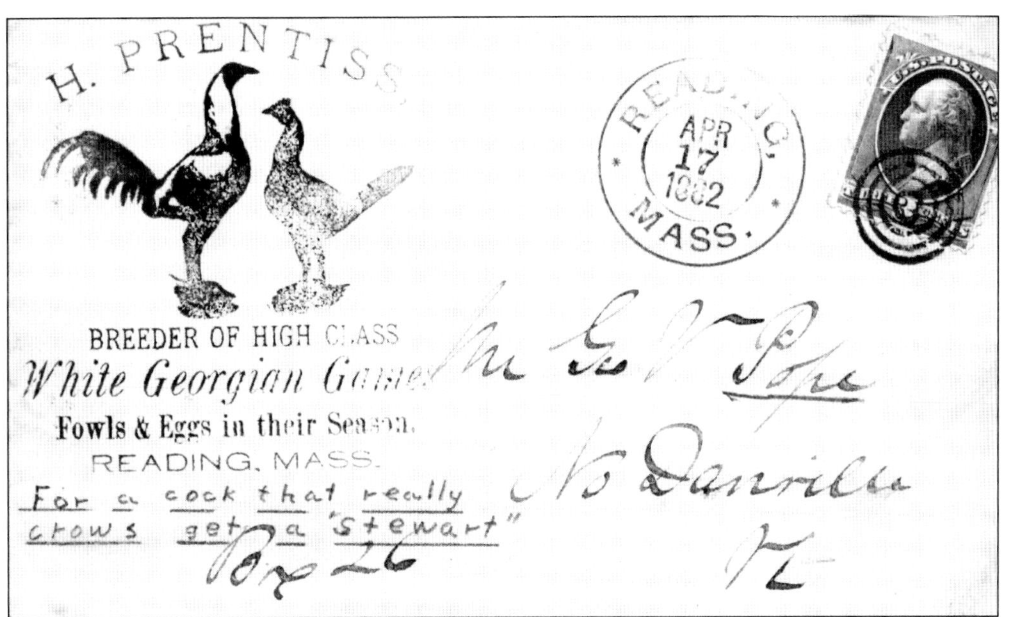

Both Harley Prentiss and his father served in the Civil War. The 1875 map shows Harley living on Highland Street, then called Love Lane. This envelope, dated April 17, 1882, advertises that he was raising white Georgian game fowl. By 1895, he was living at 44 Linden Street (new No. 54), and in 1899, he was appointed Reading's postmaster, a position he held until his death in 1905.

BASSE QUALITY
BABY CHICKS

SHIPPED ALL OVER THE UNITED STATES

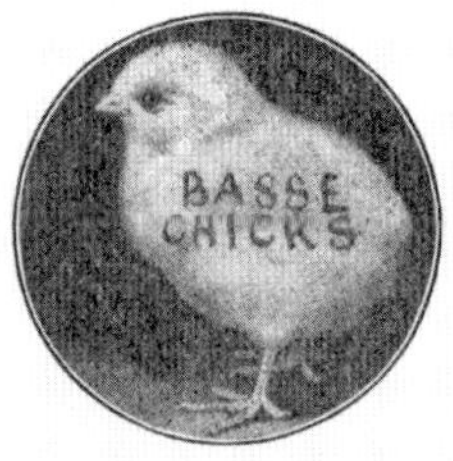

READING HATCHERY
242 WEST STREET
READING, MASS.

Telephone Reading 192-W

By 1924, the Reading Hatchery, owned and managed by Linda Basse, was located on the western portion of the Bancroft farm. The catalog shown here describes the new hatchery building and the "mammoth" incubator. By 1937, Linda was living across the street at 343 West Street. In 1949, the house and land on both sides of the street, totaling more than 40 acres, were taken for back taxes.

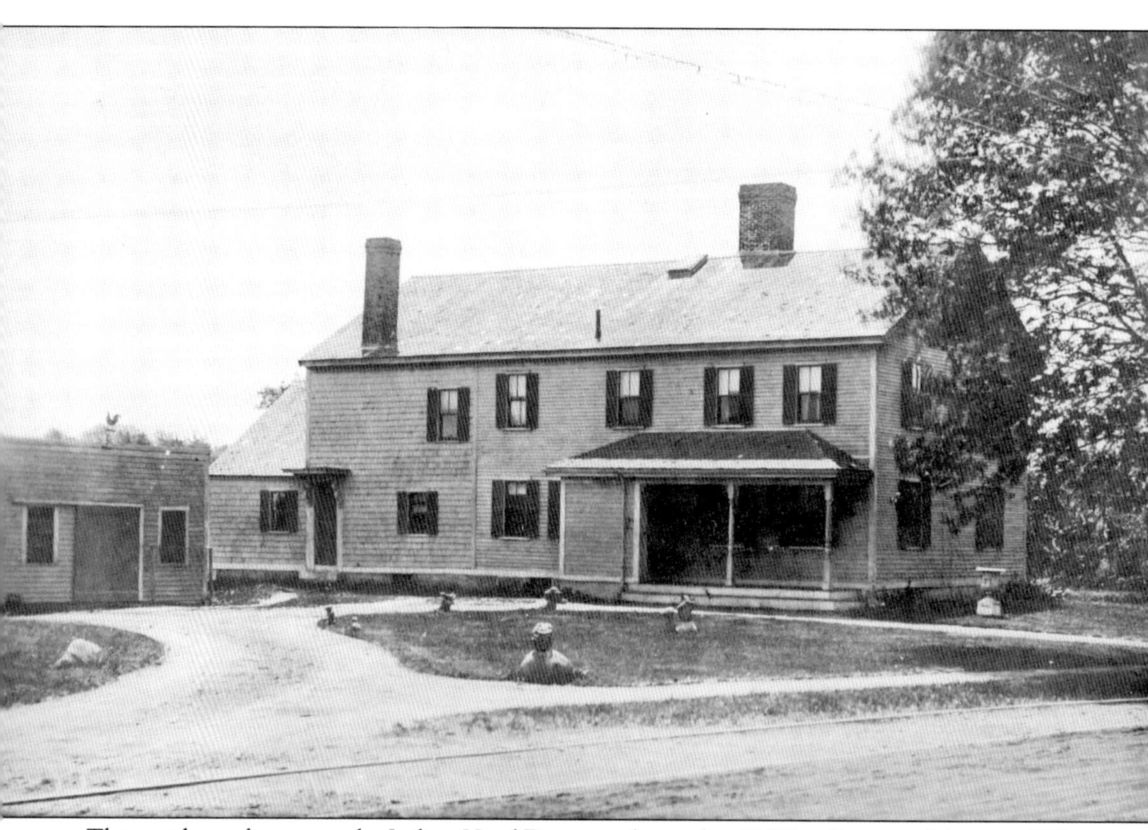

This residence, known as the Indian Head Farm, was located at 63 West Street and dates to 1798. It may include part of the original dwelling, shown on the map of 1795 as A. Weston, built on land deeded on February 17 of 1691 or 1692. The original 25 acres were bounded on the north by land of Josiah Hodgman (see page 87) at Oak Street, on the west by John Richardson's land at West Street, on the south by James Pike's land (later Hillcrest Farm and now 51 West Street), and on the east near Parker's Woods, the development in the area of Pine Ridge and Oak Ridge Roads once known as Colonial Village. Note the small rock "monuments" around the driveway. These odd stones were thought to be Indian artifacts but were more likely "washed" rocks plowed up by Charles A. Weston (1825–1899) from the field behind the house. The house was demolished in 1985 when the homes on Louanis Drive were built.

Advertising items may also be very utilitarian. At right is a thermometer from the Indian Head Farm at 45 West Street (new No. 63), owned by Willard A. Bancroft when it was demolished in 1985. This approximately 14-acre farm had several buildings in addition to the house. There was a stable, a hen house, sheds, and a large barn for the cows. Below is a combination bottle opener and milk bottle cap lifter. The front reads, "Jos. B. VanBuskirk," and the opposite side reads, "Kitchen Helps." Joseph Bacon Van Buskirk was the proprietor of the Metcalf Store, formerly known as E.C. Metcalf, at the northeast corner of Main and Haven Streets beginning in the mid-1910s. The 1921 directory describes the store as having the "largest assortment of household necessities in town."

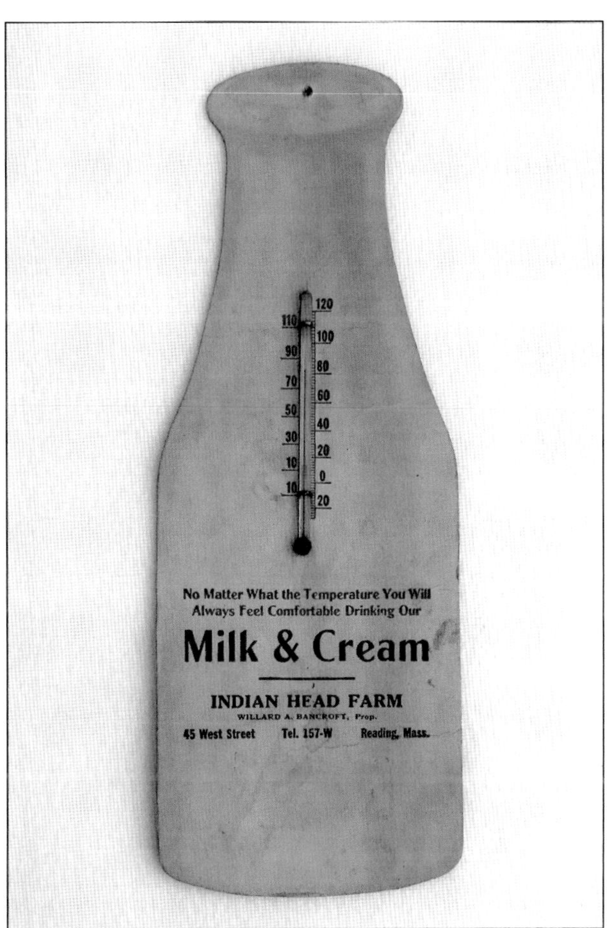

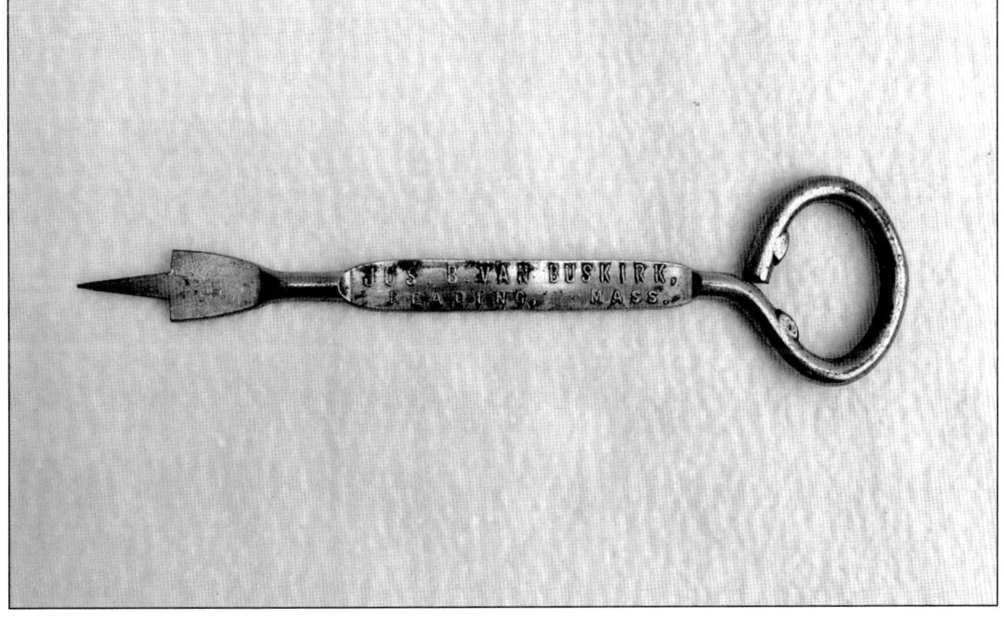

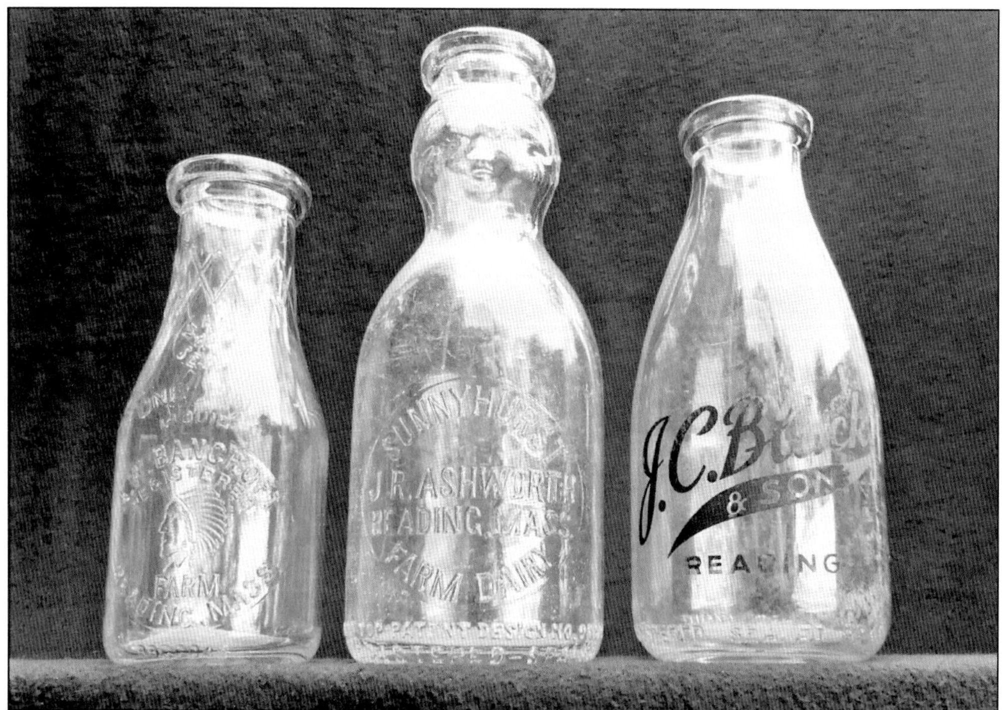

The business directories of Reading show many dairies and milk dealers. These bottles are, from left to right, A.W. Bancroft Farm, Sunnyhurst Farm Dairy, and J.C. Black & Son. The first two have embossed lettering, and the last used a process developed in the 1930s called pyroglazing. The bottle cap seat in the neck of milk bottles was developed about 1900 by the Thatcher Manufacturing Company. Below is a selection of milk bottle caps, including Chestnut Hill Farm on Walnut Street, E.W. MacLeod's Pinebrook Dairy, A.J. Beaudoin, A.W. Bancroft Indian Head Farm at 63 West Street, and Redanddotte Farm of J.C. Black & Son on Lowell Street.

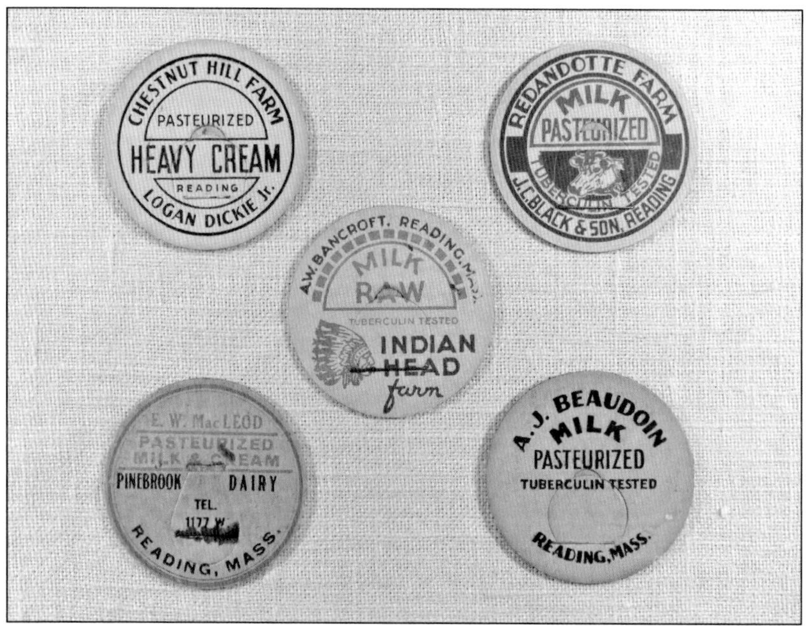

Between 1894 and 1902, Jabez Snow Hawes lived at 71 Prescott Street (new No. 123). He was born in Wellfleet, Massachusetts, and was living in Reading with his parents by 1870. His 14-page catalog, with front and back covers shown here, describes the care, feeding, and breeding of Belgian hares. Hawes moved to Leominster, where he died in 1911, and is buried at Laurel Hill Cemetery.

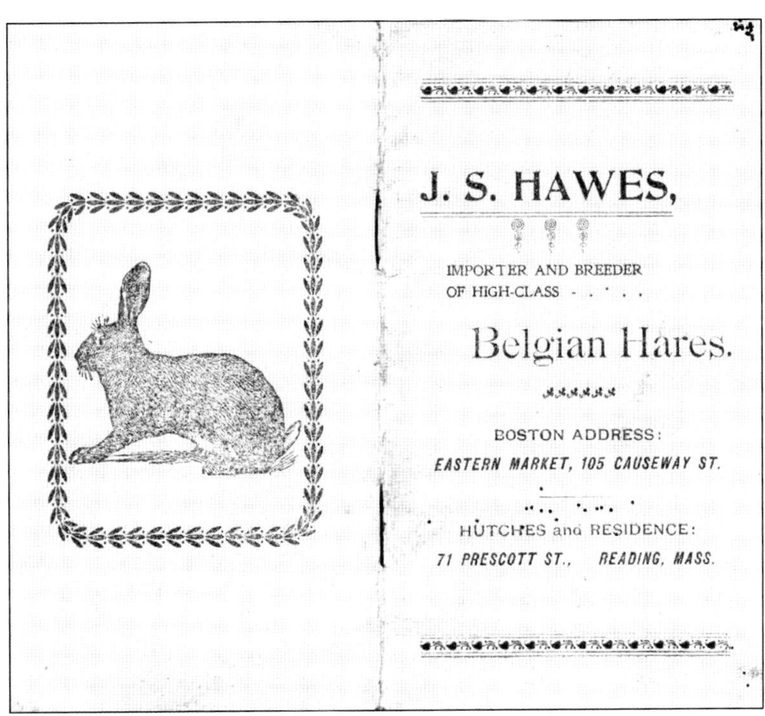

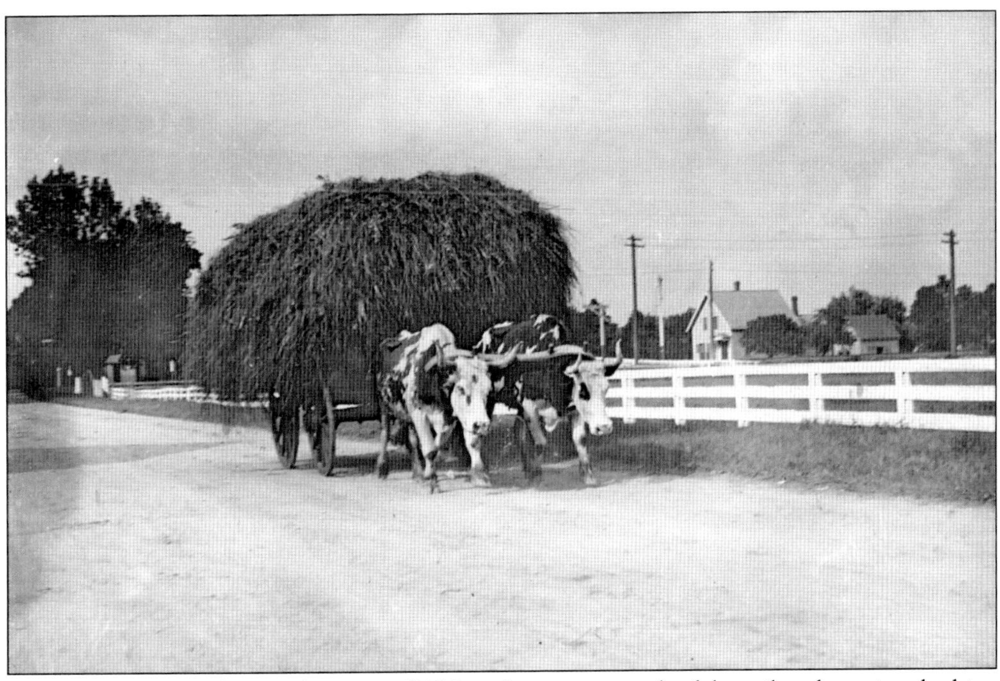

This 1898 photograph was taken near 174 Main Street, just south of the railroad crossing, looking northeast toward Ash Street. A summer cut of new hay is headed south to a barn for winter feed. The yoked pair of oxen seem to know their own way. Note that Main Street is still a dirt road, but there are electric poles and railroad signal poles.

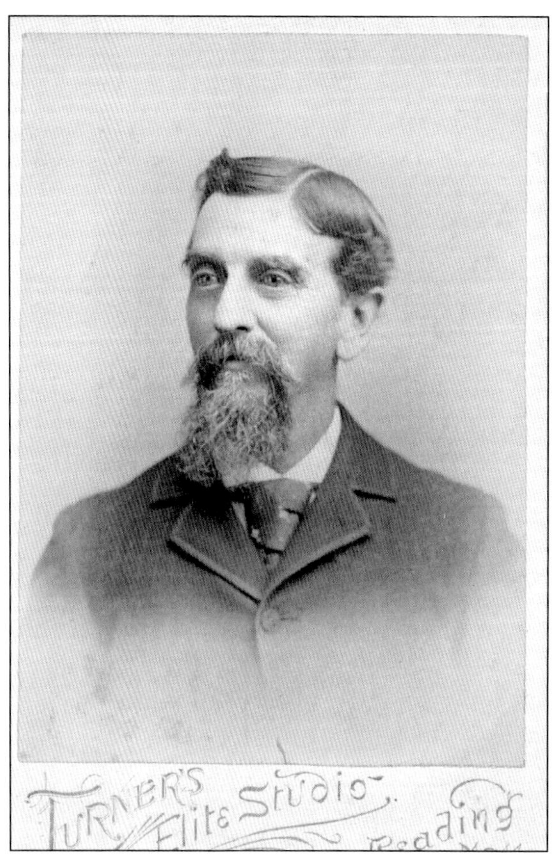

Joseph Bancroft Hopkins and his family lived at present-day 291 South Street. He was born in South Reading (Wakefield) in 1815 and was the son of Joseph Hopkins who served in the Revolutionary War. In 1905, at the age of 90, Joseph B. filed the paperwork to become a Son of the American Revolution. These are two photographs of him. The one at left, showing him as a younger man, was taken by Turner Studios of Reading. The one below shows a much older man standing in front of his South Street home. Hopkins moved to Derry, New Hampshire, before 1905 and died there in 1908. He is buried at Laurel Hill Cemetery in Reading, and his monument is made of cast zinc, which the Monumental Bronze Company of Bridgeport, Connecticut, advertised as "white bronze."

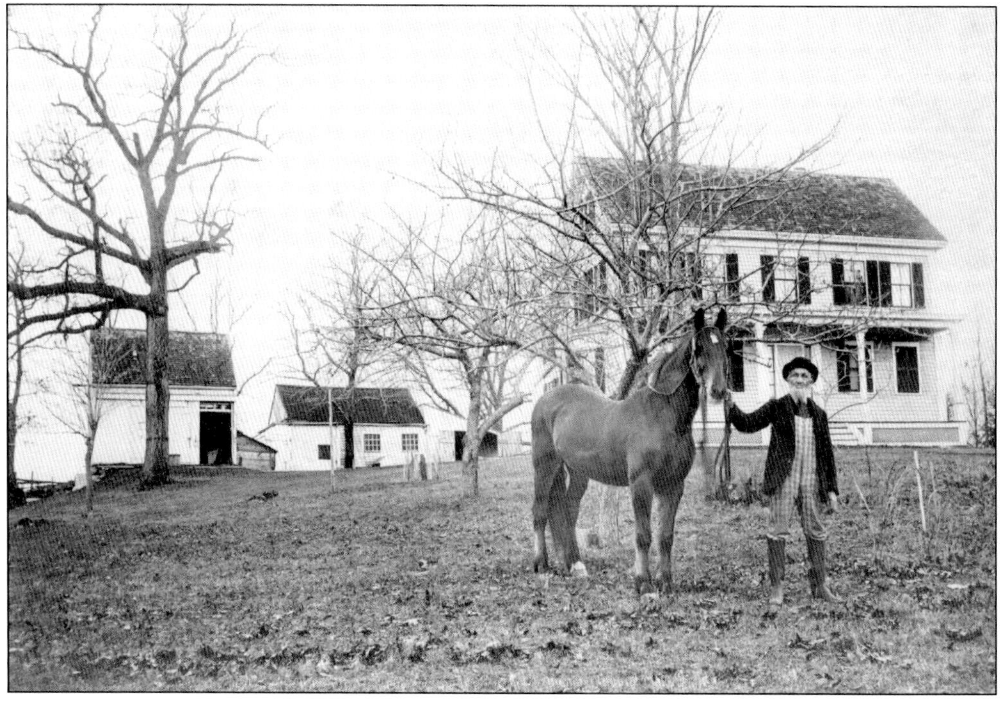

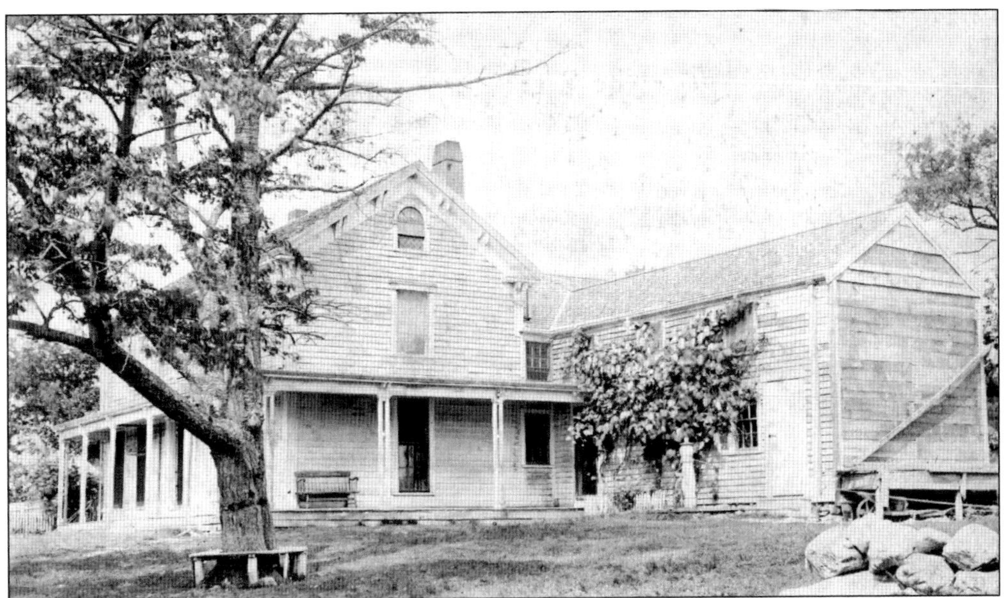

This photograph shows the house at 249 Forest Street. This Italianate home, built after 1830, was home to the Amos and Selina Flint family in 1850. The property was called the Acorn Farm in the early 20th century, and was home to Clarence DeMar in the 1940s. DeMar won a record seven Boston Marathons between 1911 and 1930.

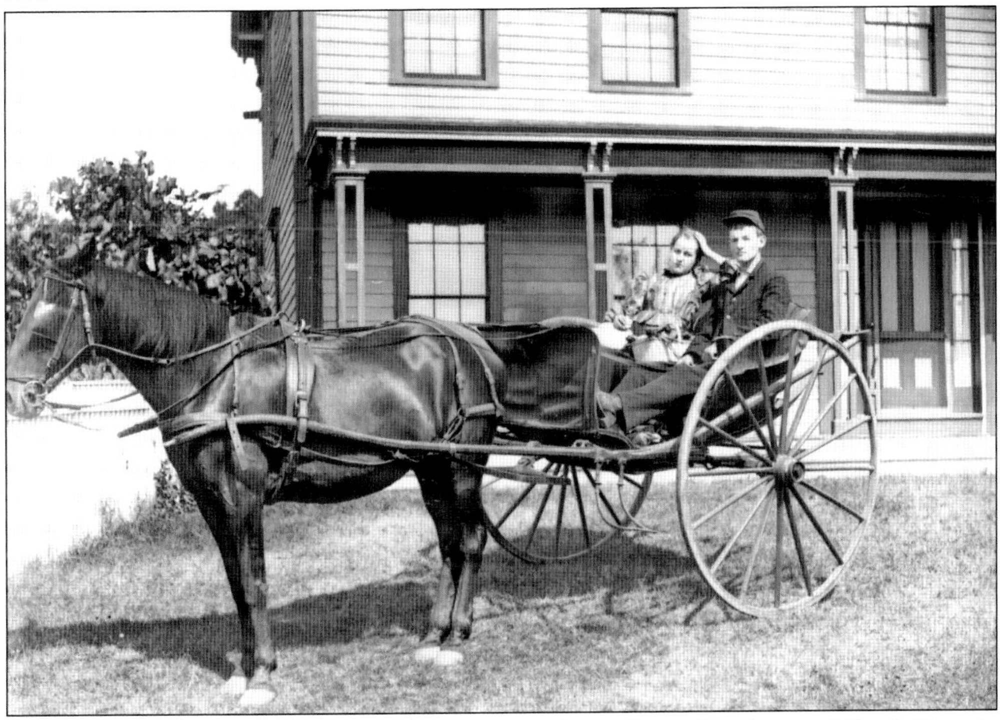

This photograph, taken from a glass-plate negative, shows Grace Goodwin and Frank Hunt in front of the home at 249 Forest Street with its unique porch columns. Frank was the son of George W. and Hannah (Hartshorn) Hunt and lived across the street at what is now 264 Forest Street. He was born in 1877, and by 1907, his occupation was undertaker.

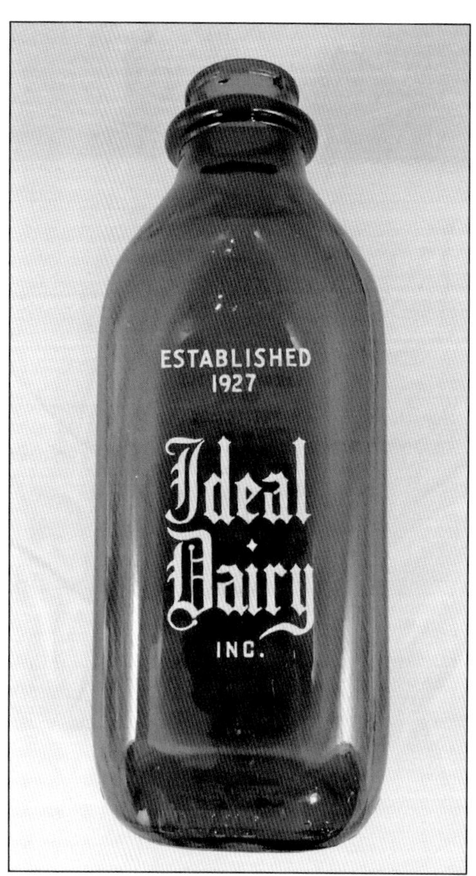

Adolph S. Larson owned over 20 acres south of the Englund property on the west side of South Main Street, which was taken for the construction of Route 128. The back of this unique Duraglass amber Ideal Dairy milk bottle reads "for the protection of the distinctive Fresh Flavor" and shows the early 1920s trend to produce homogenized vitamin D milk. Massachusetts did not require pasteurization until after 1947.

Eric Algot Florentin Mattson, born June 15, 1895, in Angnesberg, Sweden, arrived in New York on November 22, 1916. The 1918 street list shows him living at 16 South Main Street (new No. 70) with another border, Harry L. Larson, age 20, a milkman. Mattson is pictured here in an Ideal Dairy truck. He became a naturalized citizen on November 21, 1938, and listed his occupation at that time as machinist.

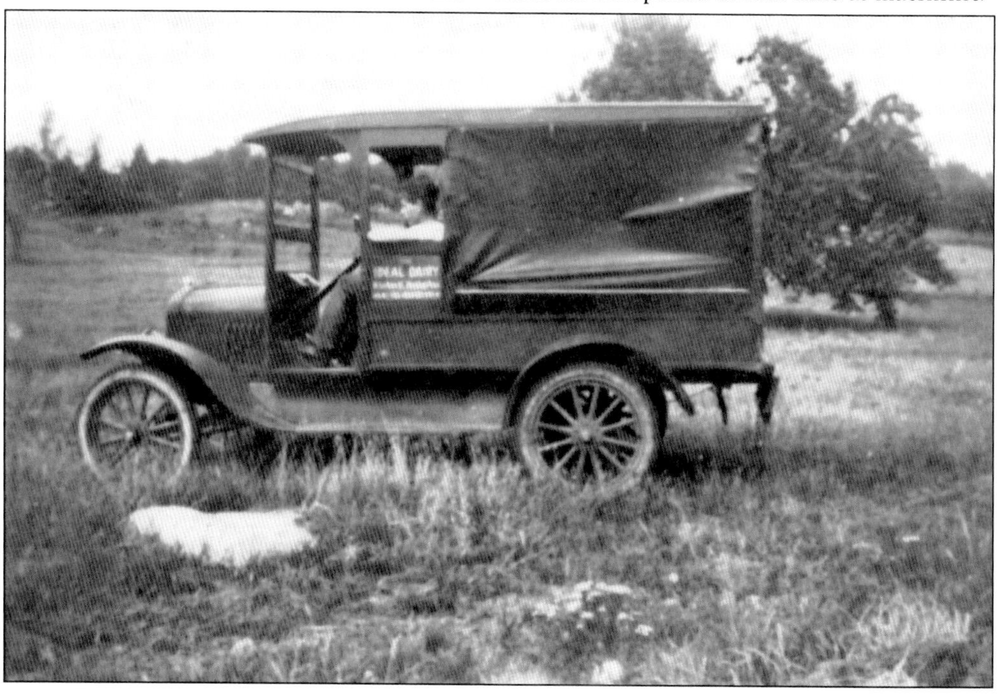

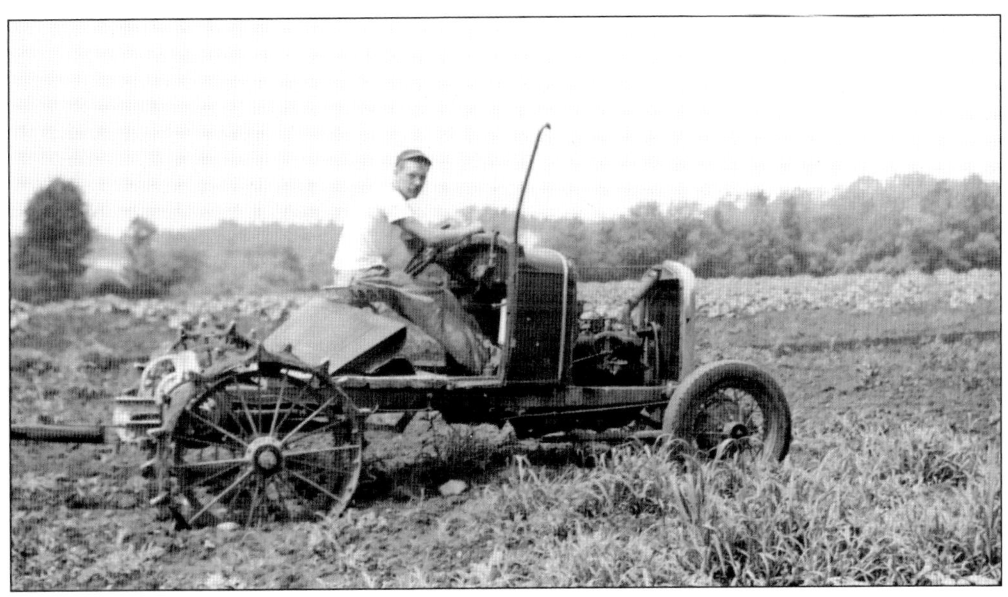

The photograph above shows Clifton "Dub" Englund cultivating squash in 1942 at the Englund farm on the west side of South Main Street. This land was later sold to the Addison Wesley Publishing Company for its headquarters. In 2011, the six-story building there was imploded to make way for Reading Woods, developed by Pulte Homes. The photograph below looks east over South Main Street and shows a sign for Dub's Turkeys. In 1951, this land became part of the Route 28 interchange with the newly constructed Route 128. The Englunds moved their house from 45 Main Street to 397 South Street to avoid its demolition.

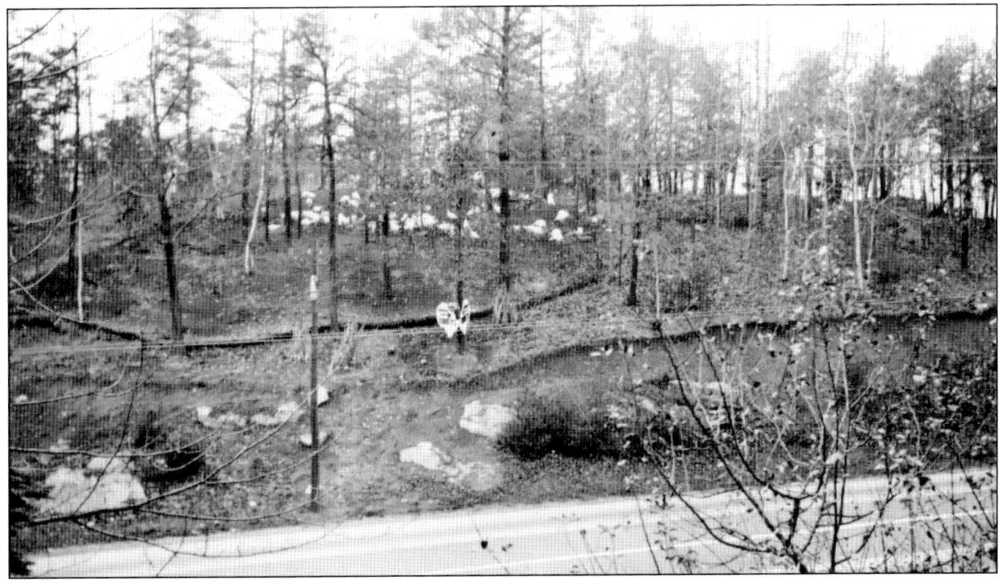

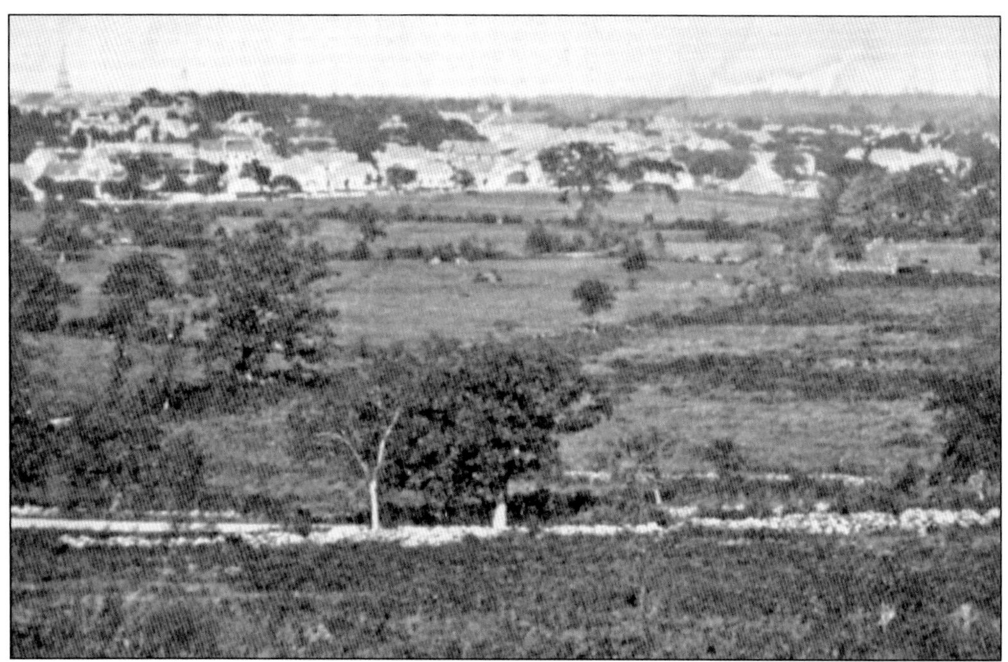

The photograph above was taken in 1871 from Scotland Hill by Horatio N. Robinson and looks toward the downtown area. Summer Avenue is at the bottom, and the open land and fields stretch down to Washington Street. Just to the right of center is the large barn formerly at Parker Tavern. The tavern itself is partially hidden by trees just to the left of the barn. Parker Tavern, shown in the early postcard below, was built in 1694 and was privately owned until 1916, when the town purchased it. The Reading Antiquarian Society, established in 1915, leased the building until 1923, when ownership was transferred to the society. In 1930, after years of restoration, the tavern was opened as a house museum, as it remains today.

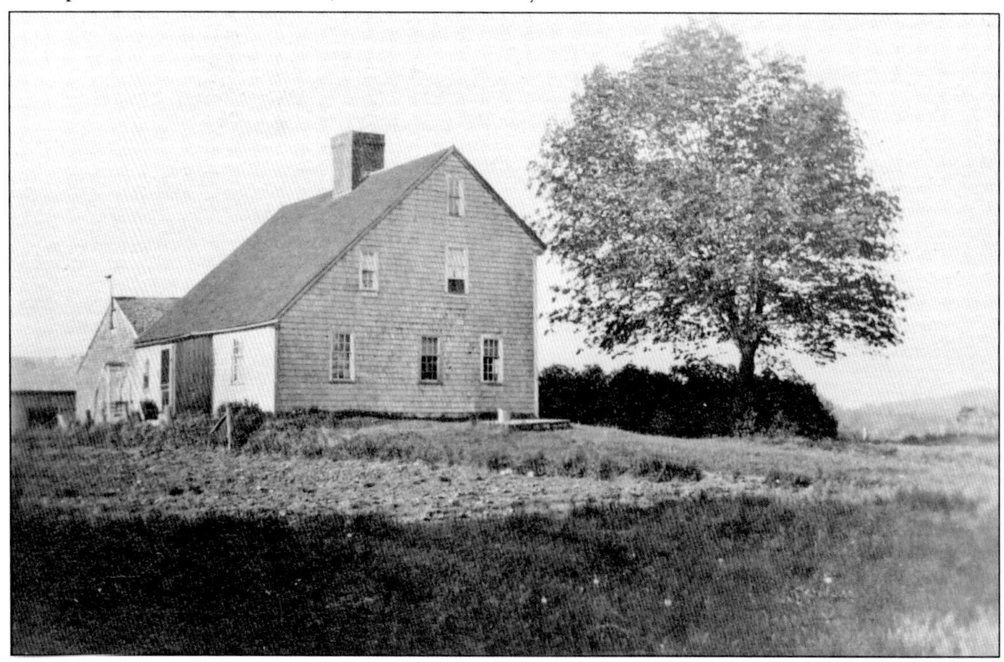

In the 1850s, Amos Cummings Jr. was responsible for development in the area of Minot Street and Center Avenue known as "Mudville." This stereoview shows Cummings's house, built before 1854, on Sanborn Street, formerly known as Bethesda Street. The house was torn down for the building of the 1906 high school, now the Schoolhouse Condominiums.

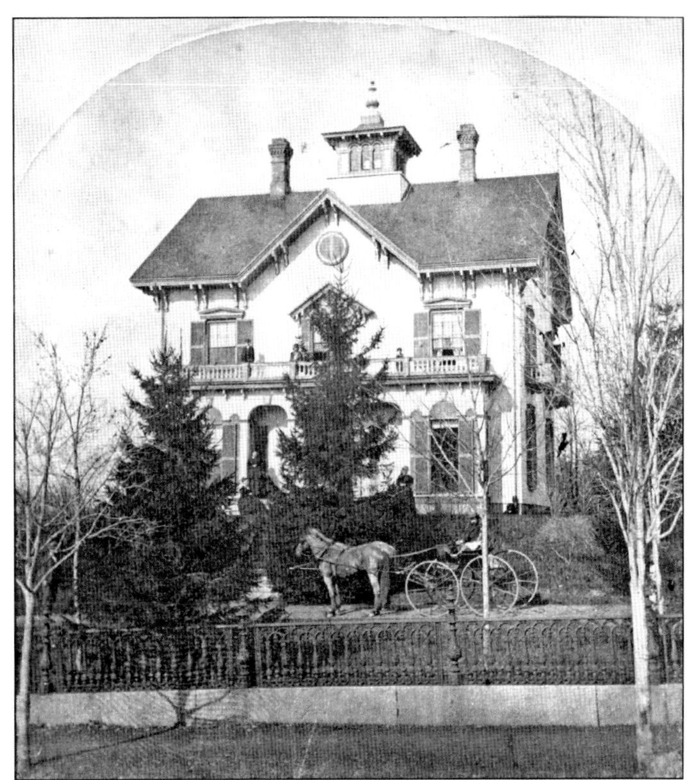

BY BROWN BROTHERS,

Office 19 Tremont Row, Boston.

VALUABLE

BUILDING LOTS

At Lake View Grove, Reading,

BY AUCTION.

On Wednesday, May 13, 1874,

At 2 1-2 o'clock, P. M.,

Will be sold about 20 Acres of Land, divided into 92 Lots, varying in size from 5000 to 12,000 square feet.

These lots are situated about eight minutes' walk from the Reading post office, churches, school-houses and station of the Boston and Maine Railroad, and close by the probable station of the proposed extension of the Lowell railroad, from its branch at Stoneham via Reading, North Reading and Lawrence to Haverhill. About twenty-five of the lots are situated on a hill covered by a walnut grove and afford fine views of Reading, Wakefield and Lake Quanapowit. There will probably, at no distant day, be extended entirely around the lake a marginal road, the Reading approach to which will be by Lake Avenue at Lake View Grove. Reading is a very desirable home for Boston business men, as it is very attractive in every respect, and is easy of access having eighteen trains each way per day—several of them express.

Terms of sale will be easy, and a guarantee payment of $20 per lot will be required at time of sale. Lithographic plans of lots and free tickets from Boston and return can be had by applying to the owner, **EMILY RUGGLES**, Reading, or to the Auctioneer.

☞ Please "put this where it will do the most good."

This postcard advertises the sale of building lots owned by Emily Ruggles, offering free train tickets from Boston to those interested in viewing the property. The lots were east of Main Street in the area of Beech Street, Eaton Street, and Lakeview Avenue, and can be seen on the 1875 and 1889 maps. Emily Ruggles owned a dry goods store (see page 66) at Post Office Square.

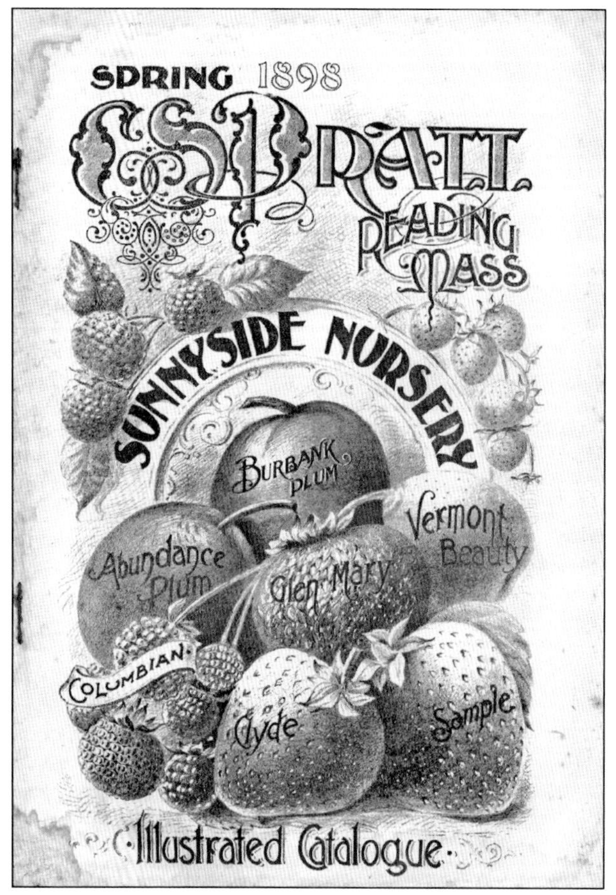

Charles S. Pratt was born in Boston, raised in North Reading, and was living in Reading by 1895 when he was operating the Sunnyside Fruit Farm. His address was "Sunnyside, off Prescott Street." The 58-page catalog at left contains a list of fruits, plants, and flowers available from the Sunnyside Nursery. The undated postcard below shows a car covered with flowers and flags, ready for a parade. An advertisement in the 1898 Reading directory says that Pratt had 25 acres devoted to strawberries and more than 50 varieties of dahlias. According to the 1900 and 1910 censuses, his home was at 154 West Street (new No. 218). "Strawberry Pratt," as he was known, advertised in 1913–1914 that he had one million plants for sale. In 1917, he moved to Princeton, Massachusetts, where he continued his nursery business.

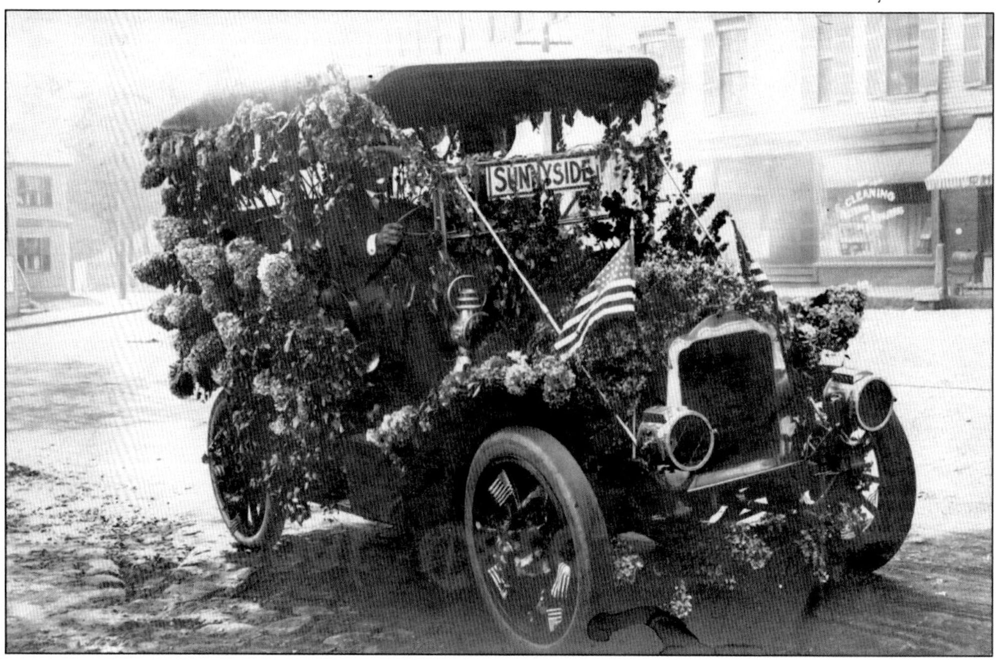

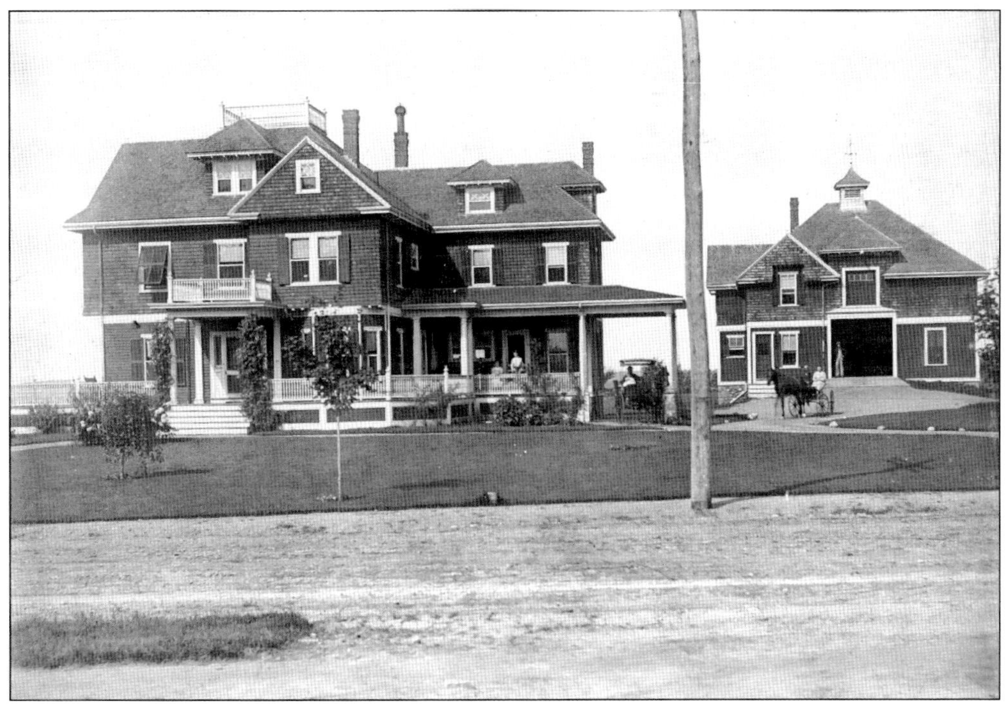

This house is an example of how homes changed over time. In 1875, Alden S. Johnson, "dealer in sand," and his wife were living at 46 West Street (new No. 66). From the 1940s through the 1960s, it was a nursing home before transitioning back to a family home with rental units. The house was torn down in the early 1990s for multiple apartment buildings, currently known as Reading Commons.

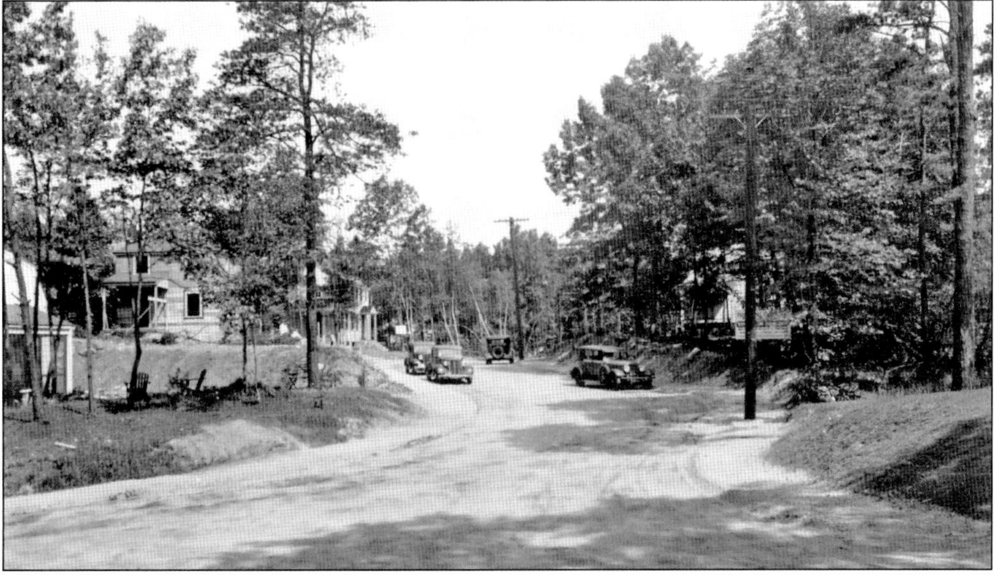

The need to create more housing in Reading led to taking both open farmland and wooded areas. Fairmount Park was developed in the 1930s and 1940s. This photograph shows construction of what would become Fairmount Road off Hopkins Street in the Bear Hill area. Kenneth Road was developed not long after.

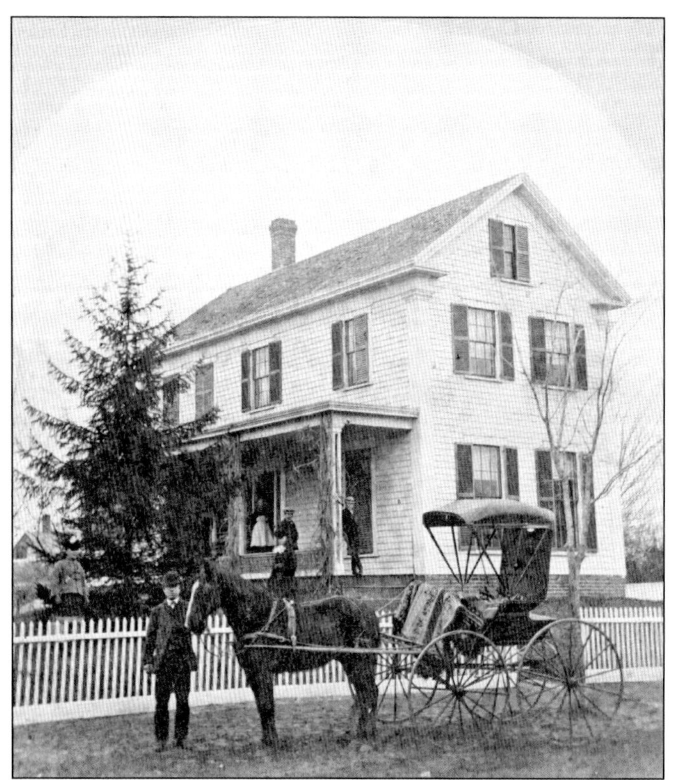

The residence of Daniel Myron and Eunice E. (Richardson) Damon at 16 Pleasant Street (new No. 76) is shown in this 1871 stereoview. The building first appears on the 1856 Middlesex County map. On a closer look at the Reading inset on the map, one can see the location of a shed that probably was Damon's blacksmith shop. The Damon family lived there into the 1890s, and then the Fisher family lived there until 1940.

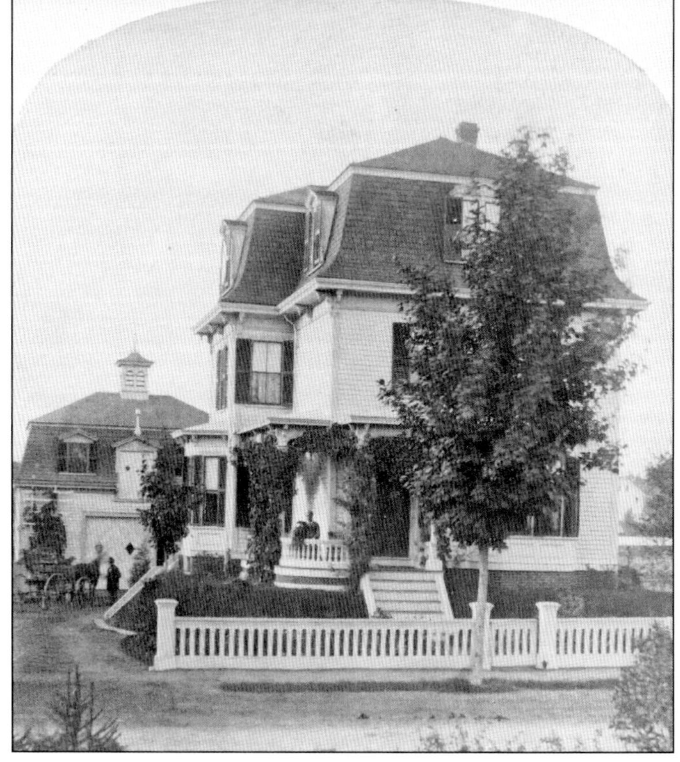

This stereoview shows the house and stable/carriage house of Henry Robinson, with their Mansard roofs, at 85 Woburn Street (new No. 155). In 1894, Robinson was named chairman of Reading's first Electric Light Board. By 1916, his son Elmer owned the house, and lived there until a fire destroyed it in January 1922. The Robinsons moved to Temple Street for two years until the current brick home was built.

This stereoview shows the home at 65 Prospect Street (new No. 81), which was built in 1872 in the French Second Empire style for Maj. Asa M. Cook and his family. The property stretched from King Street to Mineral Street on the east side of Prospect Street. Major Cook was in charge of the 8th Massachusetts Battery, Light Infantry, in the Civil War and was a member of Reading's GAR Post 194.

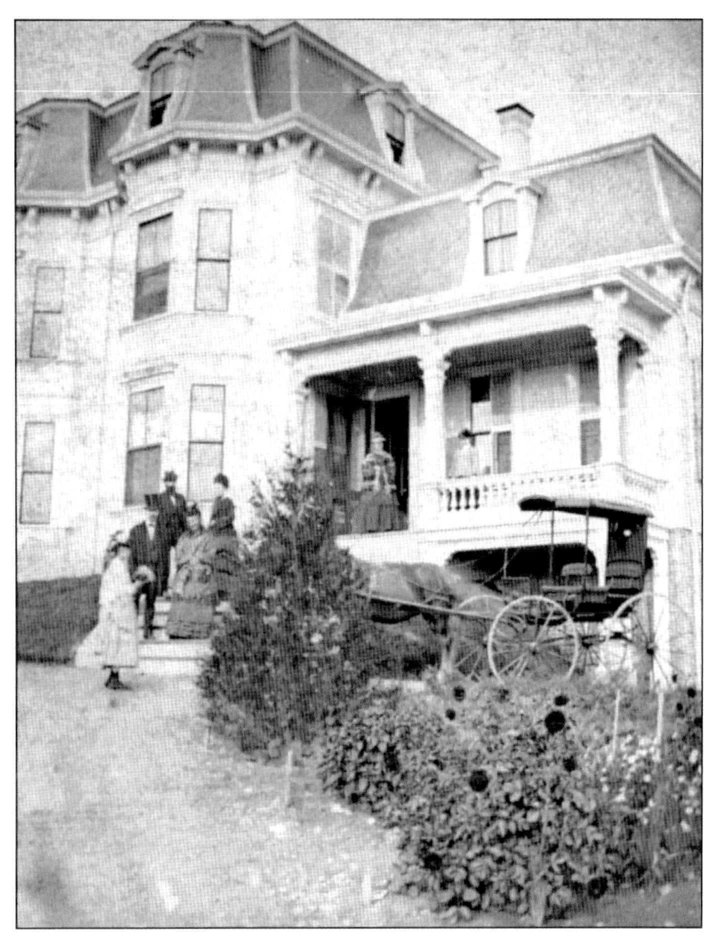

When this card was written in 1918, 18 Prospect Street (new No. 20) was the home of Frank E. and Emma Stevens. The residence was built as a simple old-style home with the veranda facing south. It was first shown on the 1889 map when it was owned by Martha J. Skinner.

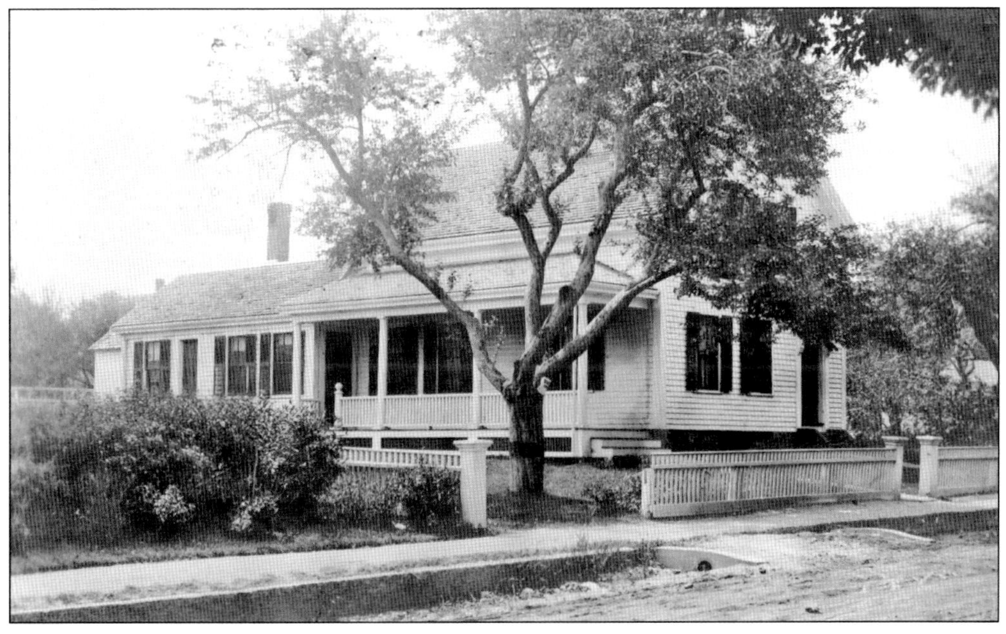

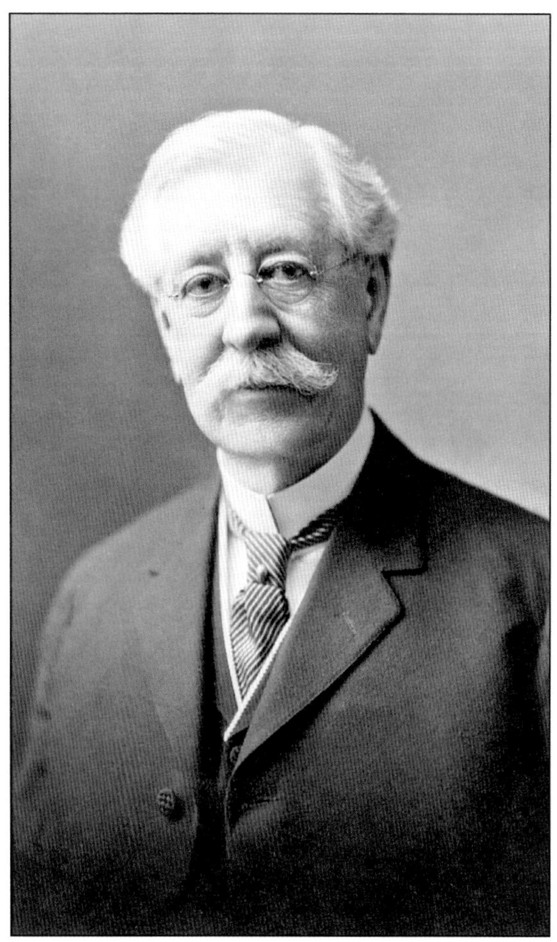

Horace Wadlin, pictured here, was born in Wakefield in 1851. He studied architecture and established his own firm in 1875. He designed many buildings in Reading including the Highland School, currently the Reading Public Library; the fire and police department, currently the Pleasant Street Center; and many houses including his own at 118 Woburn Street (new No. 206). He became chief of the Massachusetts Bureau of Statistics, the librarian of the Boston Public Library, and a Massachusetts state legislator. He also held many local positions, including on the school committee and library board. When the postcard below was printed, Woburn Street was still a dirt road. On the left is Wadlin's house, built in 1892. Pictured are the Boyle children, who lived across the street at 115 Woburn Street (new No. 207).

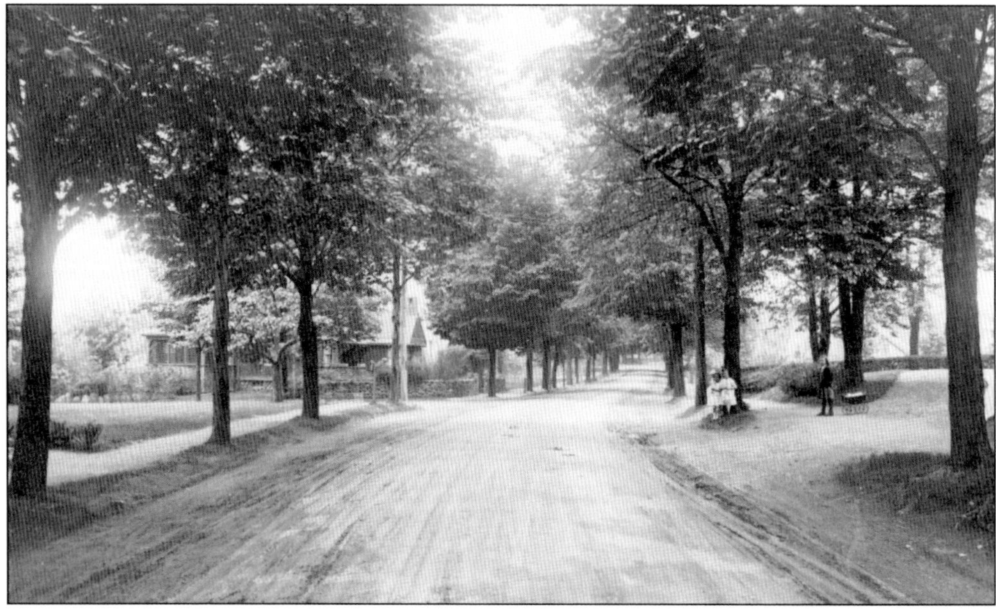

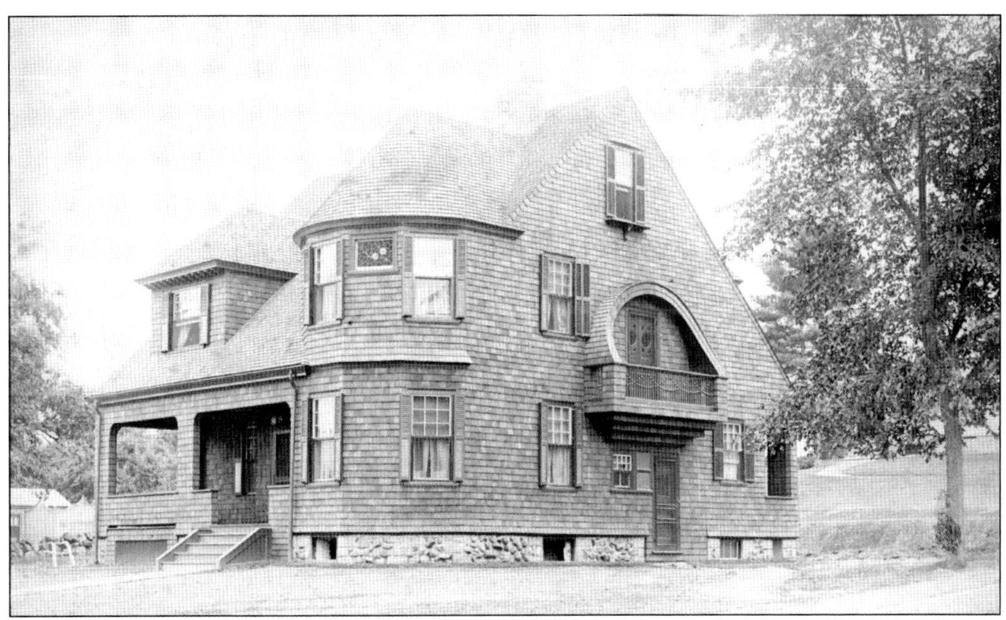

Built in 1890 at 103 Summer Avenue (new No. 159), this home was designed by Reading architect Horace Wadlin and represents a transitional style between Queen Anne and Shingle style. It was built for John Roberts and his wife, Mary. The Roberts family, including John's father, brother, uncle, and cousin, owned houses on Summer Avenue in the 1890s. The unusual second-floor balcony no longer exists.

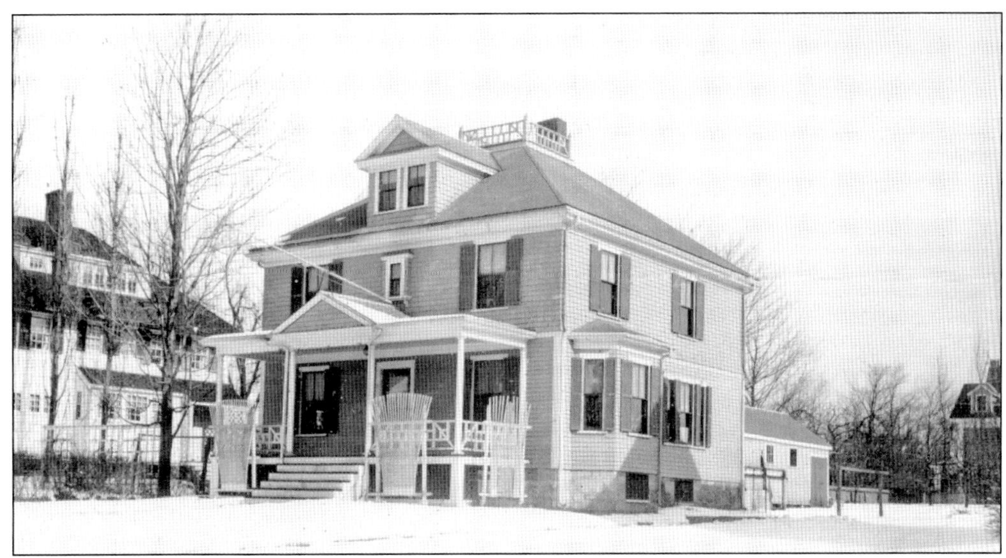

The Clapp family lived at 8 Pratt Street, and the Leach family lived next door at 12 Pratt Street. Their sons Ernest Clapp and William Leach were electricians. By 1913–1914, they were partners in Clapp and Leach, electrical contractors. In the 1920s, by now an electrical supply company, they were located in the Lyceum Building, and by the 1940s, at the northeast corner of Main Street and Chapin Avenue.

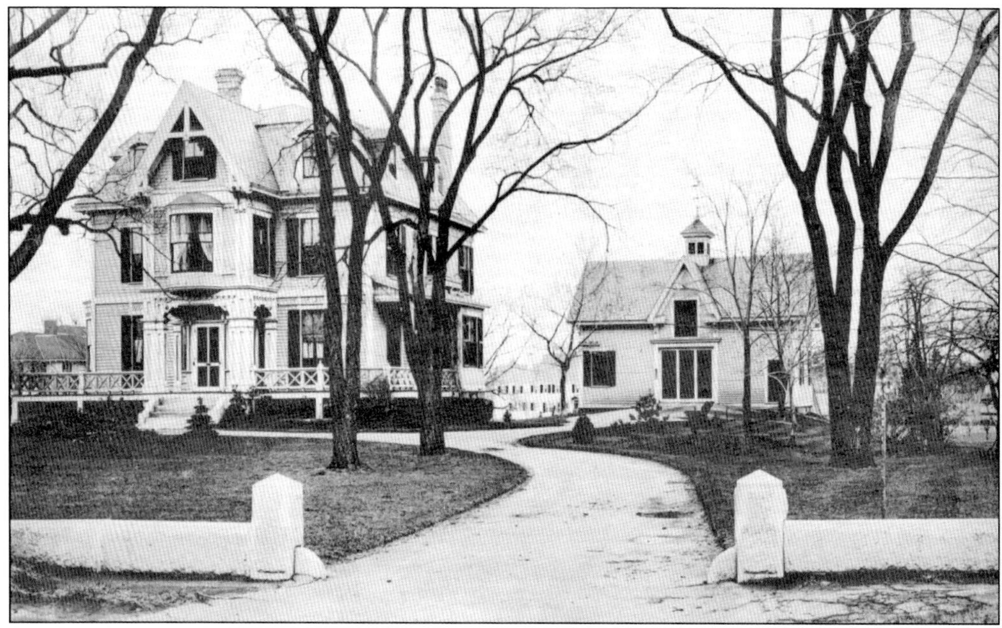

Built in 1875 by J.B. Lewis Jr., this home was later greatly altered and moved forward to become 276 Woburn Street. Lewis had his own meat business and made shoes before age 20. After serving in the Civil War, he remained in the South, made and lost a fortune selling cotton, but then recouped his losses in postwar real estate. He became the leading shoe seller in Boston and was a Prohibition candidate for governor.

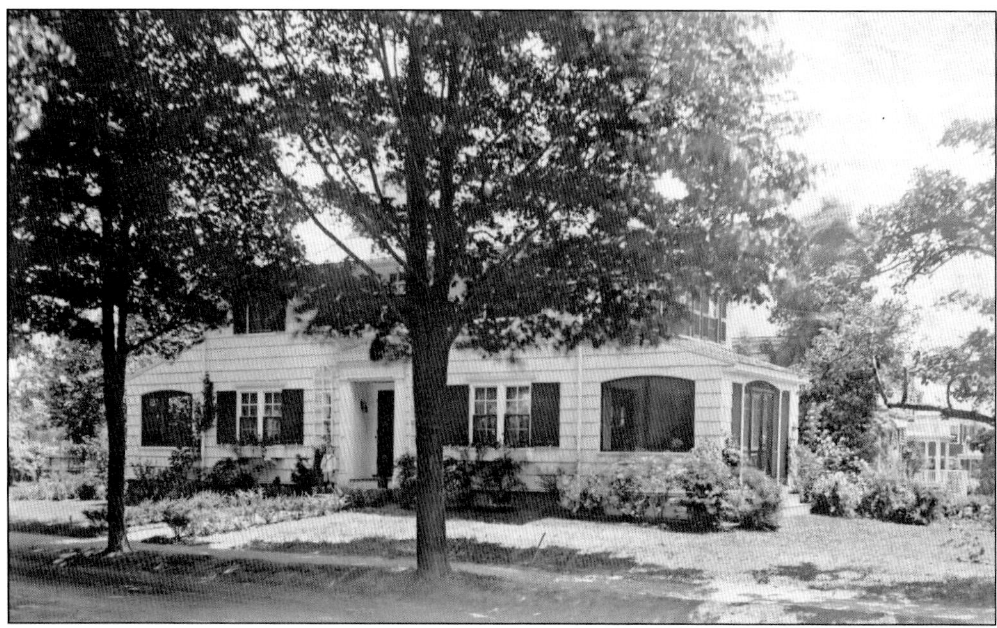

The c. 1912 home of Jesse and Marion (Howes) Morton is located at 114 Woburn Street (new No. 198) on the southeast corner with Pratt Street. Jesse was a Suffolk County superior court judge. Marion's parents were A. Newell and Lillian F. (Gray) Howes. Lillian's parents owned the house at the southeast corner of Main and Washington Streets that was torn down. The Global gas station is currently at that location.

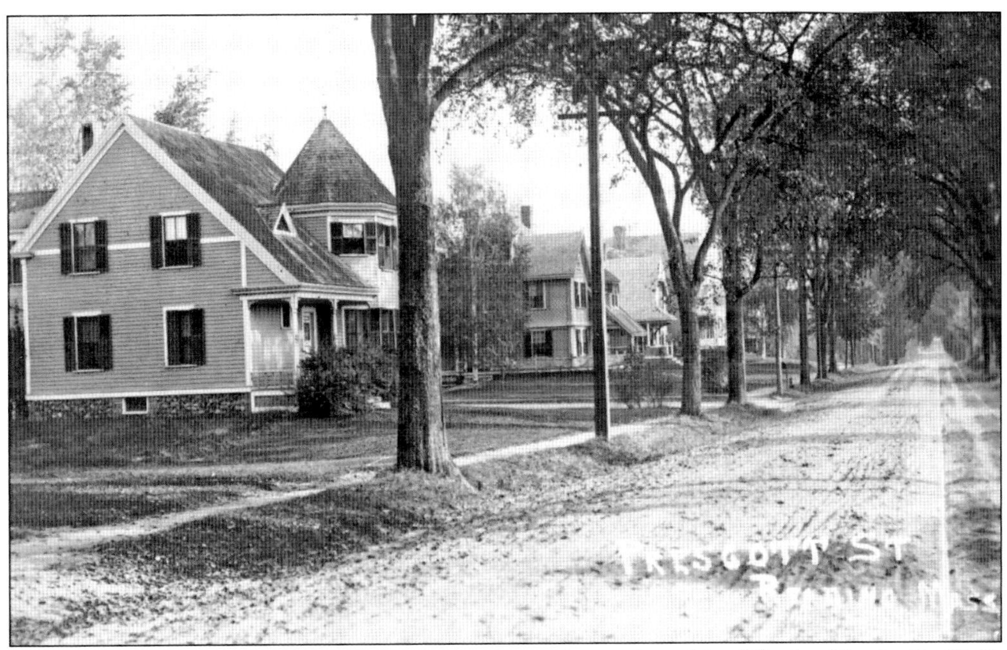

Looking east, the postcard above shows 55 Prescott Street (new No. 99), the Charles D. Wells house, built in 1894 by Friendler and Surrette. Note the trolley tracks on the south side of the street. Going from Reading Square to Woburn, the trolley went up Prescott Street, turned right onto Summer Avenue (at that time, Prescott Street ended at Summer Avenue), left onto Woburn Street, and then left onto West Street. Below, Charles D. Wells and his daughter Myrtle Delphine Wells are in their carriage drawn by Woodland. Charles was a farrier in the shop at the corner of Ash and Main Streets, now the location of Salon Fabiano. It was common for folks to use postcards as a way to communicate with friends and neighbors, especially since local mail was delivered twice daily for a time.

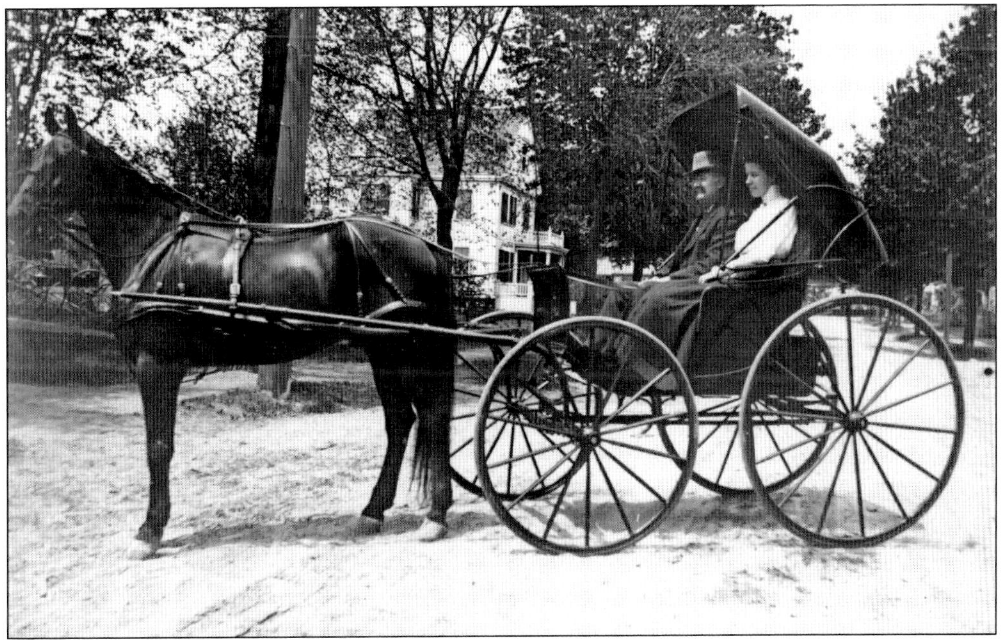

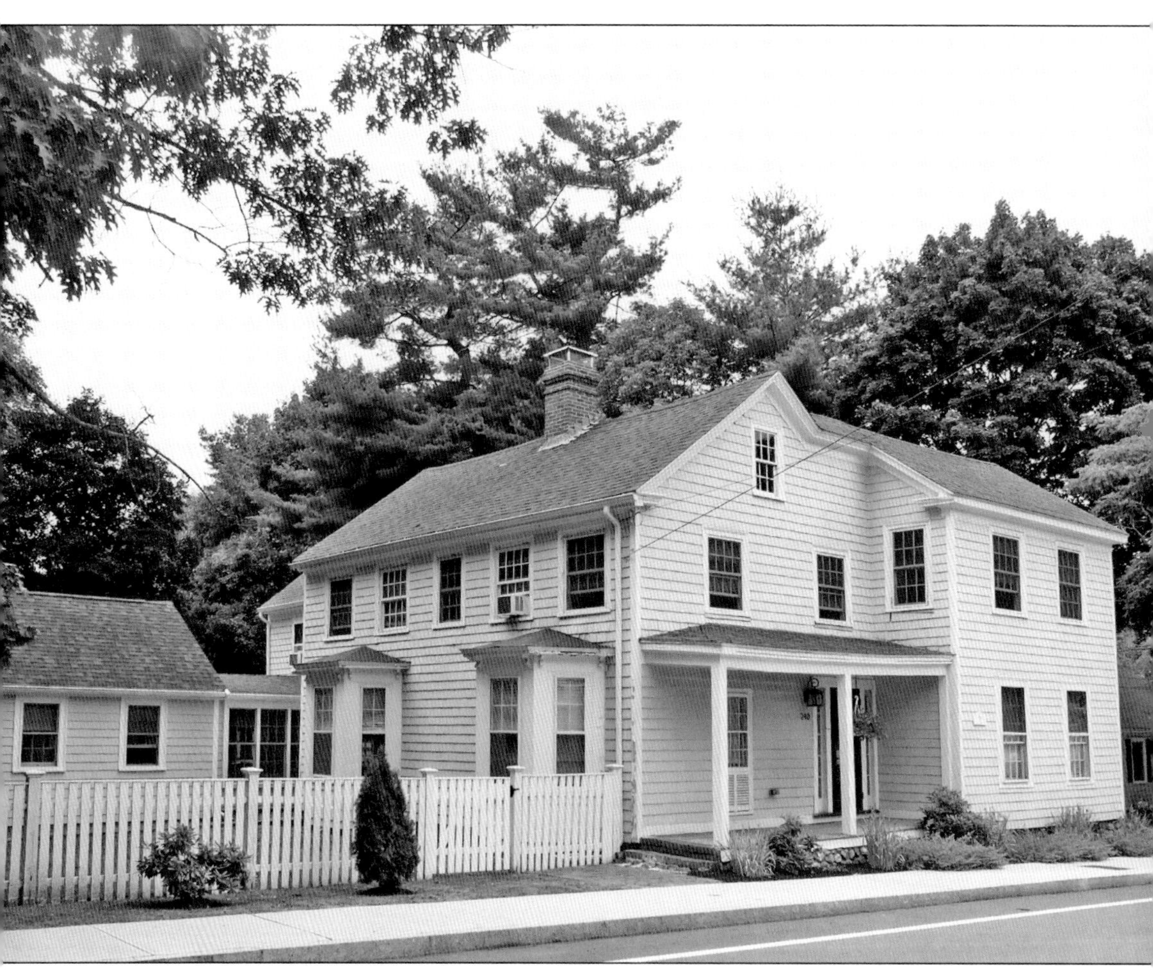

240 West Street has a mystery built into its south side. The house first appears on the 1854 map and was built sometime after 1836, when Thomas E. Coggin purchased the land from Ephraim Weston. In 1869–1870, the valuation of the house increased from $850 to $1,400. The Reading Historic District Commission was allowed to tour the house in 2013 while it was under renovation. It was discovered that an earlier two-story house, with a longitudinal summer beam and a beehive oven, had been "cut in" to the south side of the original Coggin house. The 1875 map shows the change in the footprint of the house. The floorboards also show that at some later time, two bays were added to the south side, making the building appear more contemporary to later structures. Where did that earlier part of the house come from and how old is it?

Two

Here and There

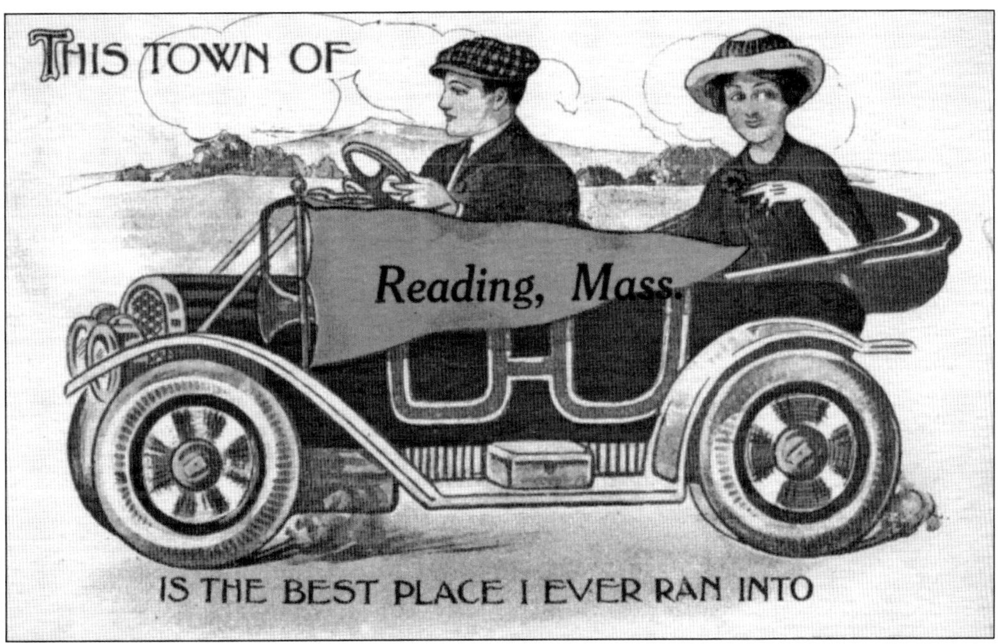

This postcard invites us to hop in and take a tour around Reading. Postcards initially cost one-half cent to mail, and were an easy way to communicate before telephones. Most of the postcards in this book are from actual photographs done on glass plates, so pick up a magnifying glass, take the time to study the pictures, and see what can be discovered.

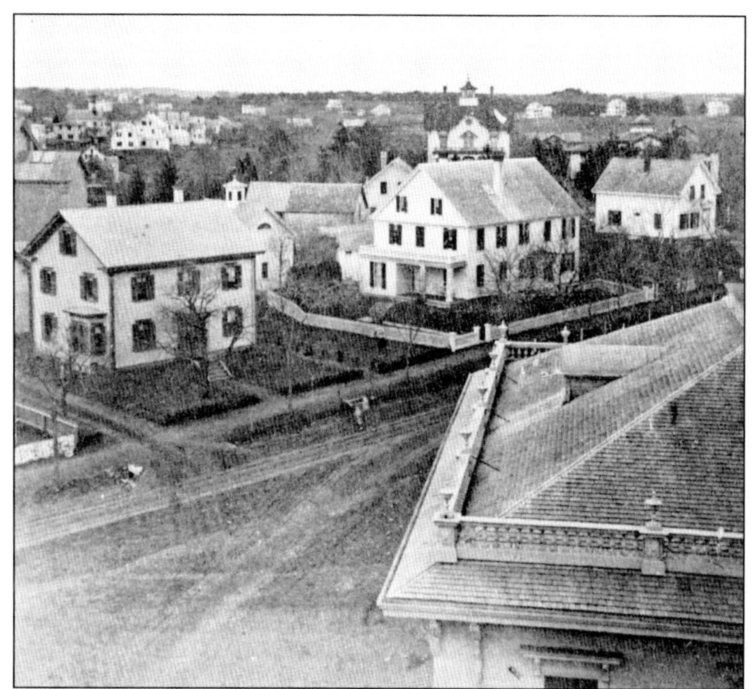

This photograph was taken between 1868 and 1887 looking over the Center School. The Brown house on the left was moved in 1916 for the building of town hall. The center property, which included the Reading Academy, was demolished to create the town hall parking lot. The house on the right was moved in 1913 to 18 Belmont Street for the building of the Christian Science church, now the Northeast School of Ballet.

Academy at Reading.
The next term will commence, in this Institution, on Monday the 16th day of April next.
Gentlemen and Ladies will be instructed in the sciences usualy taught in similar Institutions.
Instruction will also be given in the Latin and Greek, French and Spanish Languages.
Reading March 30th. 1838.
J. Bachelder, Prn

In the early 1800s, Reading did not have a separate public secondary school. The Reading Academy, a private school, was founded in 1827. This note, written by John Batchelder, first headmaster of the Academy, summarizes what would be taught during the spring term of 1838. The main focus was science and the Latin, Greek, French, and Spanish languages.

In 1843, John Batchelder resigned his position at the Reading Academy, and it was taken over by Rev. W.B. Wait and his wife, Hannah A.H. Wait. At that time, the name was changed to the Reading Seminary. The two sides of the card shown here go into great detail about the courses being offered during the four terms of the year, each 11 weeks in length.

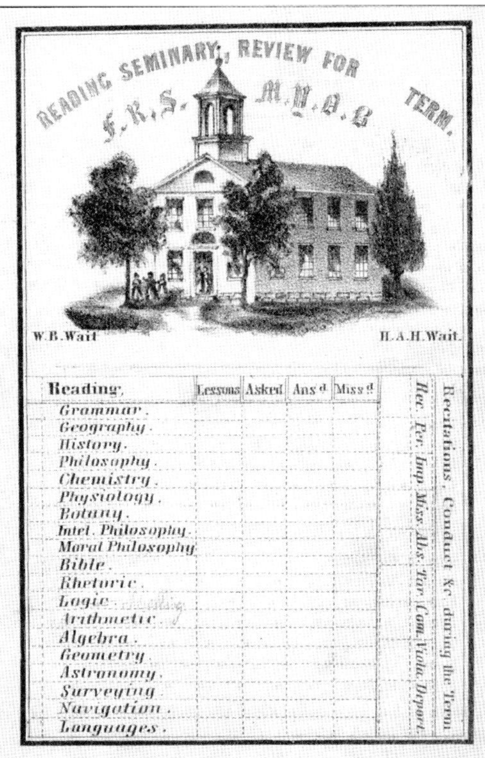

READING SEMINARY.

THIS School,—pleasantly situated in Reading, twelve miles from Boston, and nearly the same distance from Lowell and Salem, has now been in successful operation more than three years, and it may be considered as permanently established. It has already been furnished with the most essential articles of a Philosophical Apparatus, and measures are now in progress to furnish it completely, and to obtain a suitable Library. Thorough instruction given in the various branches of a complete English education, and in the Latin, Greek, French, Spanish, and Italian languages.

The year is divided into four Terms, of eleven weeks each, separated by a vacation of two weeks. The Terms commence on the second Wednesday of October, January, March, and July.

TERMS.

English,	\$4,00.
Languages and drawing, each	2,00.
Music,	8,00.
Use of Piano,	2,00.
Board per week,	1,75.

TRUSTEES.

REV. S. STREETER,	Boston.
HON. A. T. NEWHAL,	Lynnfield.
REV. H. BALLOU, 2ND,	Medford.
REV. O. A. SKINNER,	New York.
REV. E. H. CHAPIN,	Boston.
REV. C. G. BROOKS,	Lowell.
REV. C. H. FAY,	Roxbury.

Pupils both at home and at school are under the immediate supervision of their Teachers.

The Reading Seminary must have been popular since in 1848, only five years later, the school moved to South Reading, now Wakefield, in order to accommodate more students. It would be another eight years before Reading established its first public high school. That school, originally in Union Hall, moved to Cottage Hall on Main Street in the 1860s when a larger space was needed.

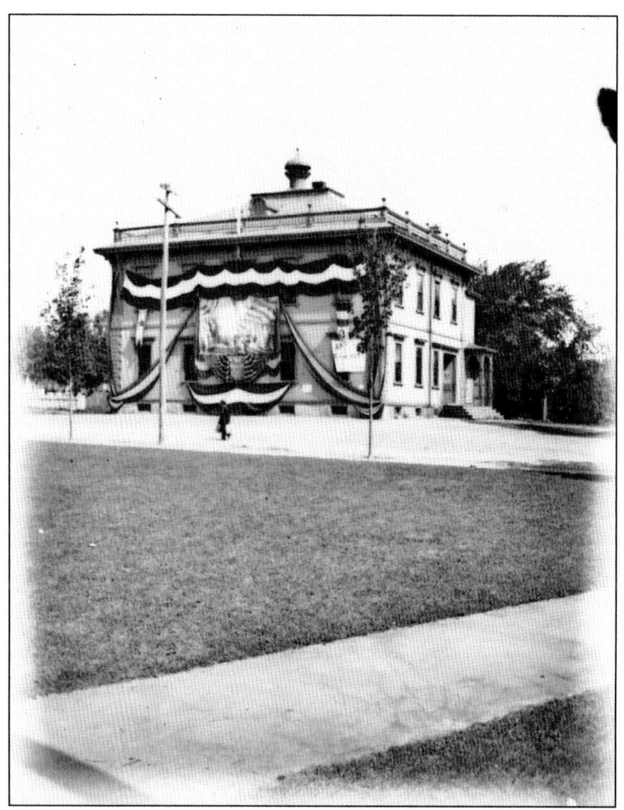

The Center School was located where the west wing of the Old South Methodist Church is now. Built in 1867, it provided the first separate rooms for secondary education. Grammar school classrooms were on the first floor, and in 1869, there was a separate room for Reading's first public library. The lavish decorations in this photograph from a glass-plate negative include a large mural celebrating the town's 250th anniversary in 1894.

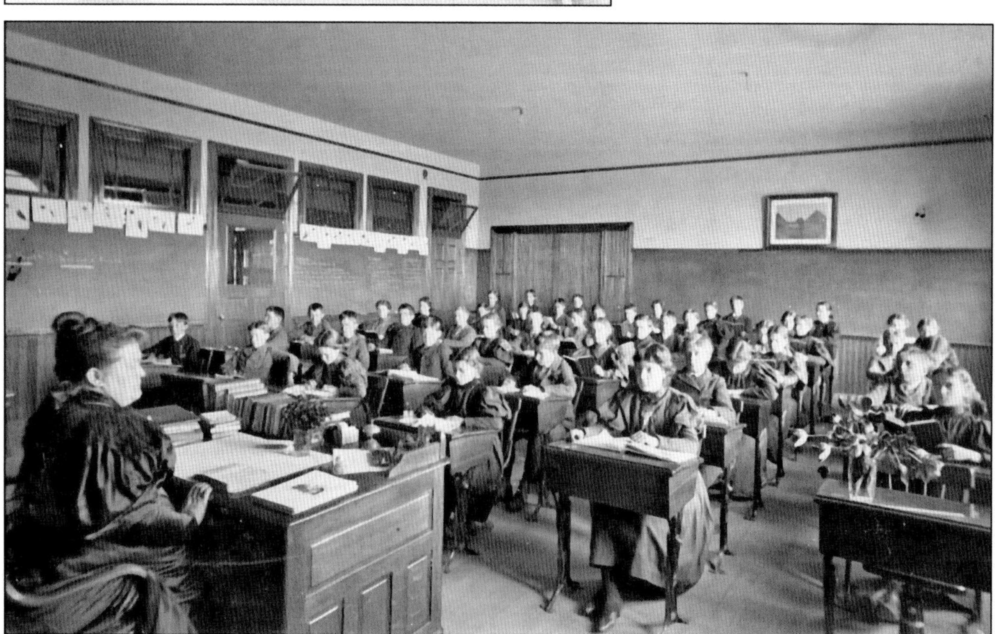

In the fall of 1896, Alice M. Barrows was teaching eighth grade at the Center School. Lula G. Scott, seated at far right, is the only student identified in the photograph. Barrows began teaching in Reading in 1880. She taught various grade levels before becoming principal of the newly opened Highland School, the present library, in 1897.

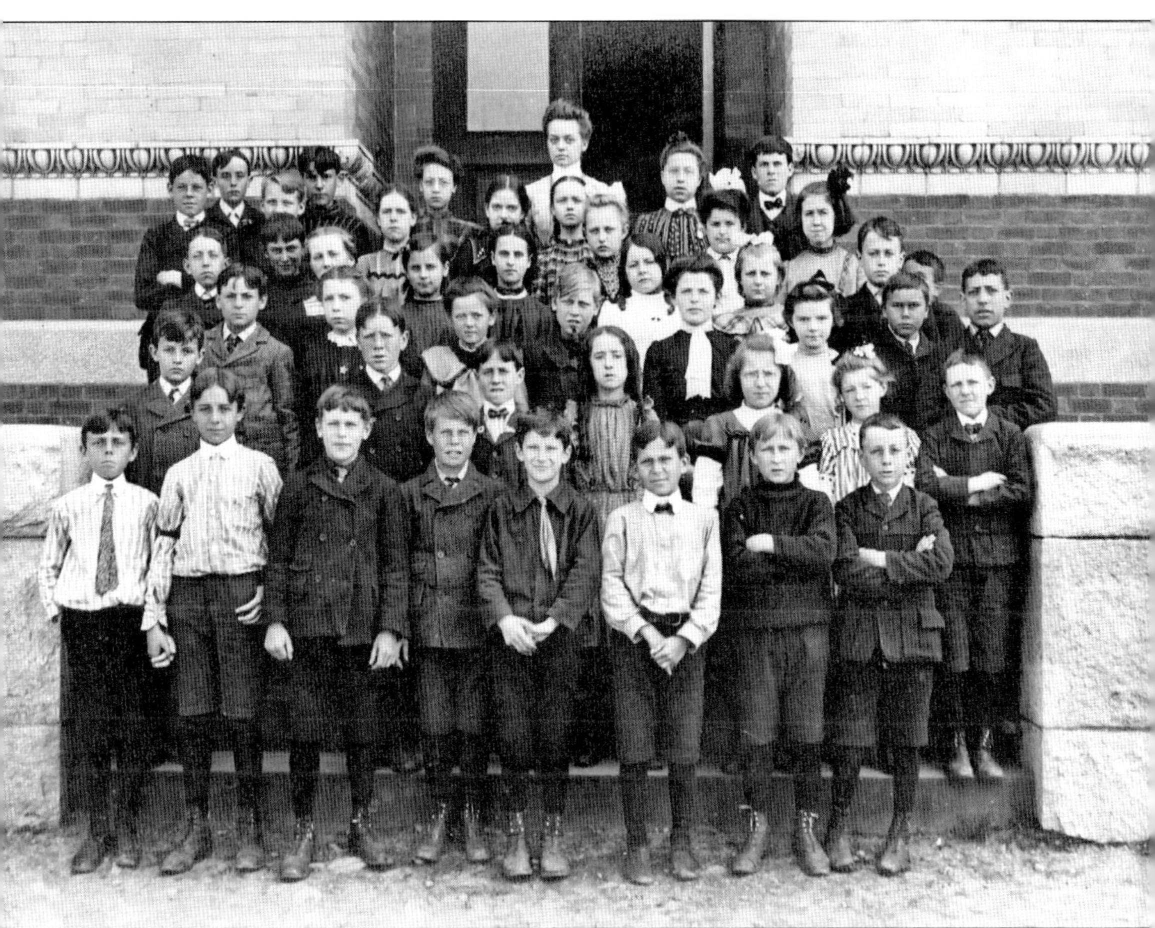

This photograph shows Florence Messer's fourth-grade class at the Highland School in 1902–1903. The names are written on the back of the photograph. From left to right are (first row) Roy Nichols, Kyle Ordway, Frank Leve, Malcolm Jewett, Albert Simons, Ralph Eames, Willie Cotter, and Leonard Doucette; (second row) Hillman Hunnewell, Otis Osgood, Ward Foote, Annie Roxbee, Phoebe Doran, Louise McKenny, and Ralph Brown; (third row) John Thorburn, Marion Flint, Mildred O'Connel, Clarence McIntire, Frieda Friedman, Madeline Pecott, James Webb, and William Meuse; (fourth row) Lyman Abbott, Arthur Bothwick, Grace Milbury, Marjorie Barbarick, Nellie Warner, Jennie Logan, Ruth MacMonagle, Fletcher Twombley, and George Dulong; (fifth row) Arthur Phebe, Paul Forbes, Bertha Wickens, Grace Stone, Pearl Mason, Vera Young, Hattie Knowles, and Elizabeth Smith; (sixth row) Charlie Kelly, Joseph Muise, Mabel Tarbox, Florence Messer, Lina Leavitt, and John Baird.

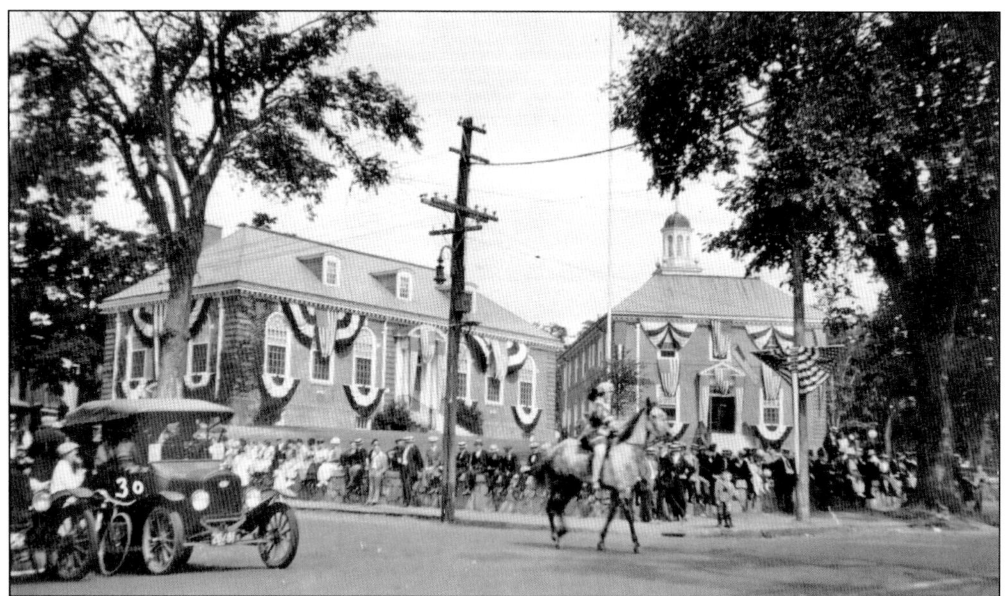

This undated real-photo postcard shows a parade at the corner of Woburn and Lowell Streets. In the background are the library, now the town hall annex, and town hall. A series of approximately 75 cards were created, and this is No. 30. Note the white number on the car at left. Perhaps a reader will know what this event was or when it took place.

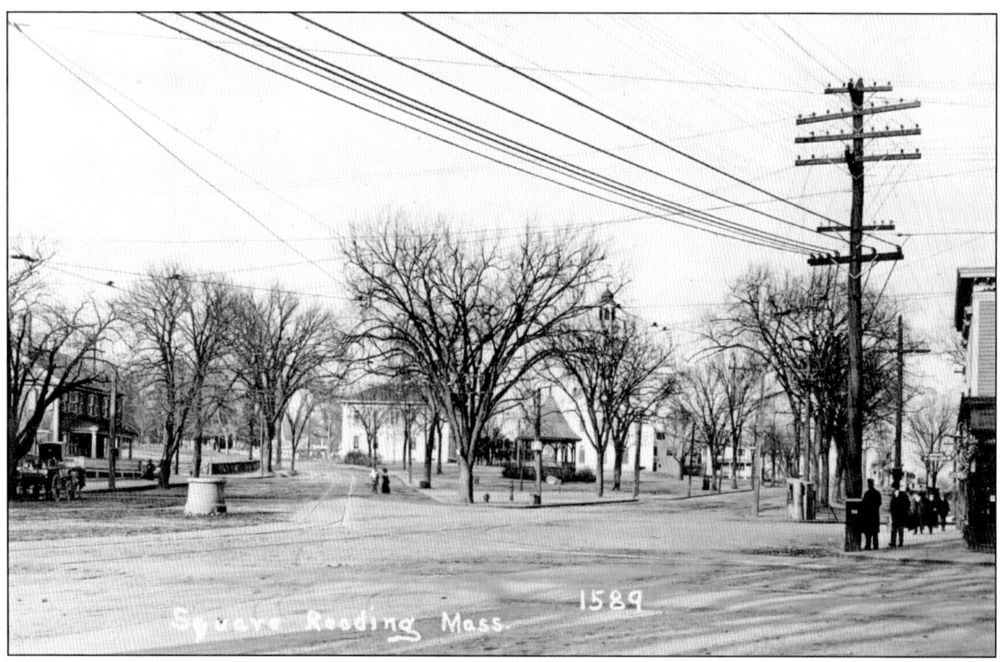

Looking north toward the common, Main Street was still a dirt road. The bandstand, designed by Horace Wadlin, and the old high school, torn down in 1957, are still there. The house on the left, at the southwest corner of Woburn Street, was built by Dr. Kendall Davies in 1836–1837. It was moved in 1913 to 18–20 Woburn Street and burned down in 2006.

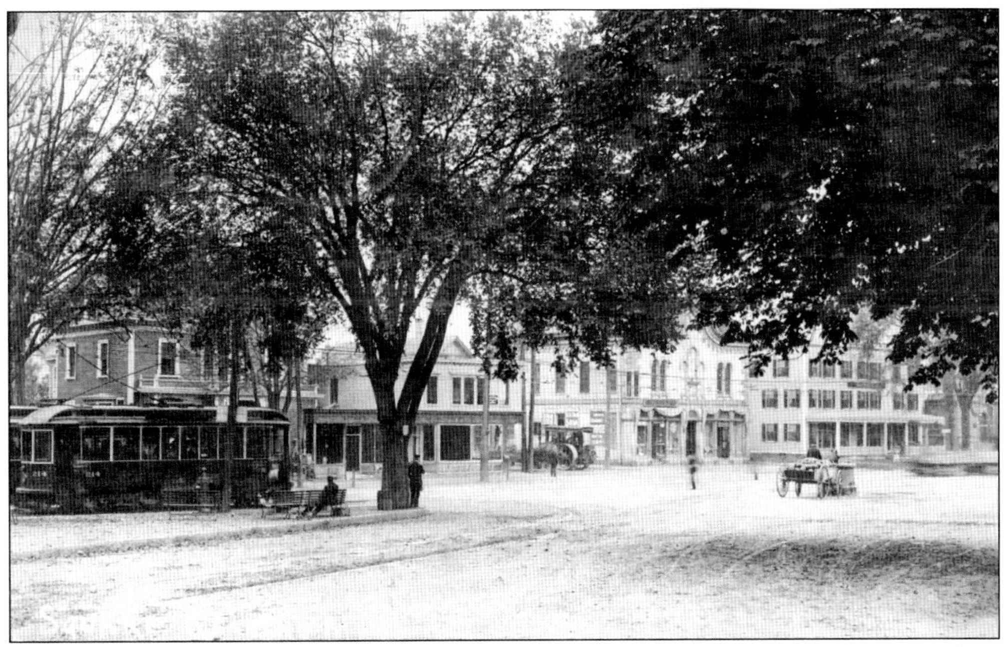

This postcard shows a lot happening near the intersection of Lowell and Woburn Streets. There are three different vehicles—trolley No. 214 on Main Street, the town grader working on Pleasant Street, and a horse and wagon pausing to get a drink at the cistern. On the north corner of Pleasant Street, A.W. Danforth's Pharmacy is seen under construction; it moved from the south corner in 1908.

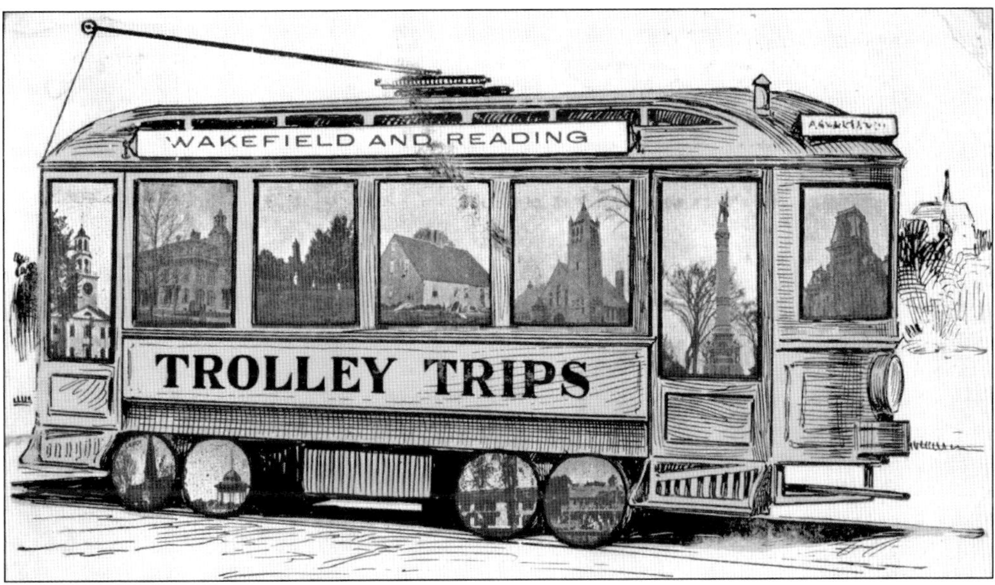

This trolley postcard was personalized to Wakefield and Reading, with photographs of local landmarks inserted into the windows and wheels. The postcard was printed in three versions with the trolley colored green, yellow, or red. In the windows are, from left to right, Old South Church (Reading), Cyrus Wakefield Mansion (Wakefield), the "rocket" water tower (Reading), Parker Tavern (Reading), Congregational Church (Wakefield), Soldiers and Sailors Monument (Wakefield), and town hall (Wakefield).

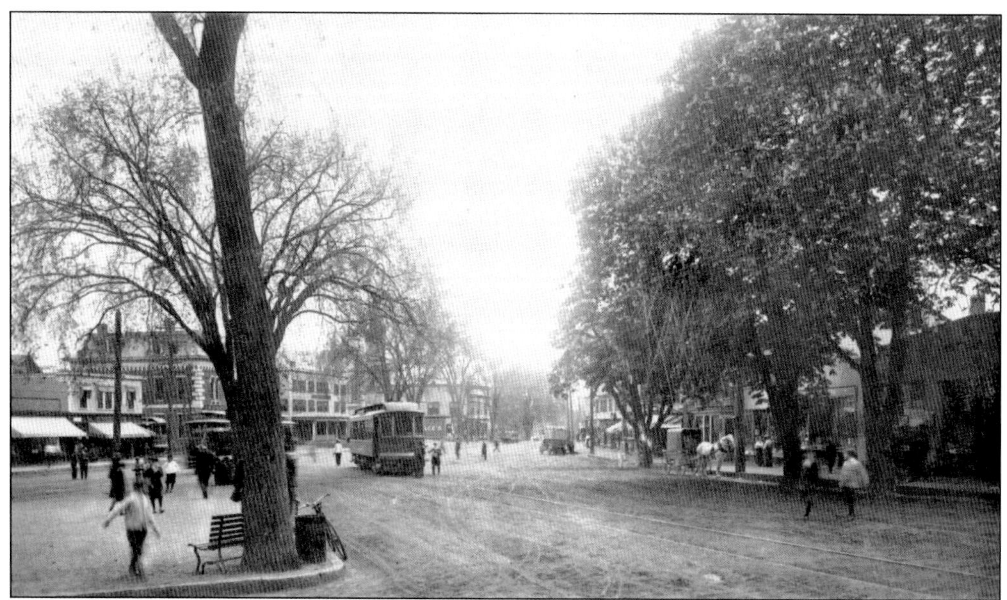

Looking south in the Square, A.W. Danforth's Pharmacy is now on the northeast corner of Pleasant Street. Five separate trolley lines met at Reading Square. One came north from Boston, and from there east to Salem, one went west to Woburn, and two others went north to Lowell and Haverhill. Police often came to search for criminals who were trying to escape capture by changing lines at Reading.

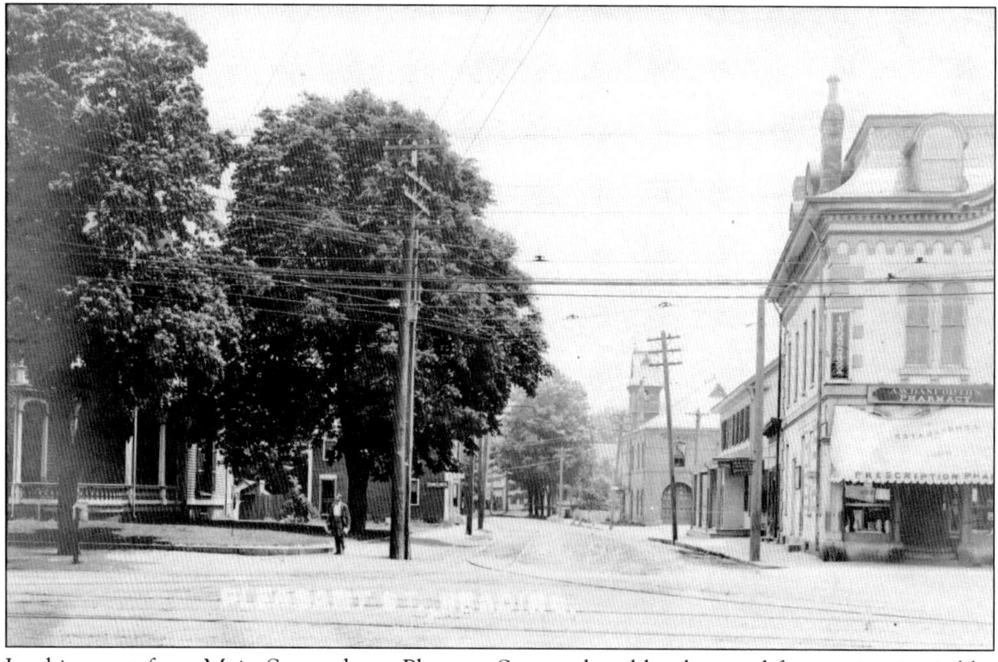

Looking east from Main Street down Pleasant Street, the old police and fire station is visible. On the right corner is A.W. Danforth's Pharmacy on the first floor of the Bank Building, where Latham Law Offices is now located. The building was erected in the early 1860s, but by 1959, the mansard roof was removed due to structural issues.

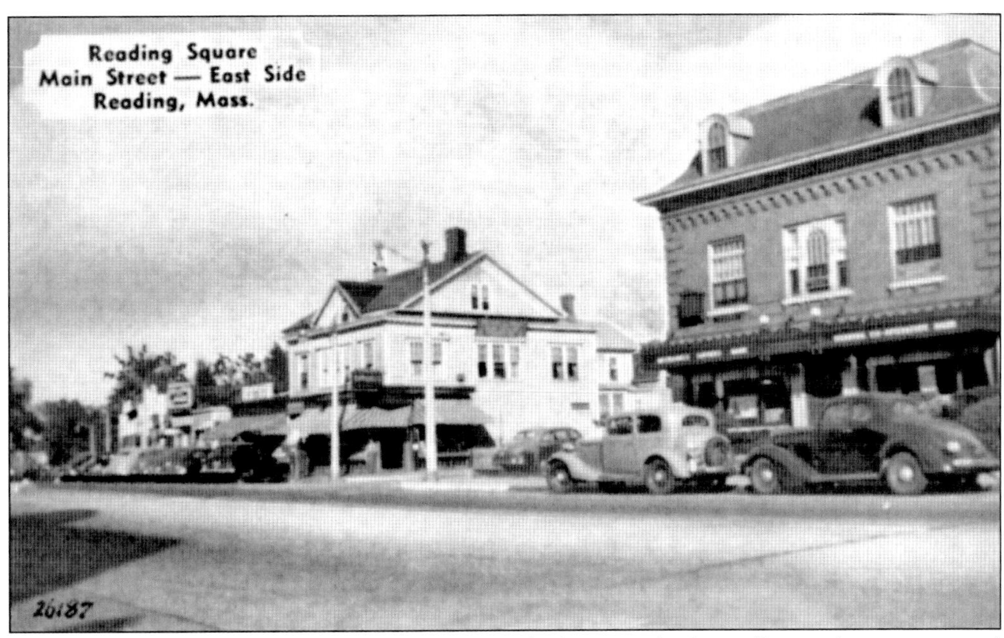

At the intersection of Main and Pleasant Streets, looking north, the trolley tracks are gone, and the electric lines are underground. On the northeast corner, the Harnden house no longer has its belvedere, but A.W. Danforth's Pharmacy was still there. The Mechanics Savings Bank and the Reading Co-Operative Bank can be seen on the southeast corner in the Bank Building, which was home to several banks over the years.

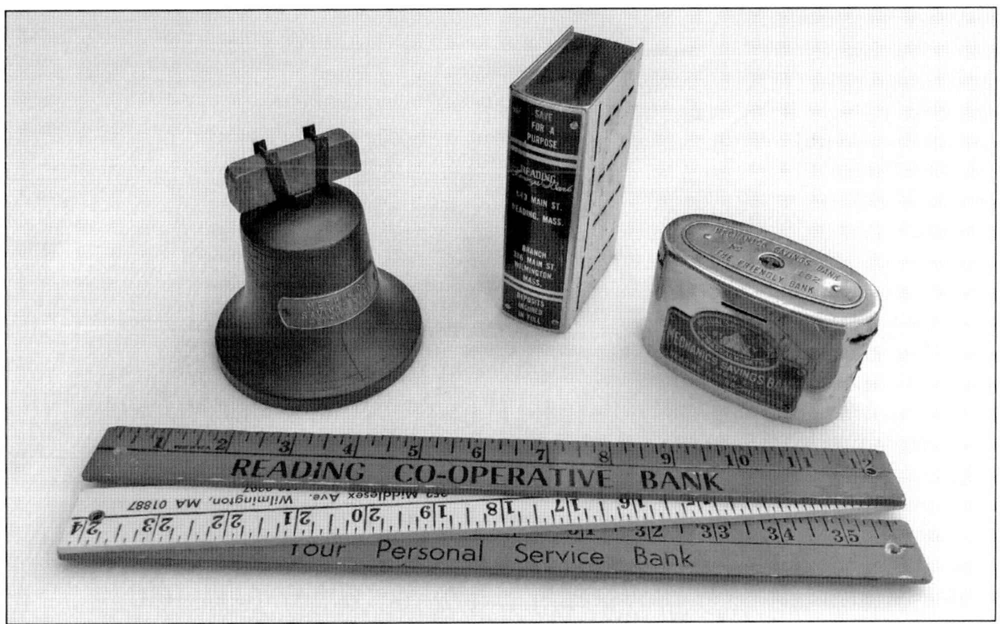

These advertising items are all from Reading banks. The Liberty Bell bank (left) and the oval bank (right) are from the Mechanics Savings Bank, which later became the Reading Savings Bank. The "book" bank shows the new address of the Reading Savings Bank after Reading renumbered its streets in 1937. The folding ruler is from the Reading Co-Operative Bank, which shared space with the Mechanics Bank until it moved to Haven Street in 1957.

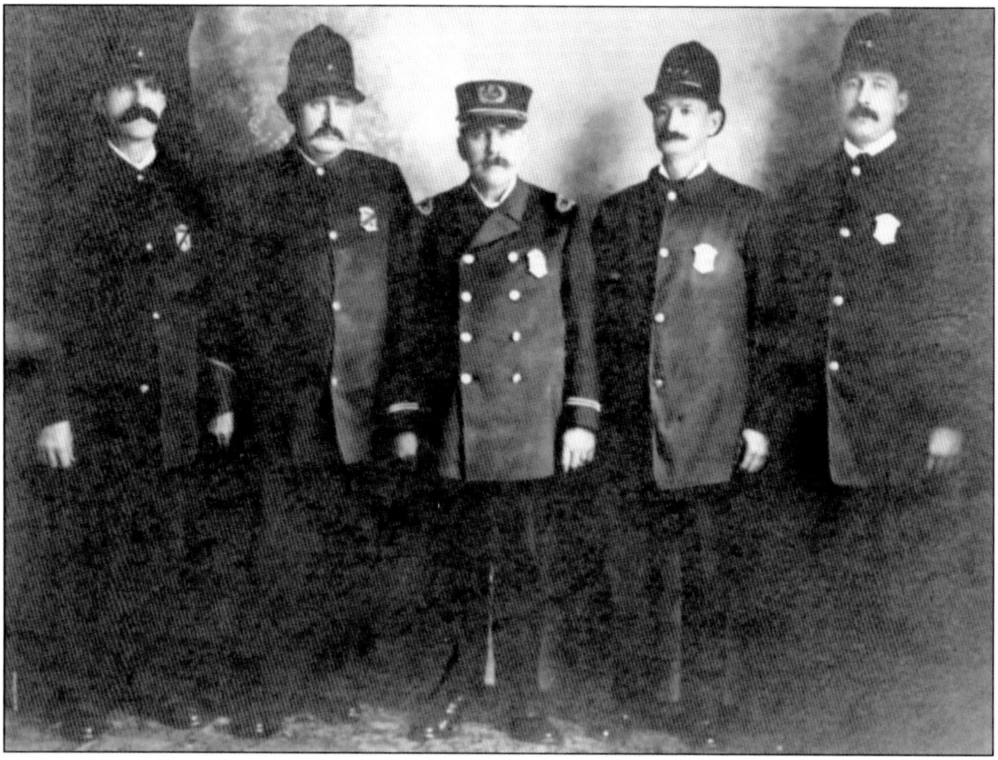

The early-20th-century photograph above shows five of Reading's finest. Future fire chief Hugh L. Eames, at center, is flanked by four police officers, from left to right, unidentified, Jeremiah J. Cullinane, unidentified, and William H. Manning. The badges below represent several different departments. Those in the top row are all from the fire department, and include one for fire alarm box 44, which was at the corner of Salem and Pearl Streets. Reading's first two fire alarm boxes were installed in 1887, and an extension to the system was made the following year. The first alarm from a firebox was from box 44 for a barn fire. The Auxiliary Fire Service (top row, right) was organized in 1941.

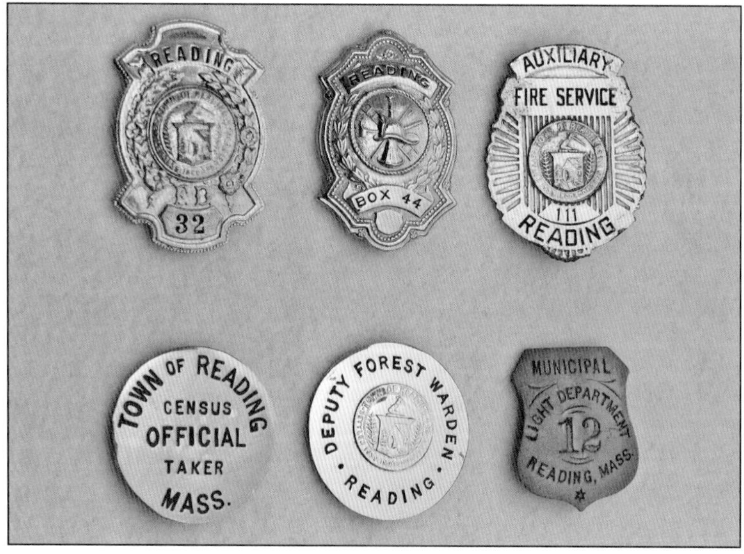

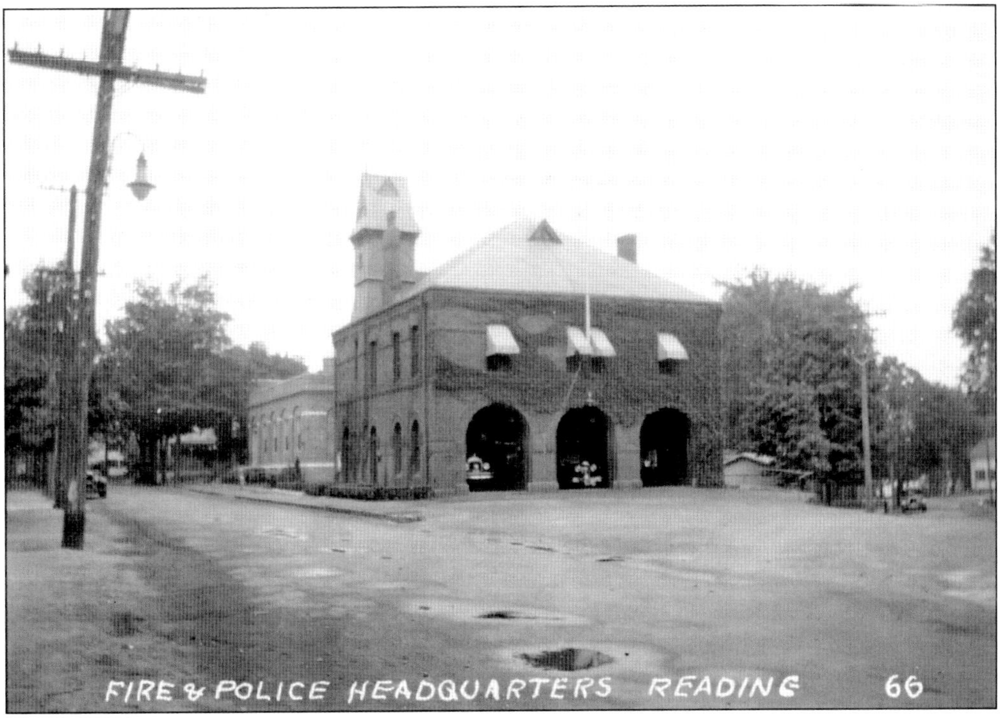

FIRE & POLICE HEADQUARTERS READING 66

The real-photo postcard above is No. 66 in a sequence of cards. The fire headquarters is the older building in the front, built in the 1880s, and the police headquarters is the newer building just beyond, built in the 1930s. A new fire department building was built on Main Street just north of downtown in 1990, and the old building was rehabilitated to become the Senior Citizen Center, now called the Pleasant Street Center. When a new police station opened on Union Street on February 28, 2000, the old police station was torn down. Reading was protected by volunteer firefighters until 1854, when the state approved a fire department in the town. Eagle Engine No. 4 was purchased and manned by a company of 60 men. At right is the announcement for the Sixth Fireman's Military & Civic Ball.

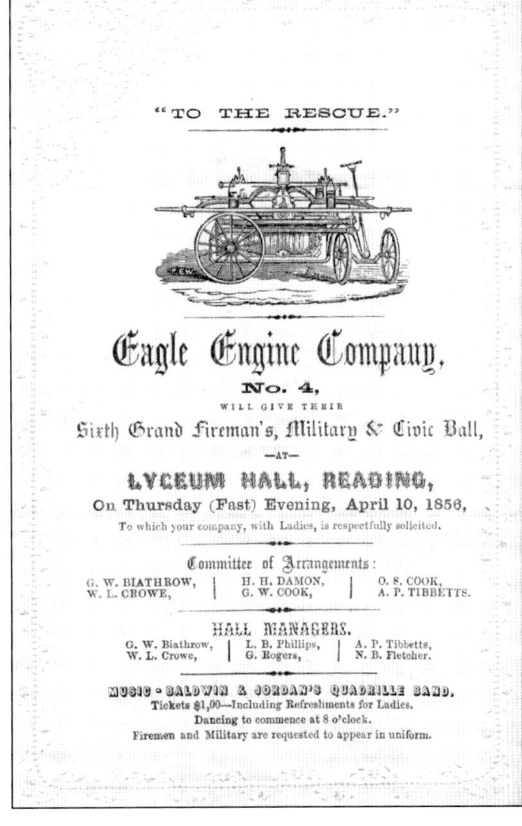

"TO THE RESCUE."

Eagle Engine Company,

No. 4,

WILL GIVE THEIR

Sixth Grand Fireman's, Military & Civic Ball,

—AT—

LYCEUM HALL, READING,

On Thursday (Fast) Evening, April 10, 1856,

To which your company, with Ladies, is respectfully solicited.

Committee of Arrangements:

G. W. BIATHROW,	H. H. DAMON,	O. S. COOK,
W. L. CROWE,	G. W. COOK,	A. P. TIBBETTS.

HALL MANAGERS.

G. W. Biathrow,	L. B. Phillips,	A. P. Tibbetts,
W. L. Crowe,	G. Rogers,	N. B. Fletcher.

MUSIC - BALDWIN & JORDAN'S QUADRILLE BAND.

Tickets $1,00—Including Refreshments for Ladies.

Dancing to commence at 8 o'clock.

Firemen and Military are requested to appear in uniform.

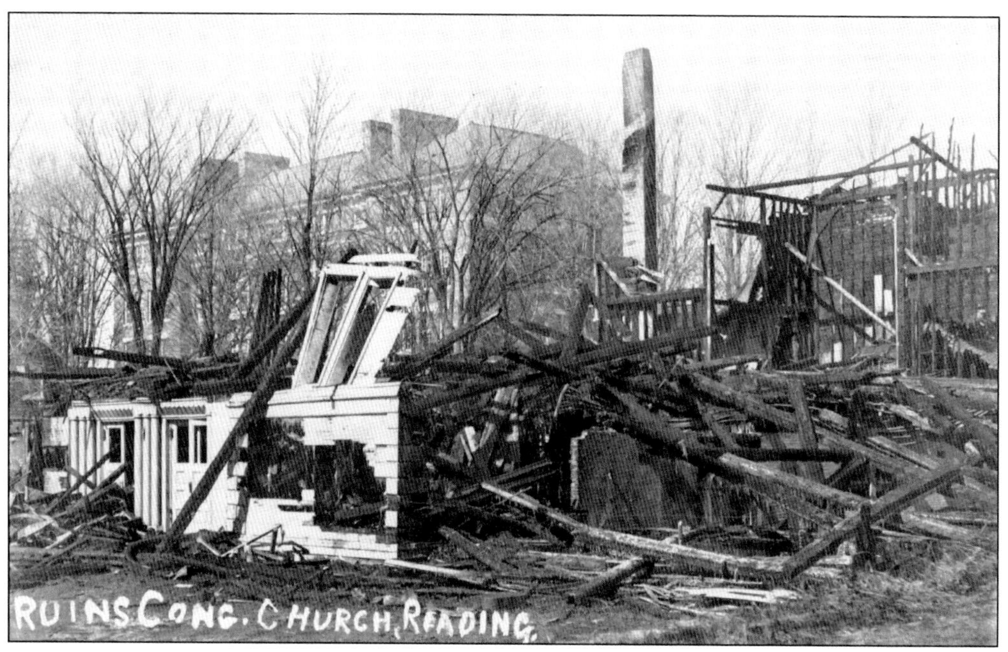

The Congregational Church originally occupied the current location of the Old South United Methodist Church on Salem Street. In 1847, a total of 23 members of the church broke away to form a separate church and built the Bethesda Church at the northeast corner of Woburn and Sanborn Streets. By 1887, the two factions had resolved their differences, decided to join together as one church, remodeled the Bethesda Church in the Gothic Revival style, and sold the church at the head of the common to the Methodists. These real-photo postcards show the ruins of the First Congregational Church after a fire on March 5, 1909. The church was rebuilt into the present stone structure designed by architects Andrews and Parker, and was dedicated in May 1911.

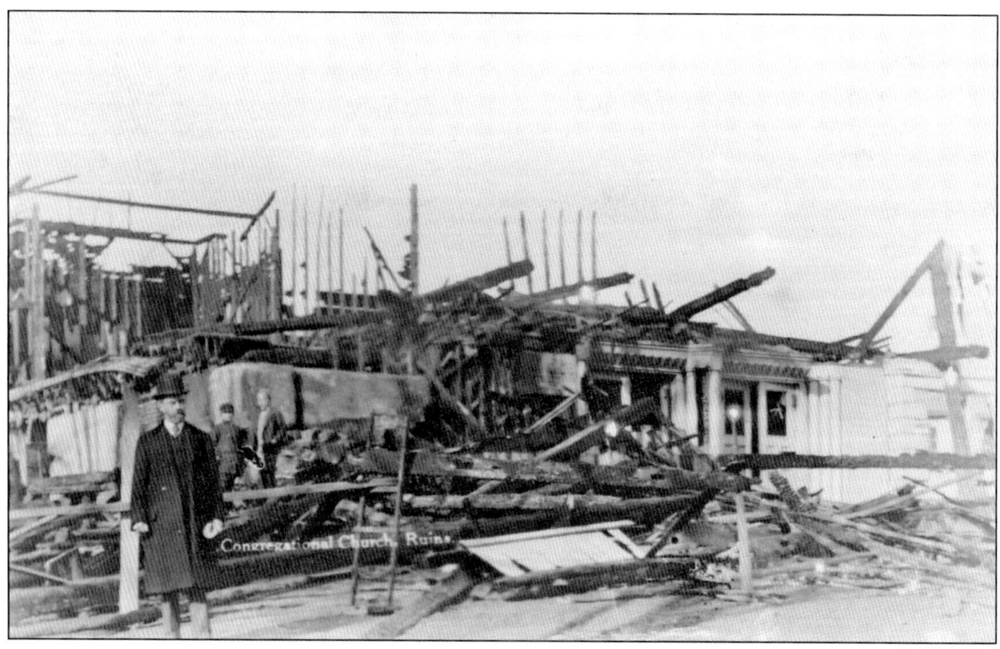

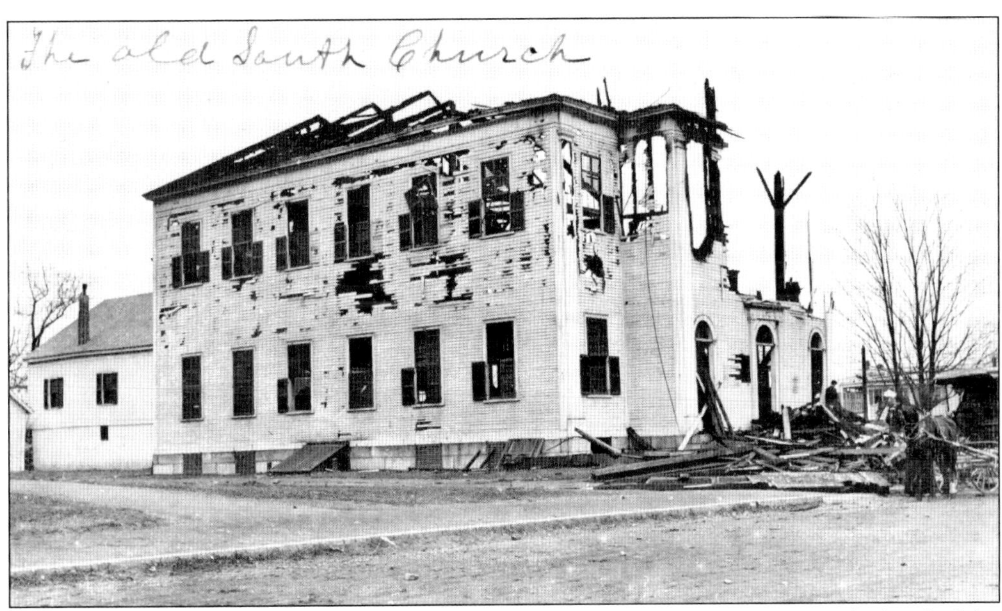

On December 9, 1911, the Old South Methodist Episcopal Church, located at the head of the common on Salem Street, was destroyed by fire. The photograph below shows the interior of the church with the pipe organ. The parishioners decided to rebuild the building to the same specifications as the original using Reading architects Adden and Parker. Townspeople contributed so that the bell tower with its clock could be built as well. One difference between the original and the new bell tower was the color of the clock face. The original had a black face, and the new one has a white illuminated face. The new church was dedicated in April 1913.

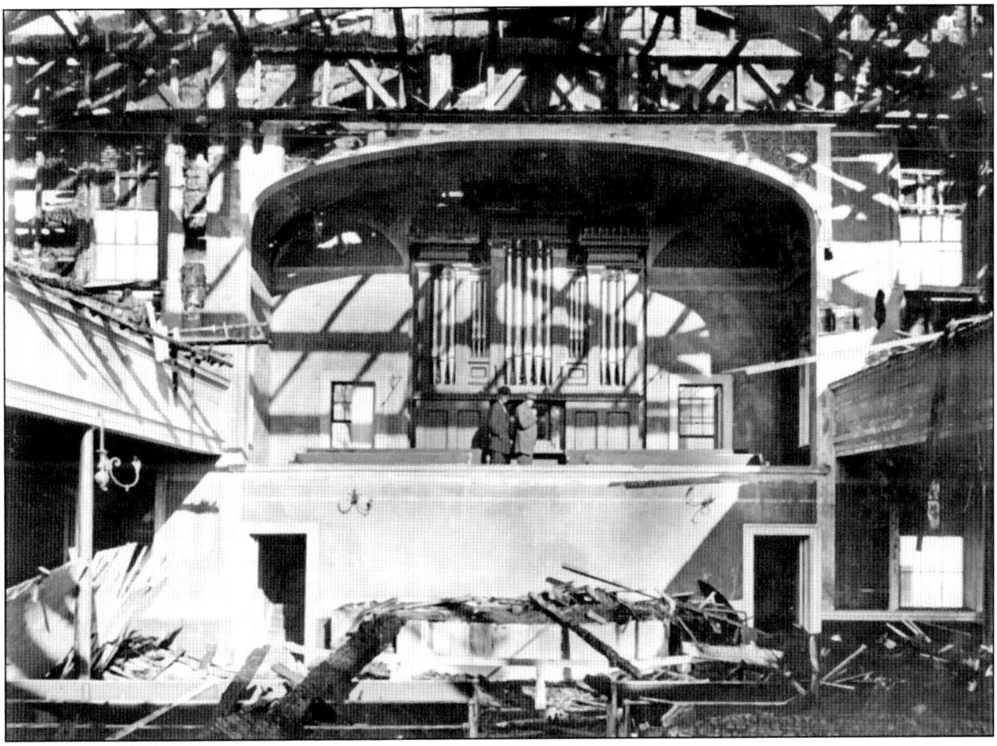

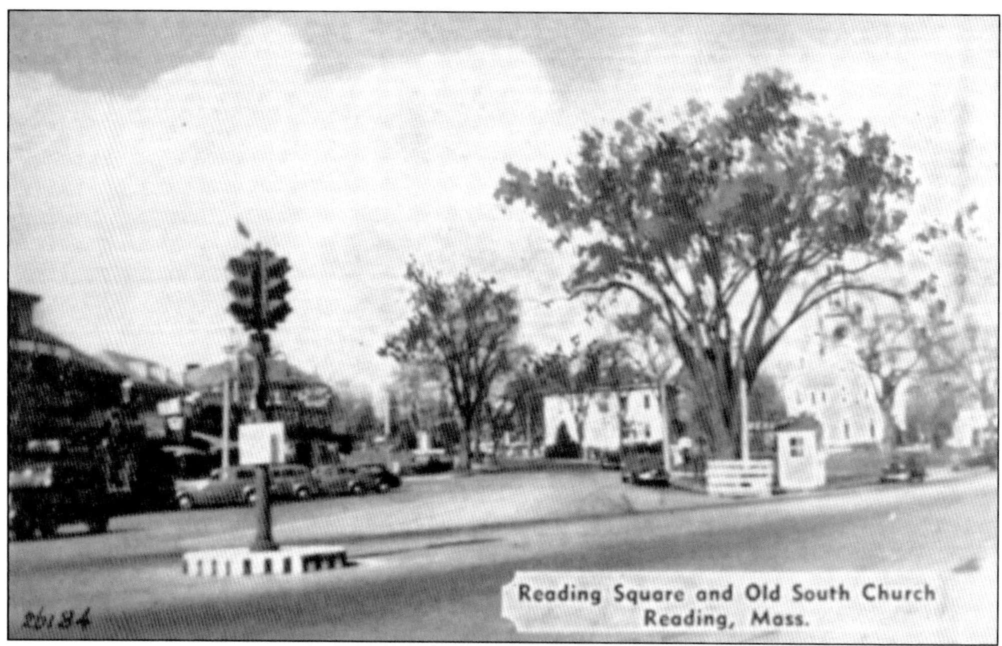

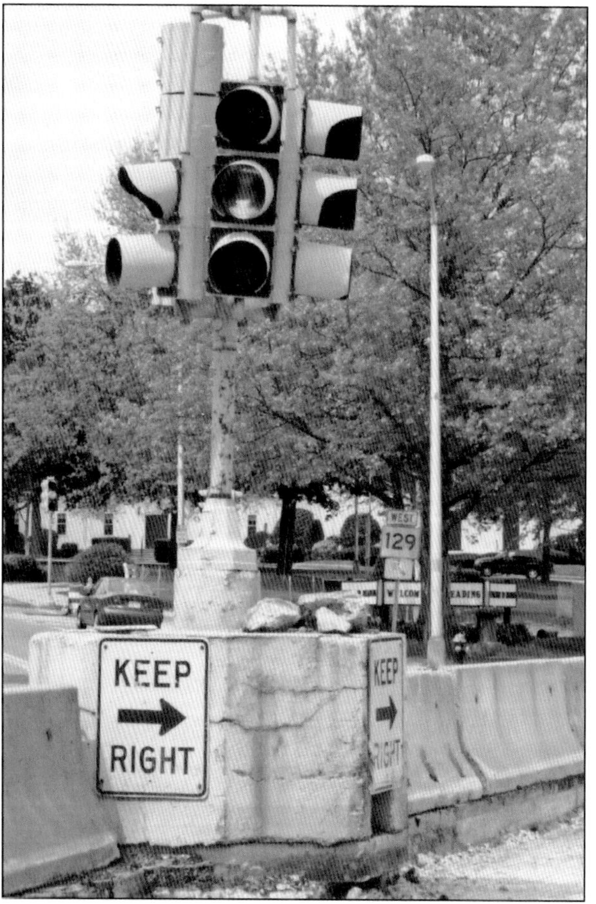

From 1927 until 2008, this light tower with four sets of three lights stood at the four-way intersection of Main (north and south), Lowell, and Pleasant Streets, south of Reading Common. Seen above is the old police officer's booth. Rumor says that the booth was moved in the 1950s to the high school and became the ticket booth at the football field. At left is one of the last days of what was by then known as "the Dummy." It was removed during the revitalization of the downtown. Many shiny fenders were saved or destroyed by varied interpretations of the combination of green, yellow, and red lights.

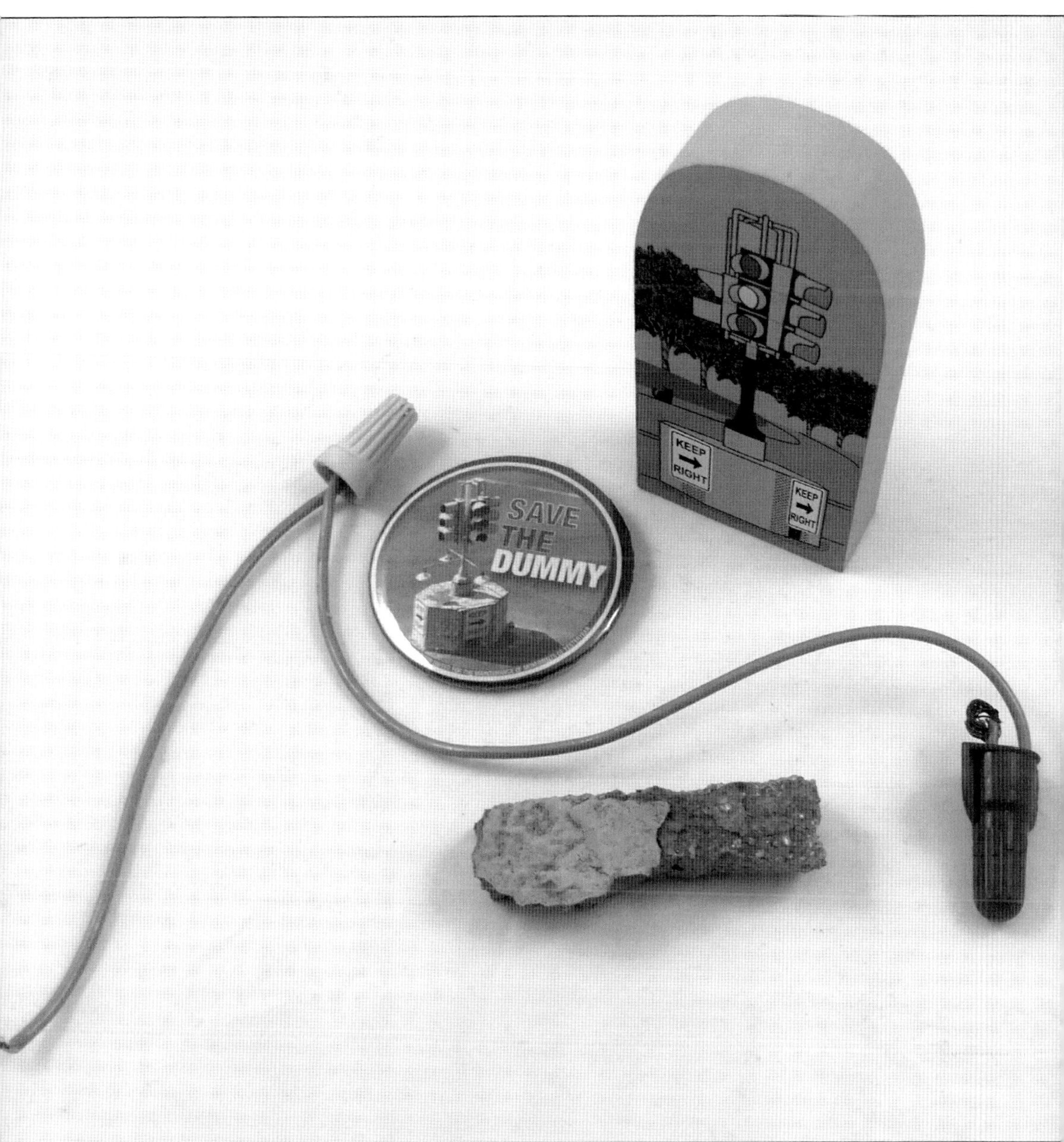

These may be the last surviving memorabilia of the Dummy, including the Cat's Meow keepsake created for the Hitching Post. Ballads were written and a YouTube video told of its history and the efforts to "Save the Dummy." On February 18, 1927, in a *Reading Chronicle* article, there was much discussion of a new tower. It said that not many years before, a three-cornered "Go to the right" sign was sufficient. Next came a sign on an iron post with two lanterns, followed by "Iron Dan," and then "Blinking Tom." The instructions to autoists were, "if it's red, stop; if it's yellow, ditto; but if it's green, step on it." Pedestrians were also instructed that "if you see a red light, stay where you are; if you see a green light, ditto; but if you see a yellow light, make a dash for it." The article also let folks know that the sentry box in front of Candyland would now have a "lever cop" instead of a "traffic cop," and that the new device would cost approximately $1,500. (Courtesy of Cat's Meow.)

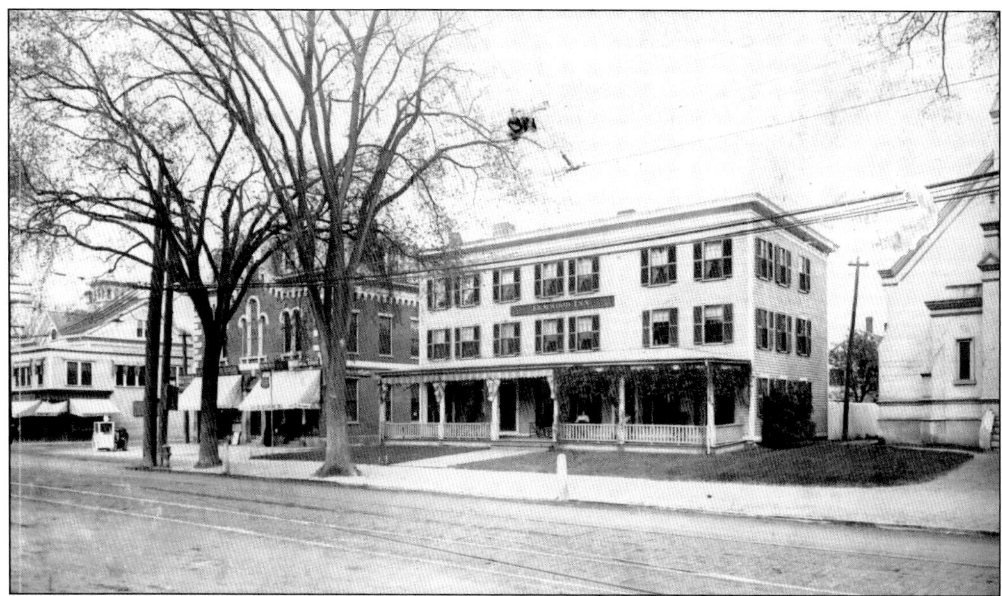

The Elmwood Inn was owned by Freedom R. Blake and opened in the early 1900s. The original building, owned by Edmund Parker in the 1830s, was greatly modified, including adding a third floor. To the right is the Christian Union Church, built in 1870 and torn down in 1920 when the congregation built the Unitarian Church of Reading at the northwest corner of Summer Avenue and Woburn Street. The Elmwood, later known as the Reading Inn, was torn down in 1963 for the construction of the George Washington Apartments. Below, the desk bell from the Elmwood, which measures almost two feet in length, includes a bucolic scene, a photograph of the Inn, pen/pencil holders, and an inkwell. Also included is an advertisement for Wendell Bancroft and Company, which was located along the west side of the railroad tracks just north of Woburn Street.

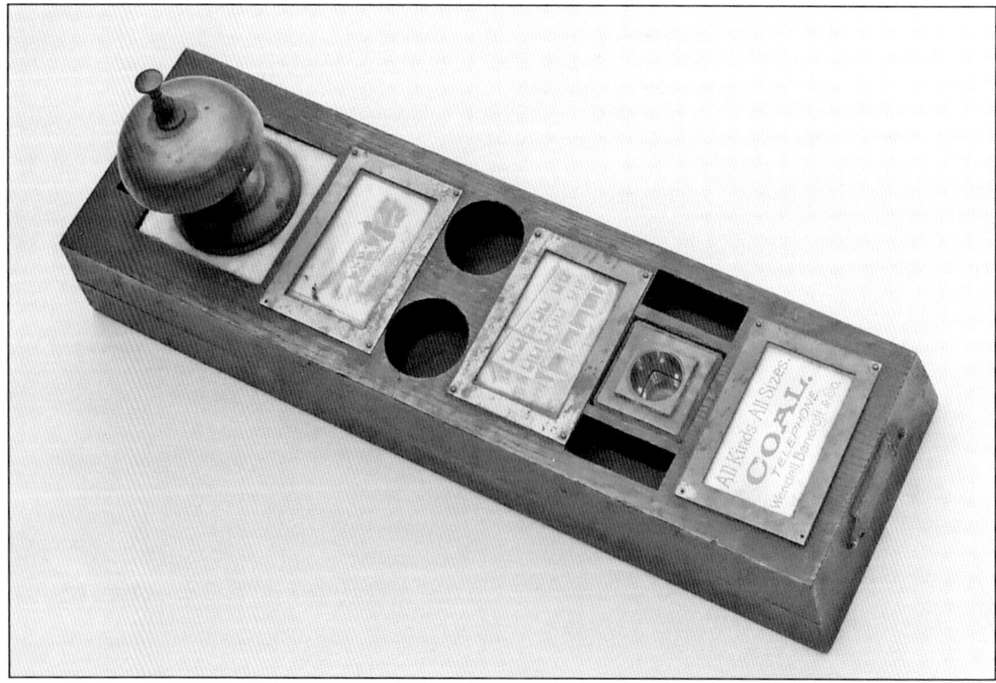

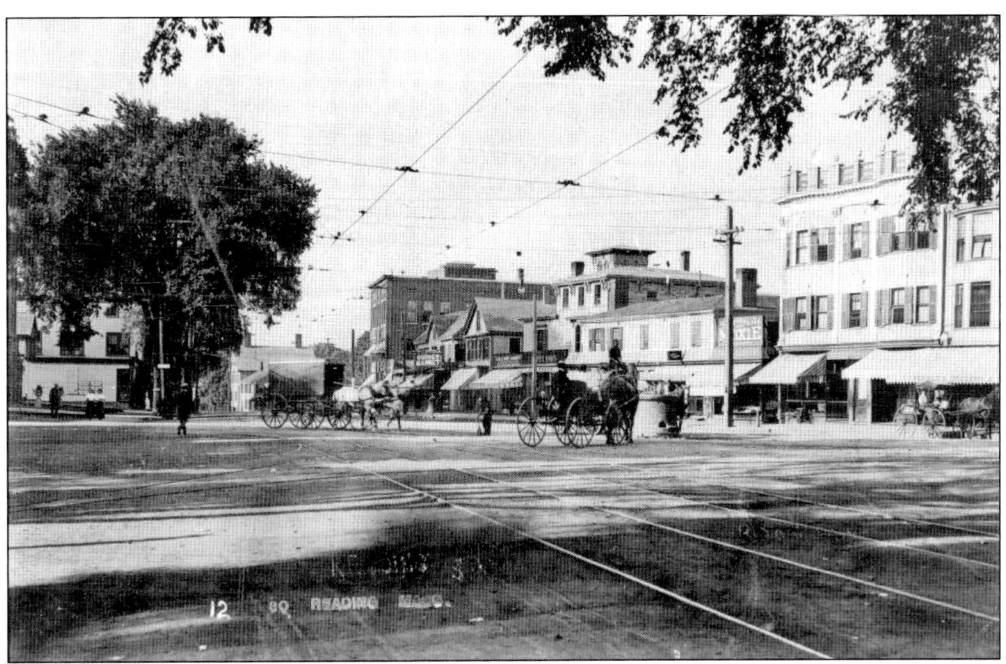

These two photographs show the west side of Main Street. Above, looking south are, from right to left, the Chamberlain and Bacigalupo Blocks, with shops on the first floor and living space above. Stephen Foster's impressive Italianate house and its tower, built in 1857, is surrounded by shops. Farther south are Quincy Market and the M.F. Charles building. The Jonathan Frost building can be seen at the intersection of Main and Ash Streets. Below, looking north, the house on the left was built by Daniel Pratt for his clock-making business. Later, it was the A.S. Nichols millinery shop, and then Quincy Market.

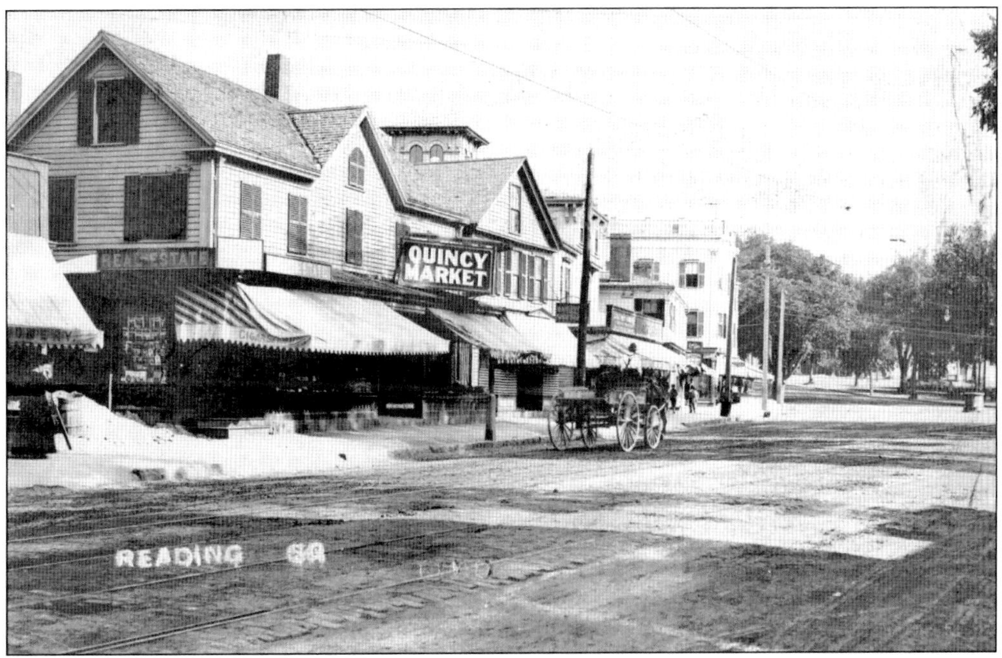

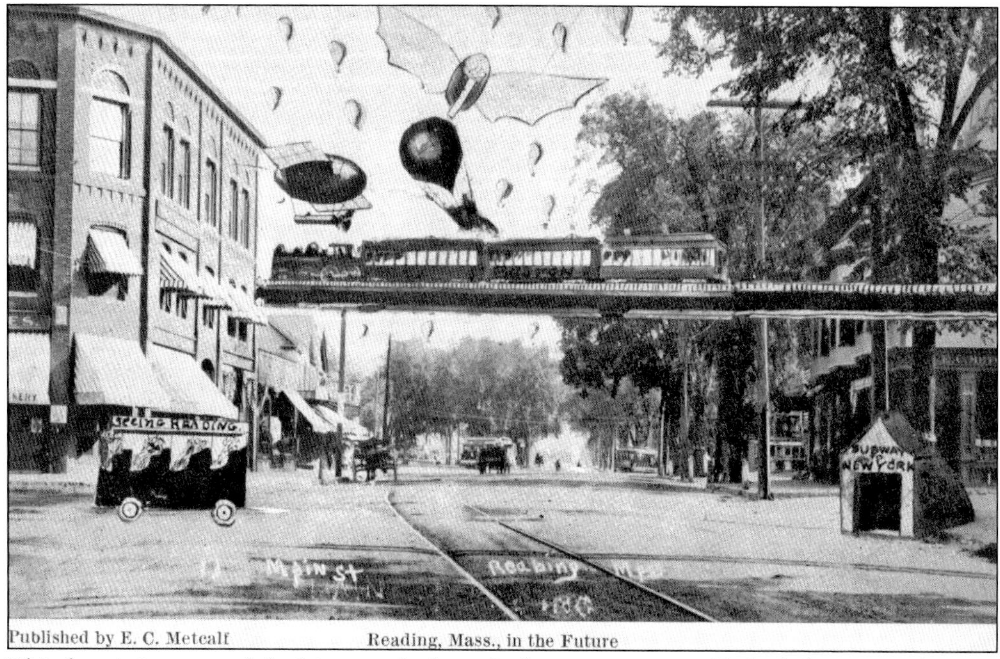

This futuristic postcard, looking north through the square, was published about 1900 by E.C. Metcalf, whose store can be seen on the right at the northeast corner of Haven and Main Streets. Edmund C. Metcalf lived at 36 Highland Street (new No. 38). A careful look identifies all sorts of flying aircraft and even an entrance to the subway to New York.

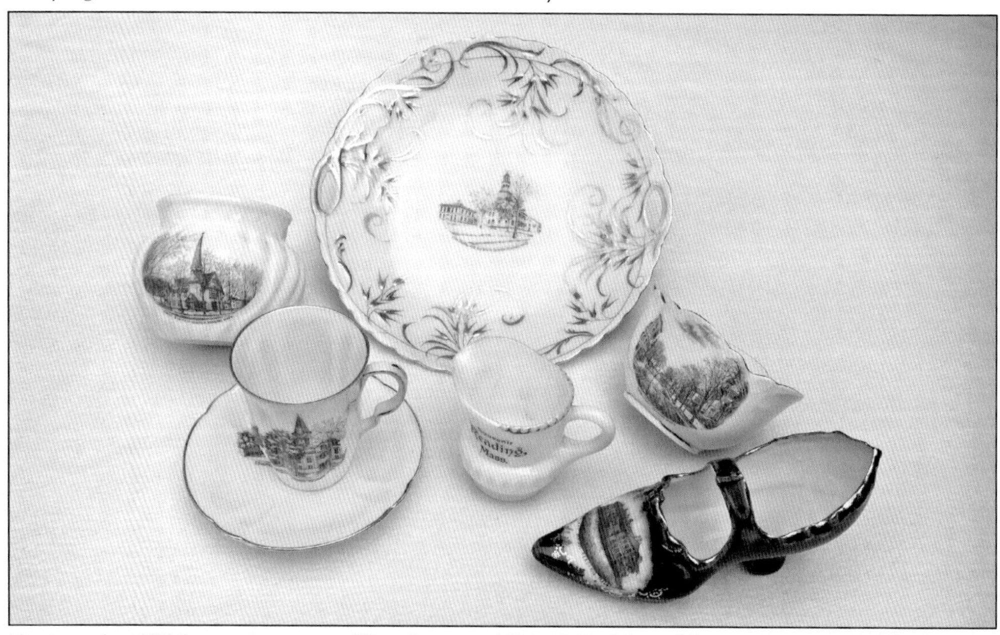

During the 250th anniversary of Reading in 1894, E.C. Metcalf's variety store sold souvenir china made in Germany. A variety of plates, cups and saucers, creamers, and sugar bowls were made with depictions of Reading's churches, buildings, and even a view looking north on Main Street, with Metcalf's store visible. Also shown is a small custard glass pitcher reading, "Souvenir Reading, Mass.," made by the A.H. Heisey Company.

This stereoview, taken before 1875, shows the Lyceum Building, erected in 1854 at the southwest corner of Main and Haven Streets. A small sign reading "Post Office" can be seen on the left end of the building, which gave the area in front of the building the name Post Office Square. Many meetings and social events were held upstairs in Lyceum Hall. The Tambone building is currently located at this site.

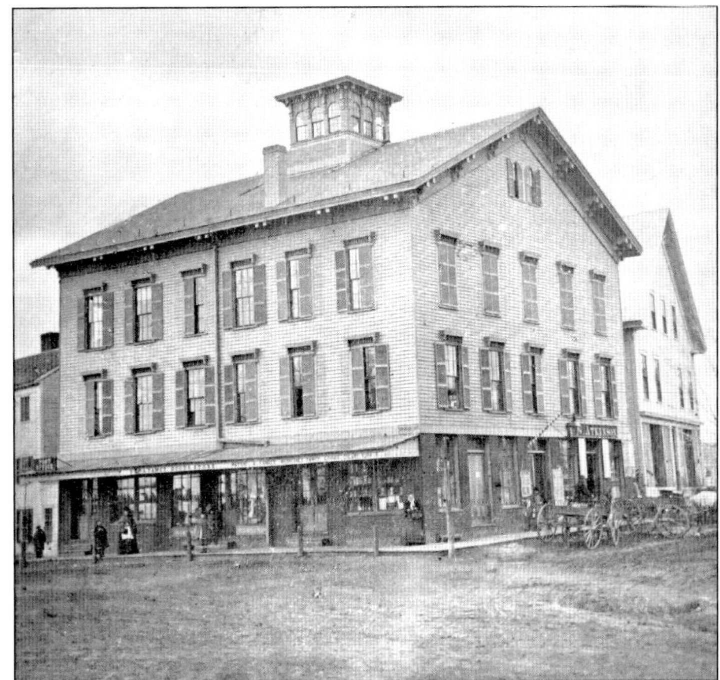

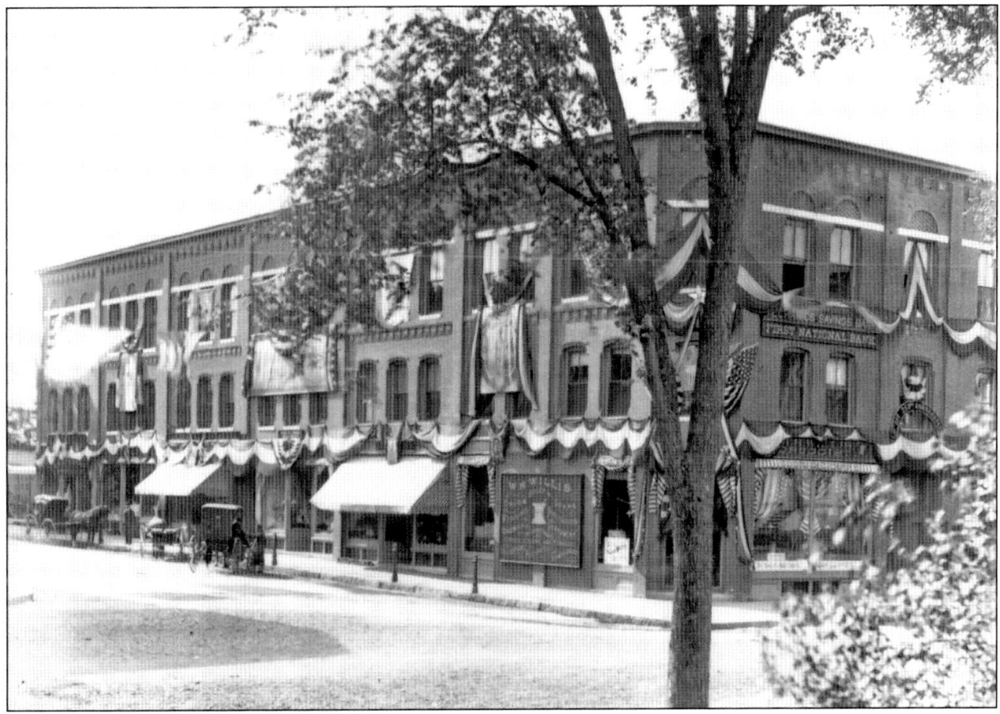

Across Haven Street is the Masonic Block, constructed in 1893 in time for the town's 250th anniversary. W.H. Willis's pharmacy moved across Haven Street to occupy this corner location. The Mechanics Savings Bank and the First National Bank were on the second floor. The Good Samaritan Lodge occupied much of the third floor until it moved in the 1970s, when this building was renamed the M.F. Charles building.

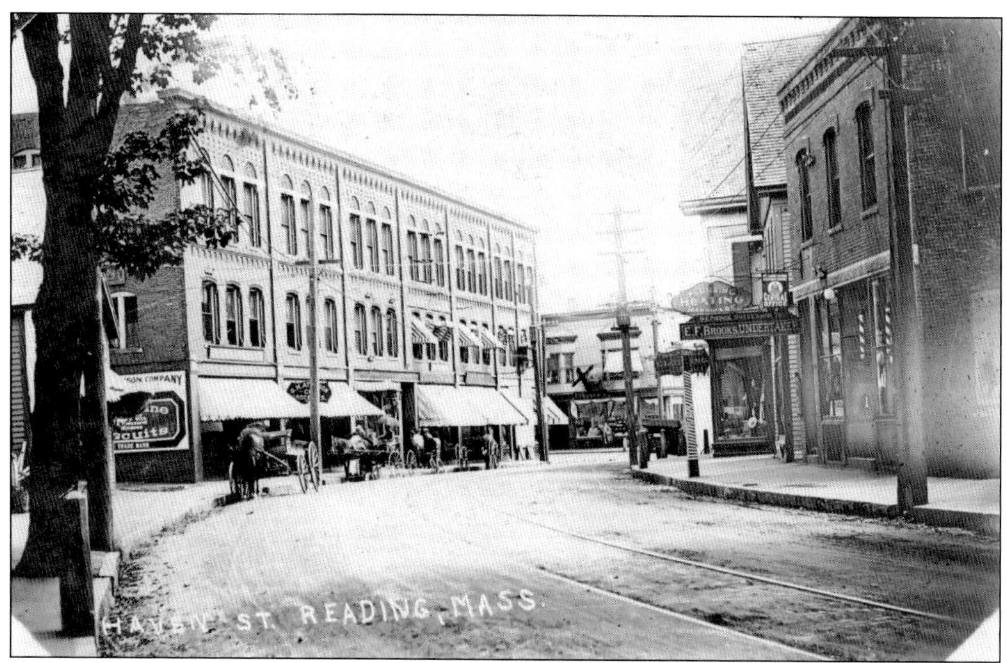

The postcard above, postmarked 1911, looks east up Haven Street toward Main Street. The writer, "ECM," points out a small hand-drawn "x" on the building across Main Street, to point out "our store"—E.C. Metcalf. Coming down Haven Street, the three buildings on the south side are the corner of the Richardson-Gowing building, the Francis Brothers building with its "Plumbing, Heating and Hardware" sign, and the brick building "G.E. Pierce Successor to E.F. Brooks Undertaker." The third building also houses the central office of the telephone company. J.B. Crosby and Company occupies that location today. Across Haven Street, G.H. Atkinson's grocery store has moved from the Lyceum Building into the Masonic Block. The store remained open until 1956. Shown below are a gallon jug and half gallon jug from that store.

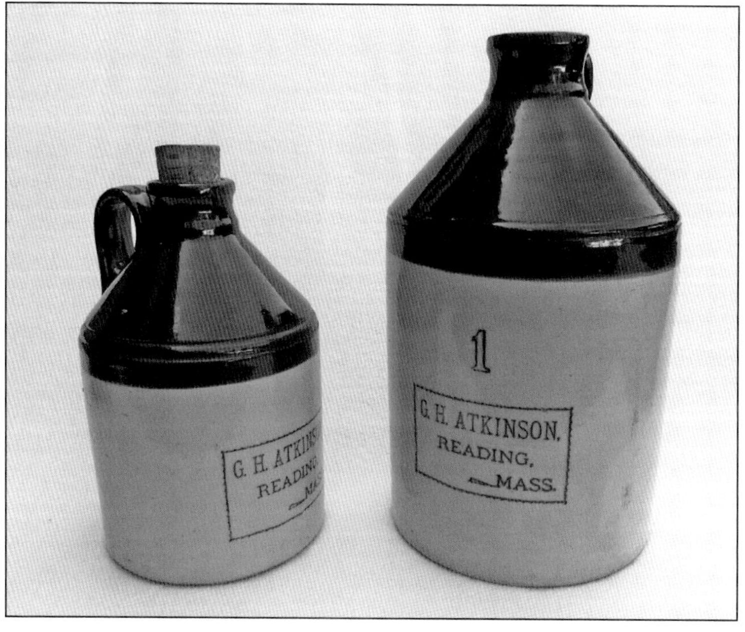

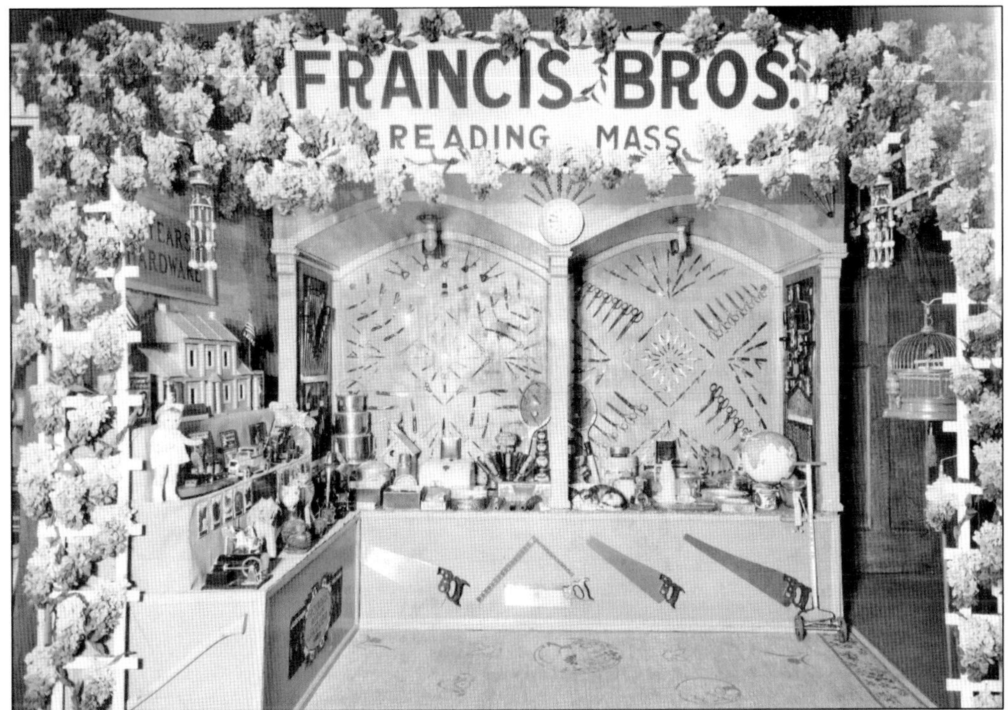

Francis Brothers Hardware on upper Haven Street, in business by 1890, was owned by Albert J. and Richard W. Francis. In 1890, Albert was also listed as president of the Beattie Zinc Works Company in Reading. Carl Sawyer operated Francis Brothers after the deaths of the brothers in 1928 and 1933. This was the store's elaborate exhibit at the Board of Trade Exposition in March 1930.

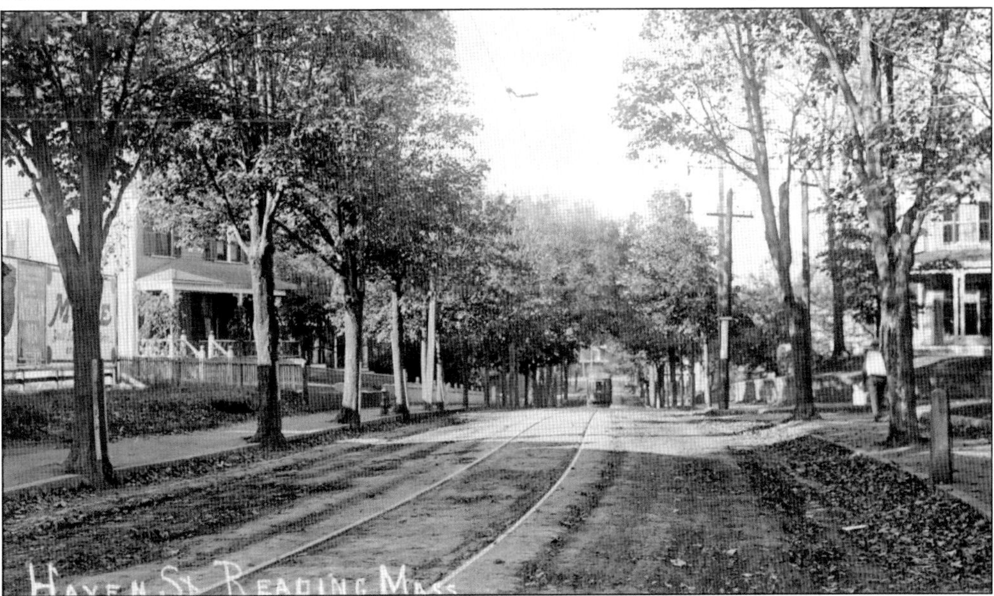

Taken from the top of residential Haven Street, this photograph looks toward the depot. Notice the large Moxie billboard on the left. The Gilman D. Kingman house at right stood at the corner of Sanborn Street. It was moved up Sanborn Street in 1916 for the building of the new post office. In 2017, postal services were moved across the street into the Eastern Bank building.

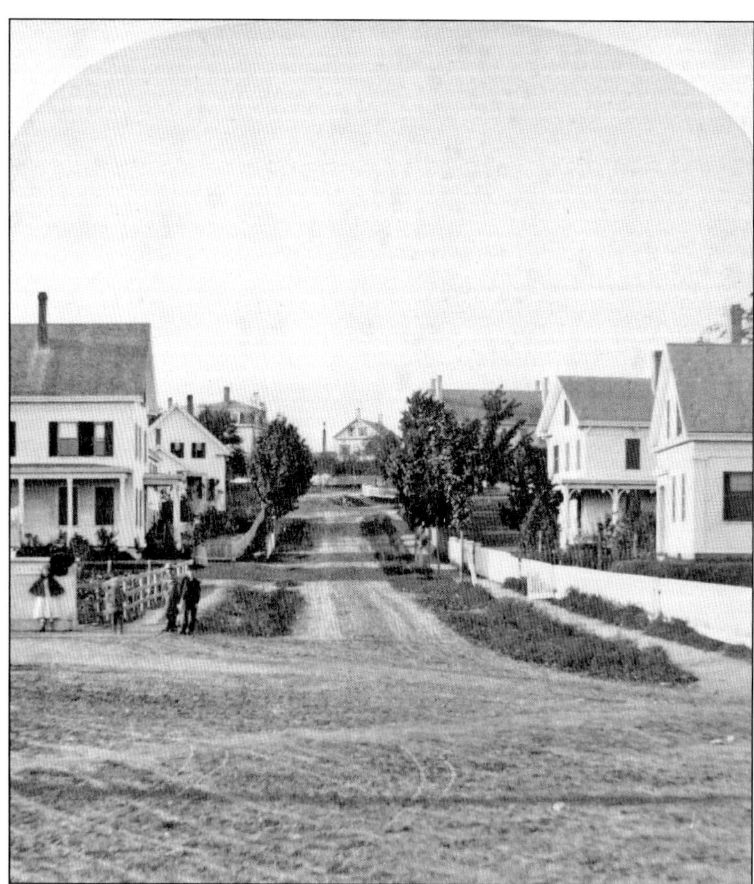

This stereoview from the 1870s, by H.N. Robinson, looks up Chute Street from the intersection with Haven Street. The first house on the left was owned by the Moulton family from 1870 through at least 1916. The third house visible on the same side of the street was the Mansard-roofed home of J.S. Temple at 34 Chute Street (new No. 42). The house at top center is 40 Chute Street (new No. 50).

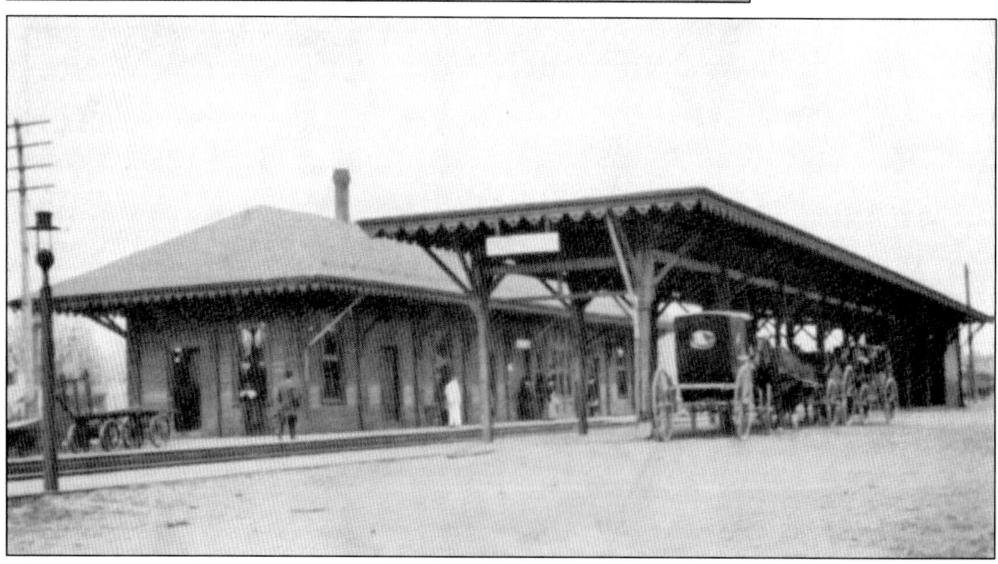

The original Reading Depot was built in 1845 when trains first came to Reading. It sustained damage from a fire in 1868, and the current building was built two years later. Shown here is the carriage and baggage drop-off structure across the tracks from the depot. Note the matching scalloped trim boards on both buildings. At one time, as many as 46 trains passed by daily.

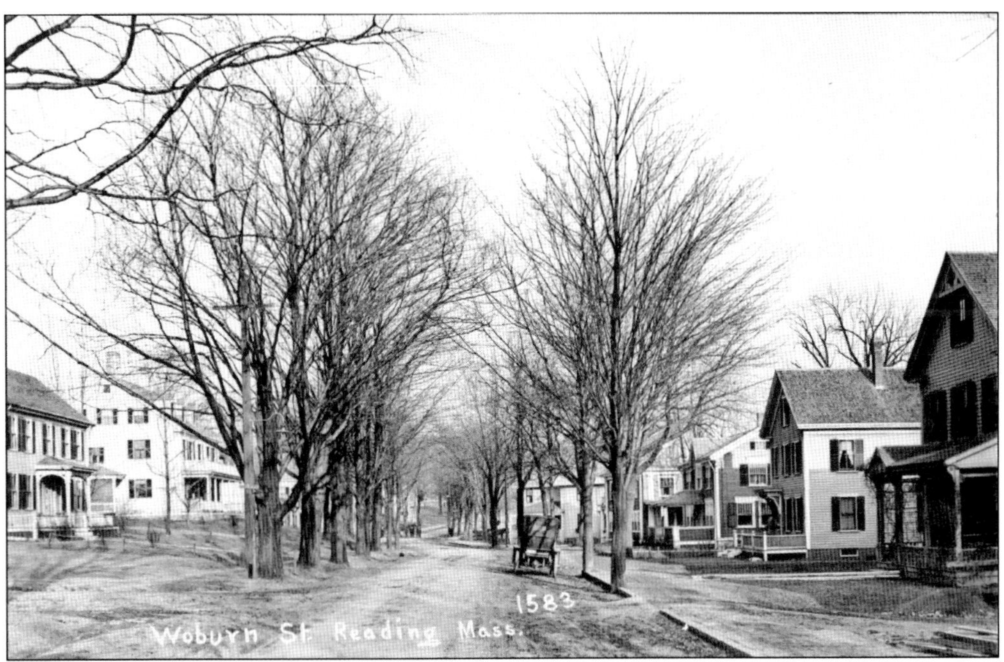

The photographs for these postcards were taken on tree-lined Woburn Street. Postcards were often printed in a series, and the card above, No. 1583, looks east from the intersection with Bancroft Avenue. Amos Potamia, a freed slave, purchased the third house on the right in 1813, now 68 Woburn Street. He lived in Reading until his death in 1858 and is buried at Laurel Hill Cemetery. On the left are 69–71 and 65–67 Woburn Street. In the 1870s and 1880s, Carroll D. Wright lived at 65–67 Woburn Street. He was the first commissioner of the Federal Bureau of Labor, and in 1905 was named the first president of Clark College in Worcester. The card below, No. 1585, again facing east, was taken just west of the future location of Wenda Street.

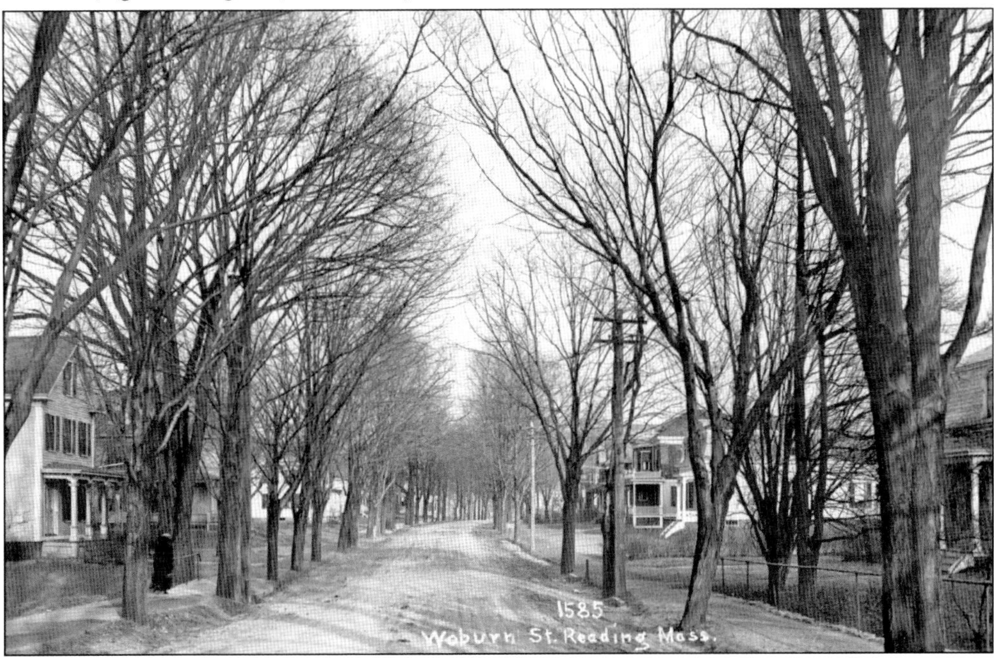

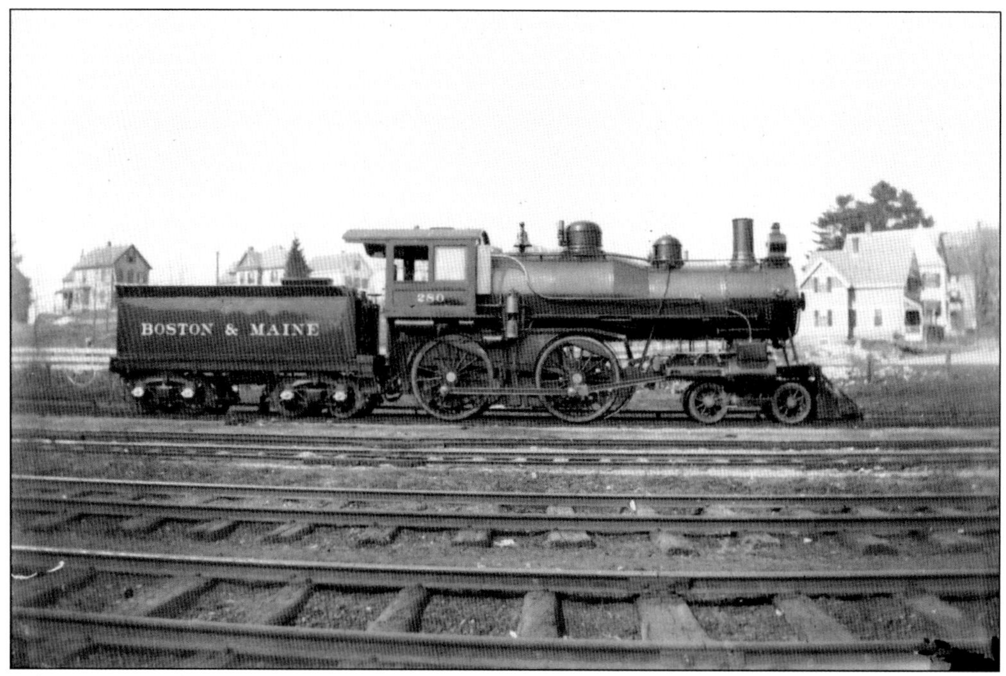

Taken in 1893, this photograph looks east across five sets of railroad tracks. Engine No. 280 of the Boston & Maine Railroad is facing south parallel to Vine Street. To the right of the engine are 127 and 125 Middlesex Avenue, with its distinctive square tower. The houses on the left are, from left to right, 23, 17, and 15 Mineral Street.

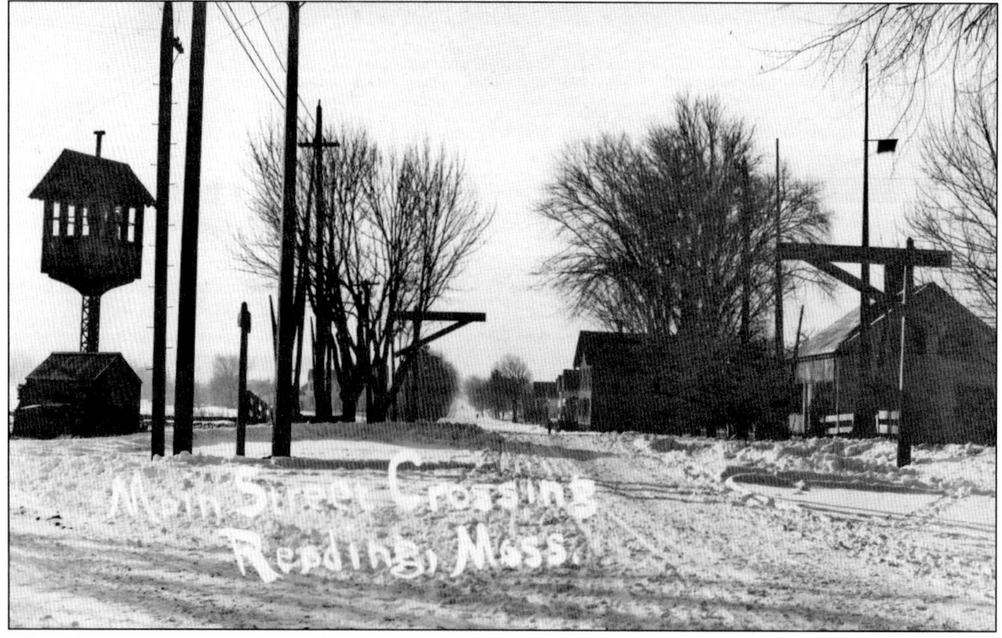

This photograph was taken at the Main and Ash Streets railroad crossing, looking south on Main Street. The roads are snow-covered, but the crossing tower stands guard over the area. The first house on the right was owned by Kirk Sweetser and then the Nichols family. The Simoniz Car Wash is now at that location.

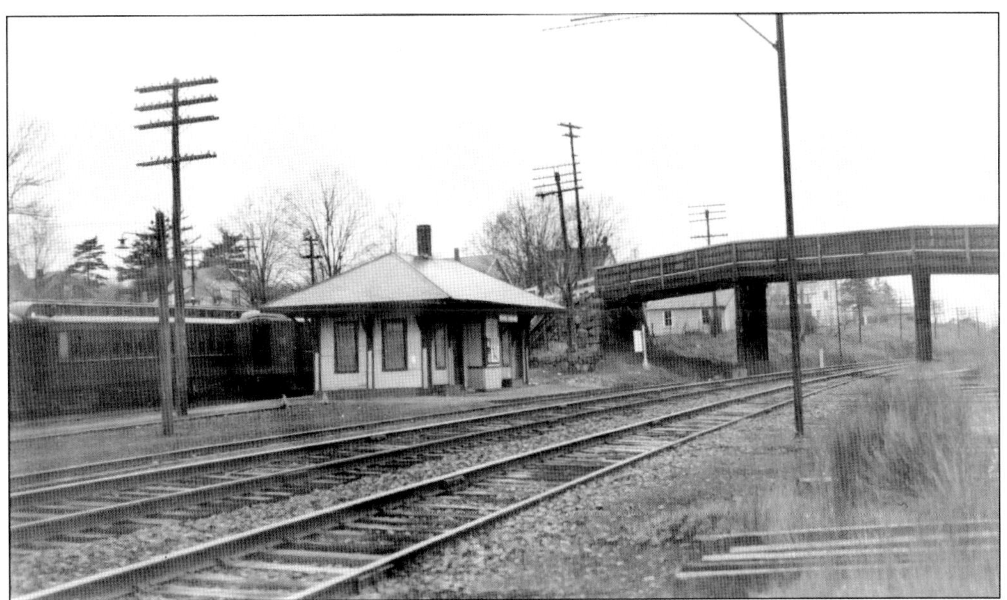

The Highlands Station was built in 1874 next to the tracks near the west end of the Mineral Street Bridge, where Tannerville is located today. The arrival of the railroad to Reading in 1845 meant a housing boom along Summer Avenue and up onto Prospect Hill, as well-to-do businessmen built homes, with the train providing easy access to their Boston businesses.

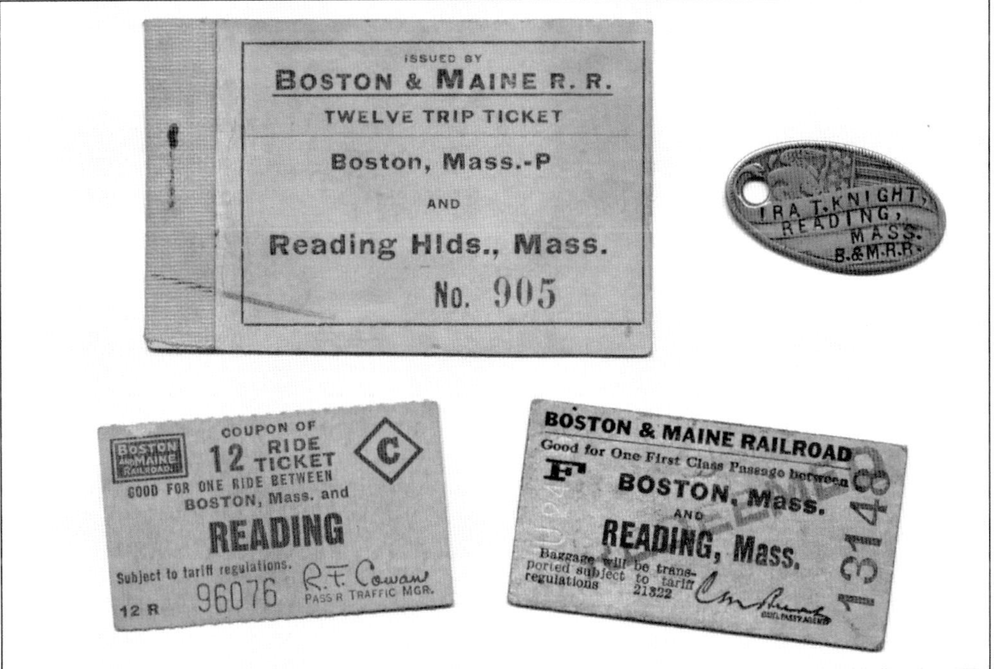

Most of this collection of Boston & Maine Railroad tickets for travel between Boston and Reading have dates stamped on the back. The uncommon Reading Highlands booklet, with two tickets still remaining inside, is dated May 1, 1911, and is stamped with "Union Station, Boston," which was demolished in 1927 for the building of the current North Station. The railroad employee tag at upper right belonged to Ira T. Knight.

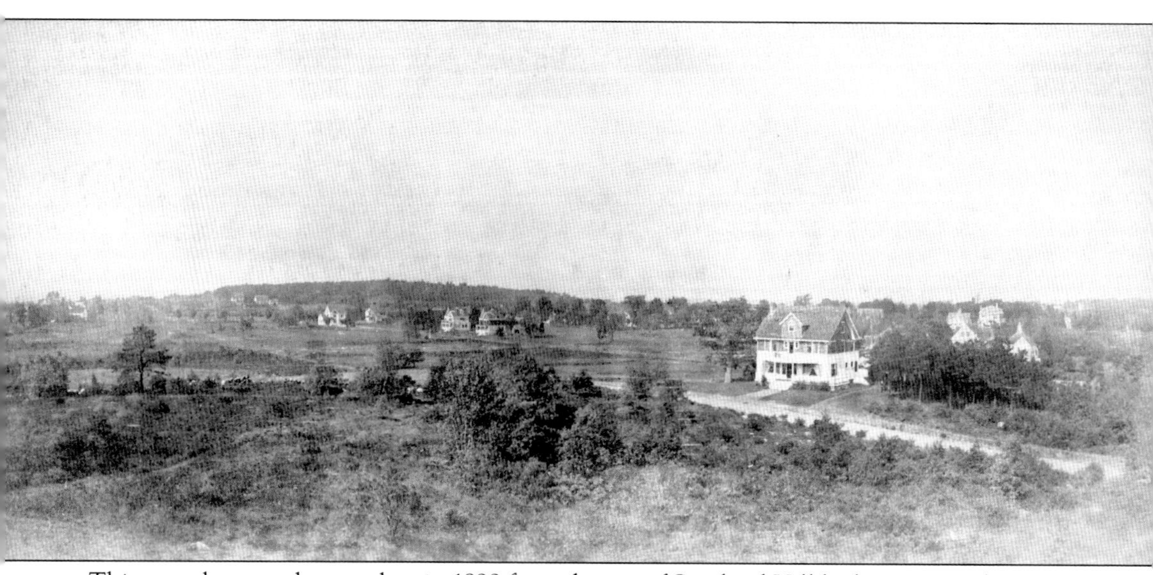

This rare photograph was taken in 1899 from the top of Scotland Hill looking west. The area is largely undeveloped. The large residence at center right is currently 35 Scotland Road. The front roof dormer has since been removed. Moving to the right, the house and barn in the distance is J.B. Lewis Jr.'s home on Woburn Street (see page 32), and slightly to the right is the house and barn, with its unique tower, now 33 Howard Street. Moving to the left from 35 Scotland, four houses on Howard Street are visible. Present-day 73, 77, and 95 Howard Street are on the north side of the street, and 92 Howard Street is on the south side. 168 West Street is blocked from view by 95 Howard Street. Farther to the left and on the hill is the Reuben Weston house on County Road. At that time, the trolley from Reading Square traveled on West Street to take folks to Woburn.

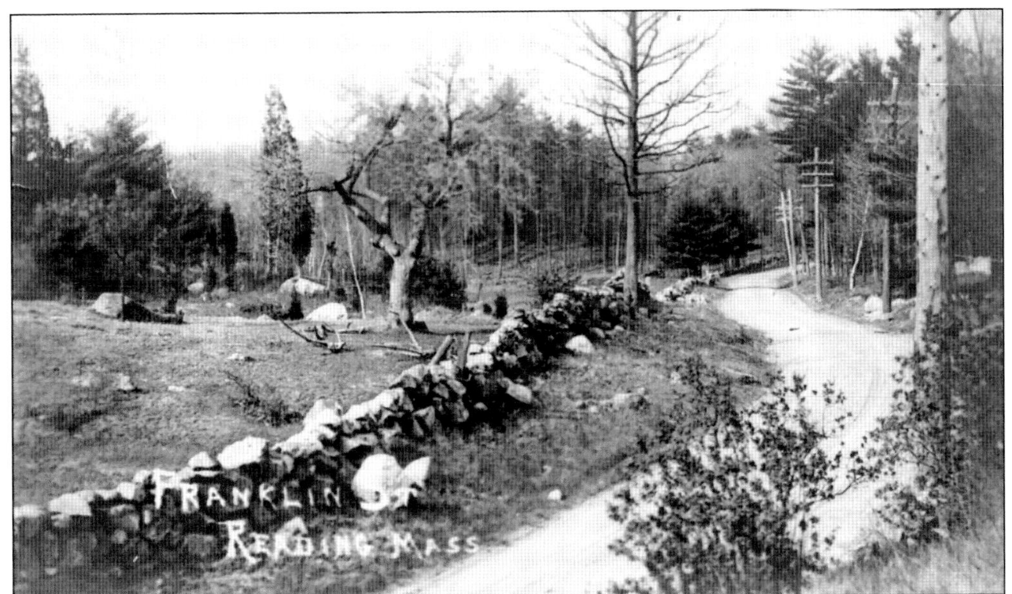

A rural road, yes, but this postcard clearly identifies it as Franklin Street. The date is not known, but the card was postmarked June 1910. The photograph was taken looking east near 315 Franklin Street. C.L. Scott, credited for this picture, may be Cora L. Scott, who was living in Reading in 1910 and gave her occupation as photographer.

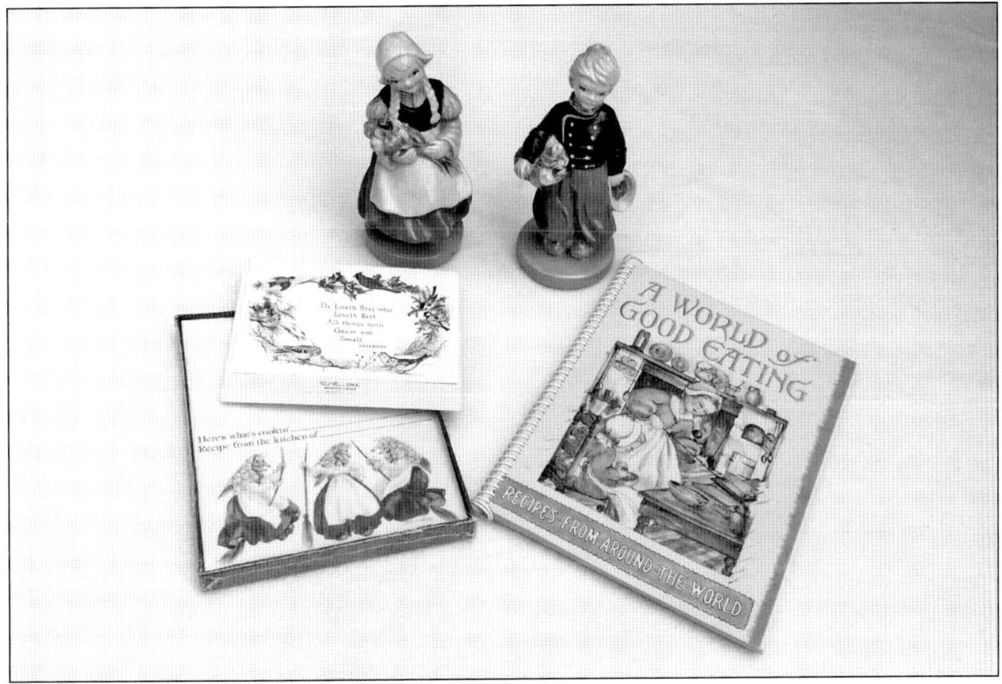

Reading has been home to many artists over the years. Ellen Nelson and her husband, Fred, lived at 420 Franklin Street in a historic half-house. Ellen was a talented artist and sculptor. She founded the Red Farm Studio Card Company in 1947. Her oil paintings and figurines were sold in area shops, and her detailed illustrations were used in cookbooks, coloring books, and on recipe and note cards.

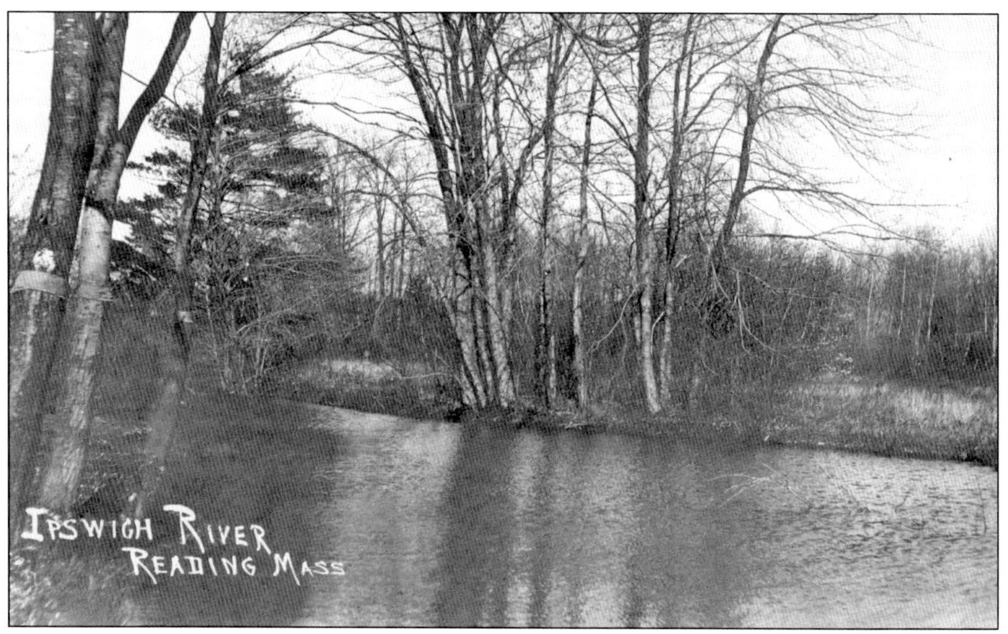

The first land grants that established Reading were given in 1639. In 1651, an additional two-mile grant added land from the Ipswich River north to Andover. When the North Parish separated as North Reading in 1853, the Ipswich River became the boundary between Reading and North Reading. The headwaters for the Saugus and the Aberjona Rivers are also located within Reading's bounds. Shown here are two postcards of different sections of the Ipswich River. On September 30, 1992, a tanker truck overturned, spilling gasoline onto Interstate 93 and causing concerns for the river and Reading's water supply. In more recent years, overuse had affected the water level in the river, but since Reading joined the Massachusetts Water Resource Authority as its water supply, monitoring by the Ipswich River Stream Team has shown that the river has returned to much healthier levels.

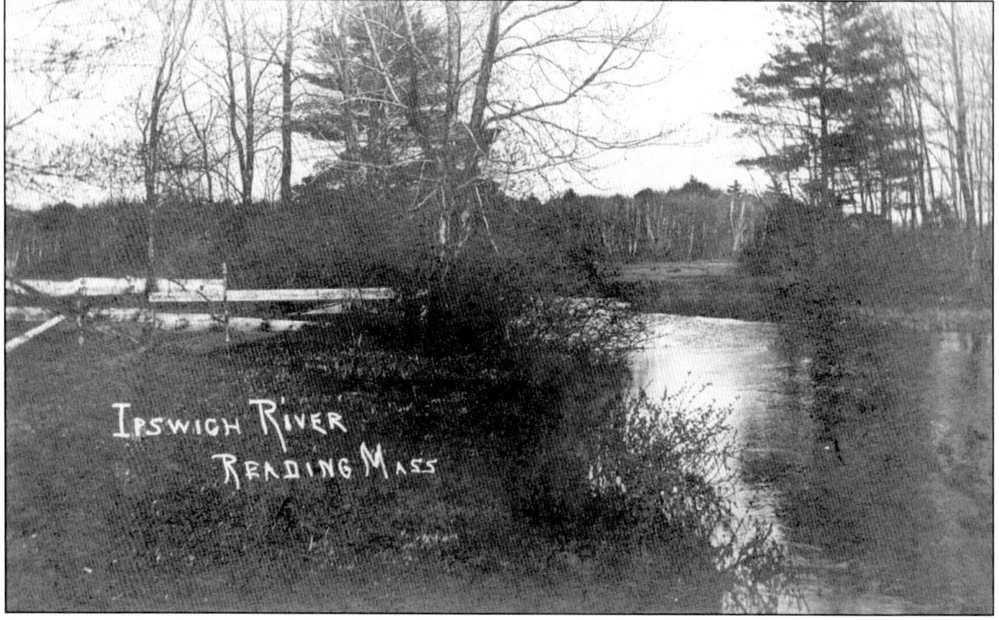

Three

Reading at Work

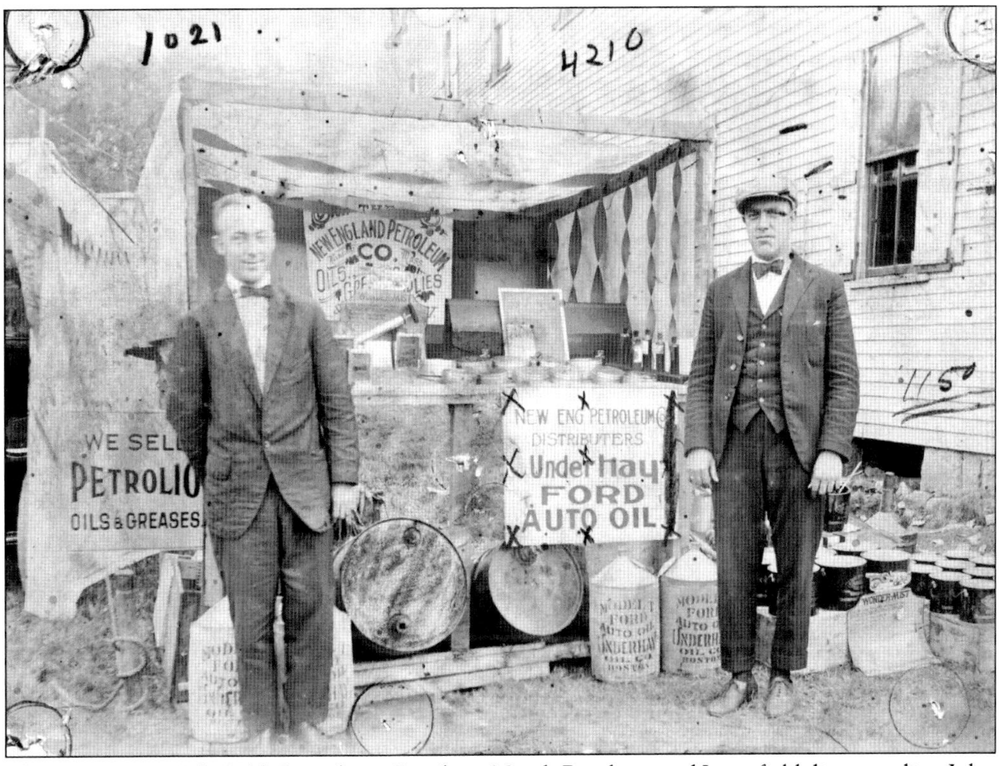

The 1917–1918 Wakefield, Stoneham, Reading, North Reading, and Lynnfield directory lists John A. Loring and Stanley R. Stembridge (right) as owners of the New England Petroleum Company, at 185 Main Street, in the Manning Block. Later, Stanley was the proprietor of a service station at 59 High Street, at the corner of High and Chute Streets, the current location of the Green Tomato in the Bryant building.

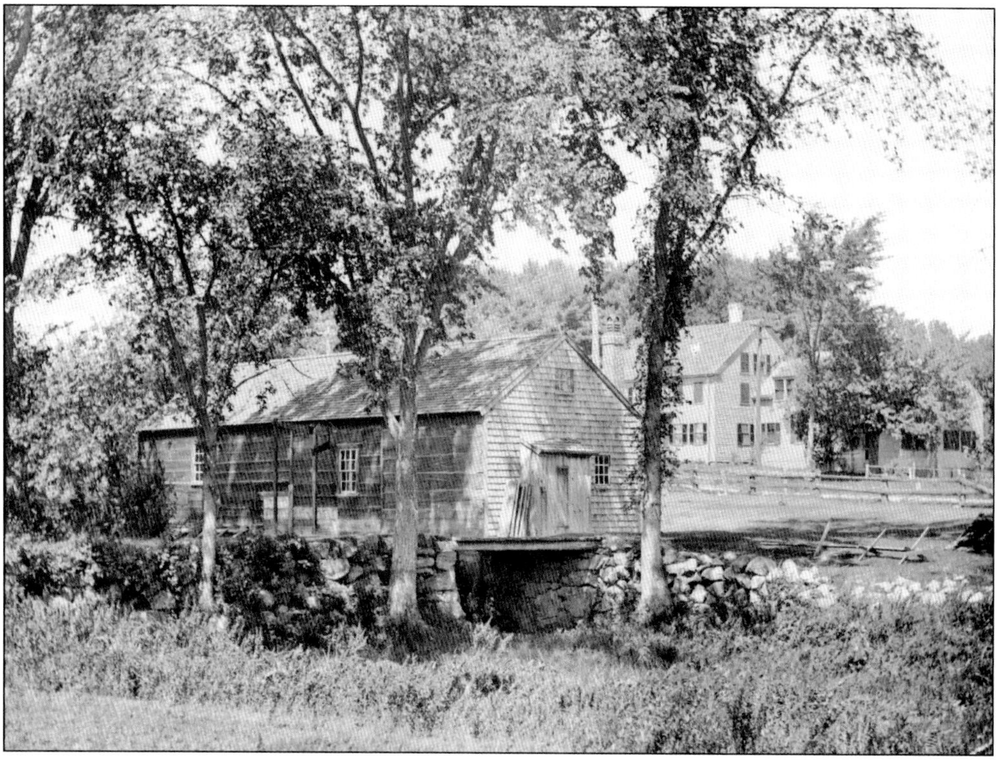

The Slab City Mill was built by Joseph Eaton between 1708 and 1722 and was located on what is now Grove Street, near the intersection with Forest Street. The area was called Pine Playne in early town records. Before development, Birch Meadow was a large flat area surrounded by pine trees with a brook running through it. At one end there was a dam, and the area would be flooded each fall and winter so it could be drained in the spring to turn the wheel at the mill. The view above shows the back of the mill and looks toward the home at 107 Grove Street. The photograph below, taken by Adelbert H. Carter, shows a downstream view of the mill.

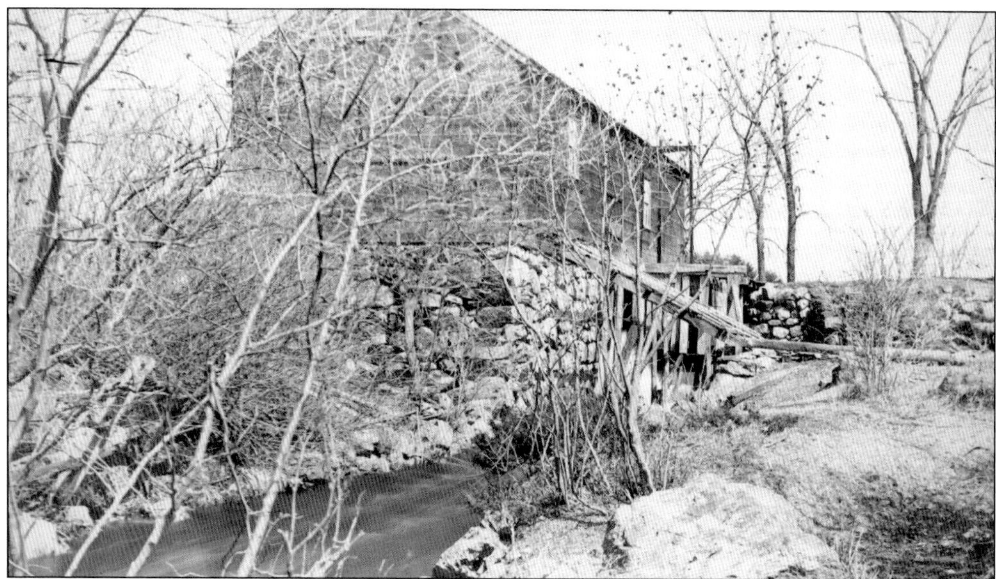

Office, Residence, and Home Grounds of JACOB W. MANNING, Reading, Mass., 60 to 80 rods from two Depots, on Boston & Maine R. R.

Electric cars from Wakefield to Lowell within 15 rods of the office, and directly pass the Nursery, which is 12 miles from Boston and 14 from Lowell.

Jacob Warren Manning moved to Reading in 1854 when he purchased land for his Reading Nursery. At one time, the nursery included all the land from the intersection of Vine and High Streets to Middlesex Avenue, and shipped plants all over the world. The 1875 map of Reading shows the location of Manning's various plantings. The image above is from the back of the Reading Nursery's 1899 advertising brochure and shows details including Manning's large Queen Anne–style home and office at left. At far right, the Highlands Station is visible along the railroad tracks, and on the hills to the west are the houses along Prospect Street. Manning and his son Warren H. did the plantings for the Massachusetts building at the 1893 Chicago World's Fair.

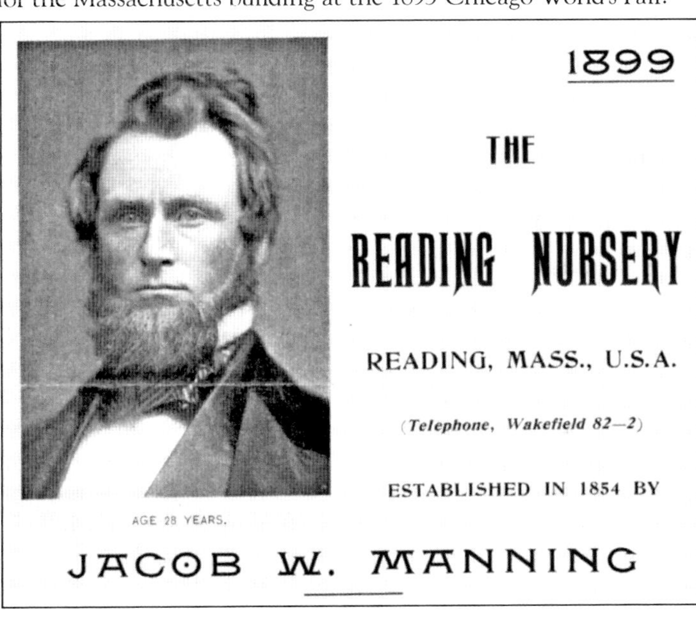

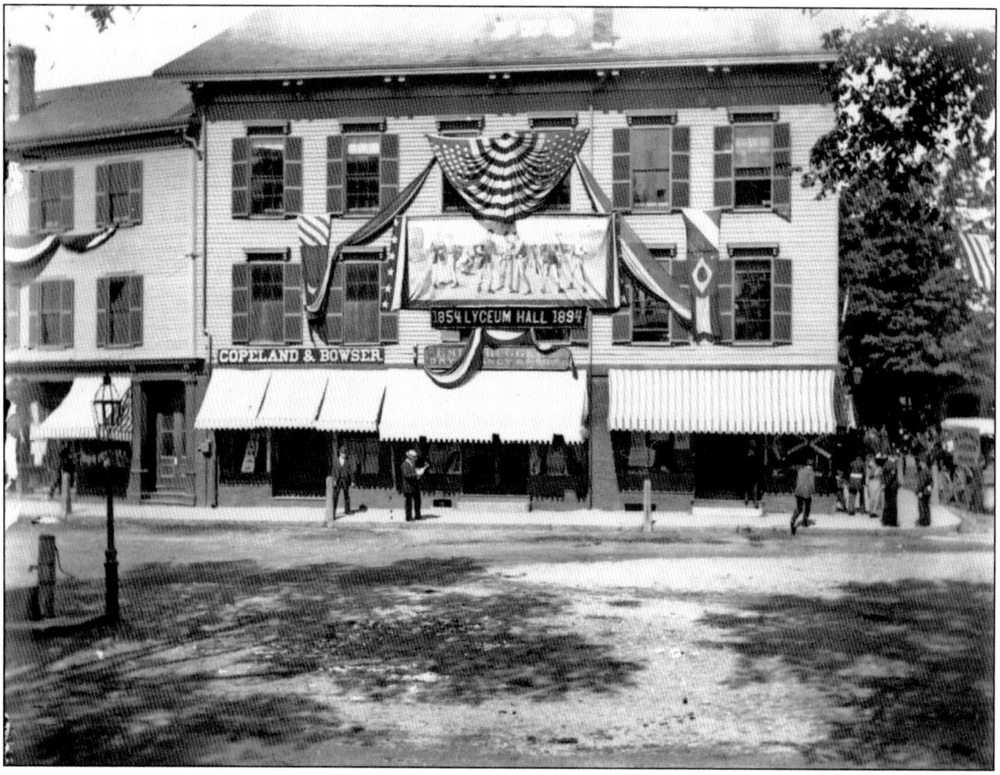

This photograph of the Lyceum Building is from a glass-plate negative. The decorations are for Reading's 250th anniversary, which coincided with the 40th anniversary of the building. The addition to the left was built in 1875. The stores on the first floor included Copeland & Bowser and the Emily Ruggles store.

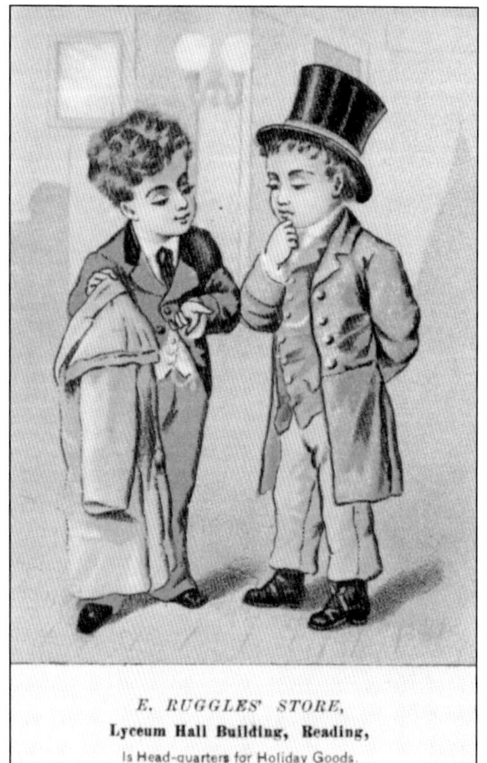

This advertising card is for the E. Ruggles store, which sold dry goods, small wares, ladies' finery, and toys. Emily Ruggles was a real estate developer (see page 25), a leading member of the Christian Union Church, a teacher for one year at the Slab City School, the first woman elected to the school committee (though she declined to serve), and a very committed member of the women's suffrage movement.

This bill, dated January 11, 1817, is for money owed to blacksmith Nathaniel Dinsmoor for services including shoeing oxen and horses, making chain link and hooks, and laying plowshare. Dinsmoor was born in July 1792 in Windham, New Hampshire, moved to Reading, and in April 1817 married Harriet Parker, daughter of Amos and Betsey Parker. It is very likely that the Amos on this biil is Dinsmoor's father-in-law.

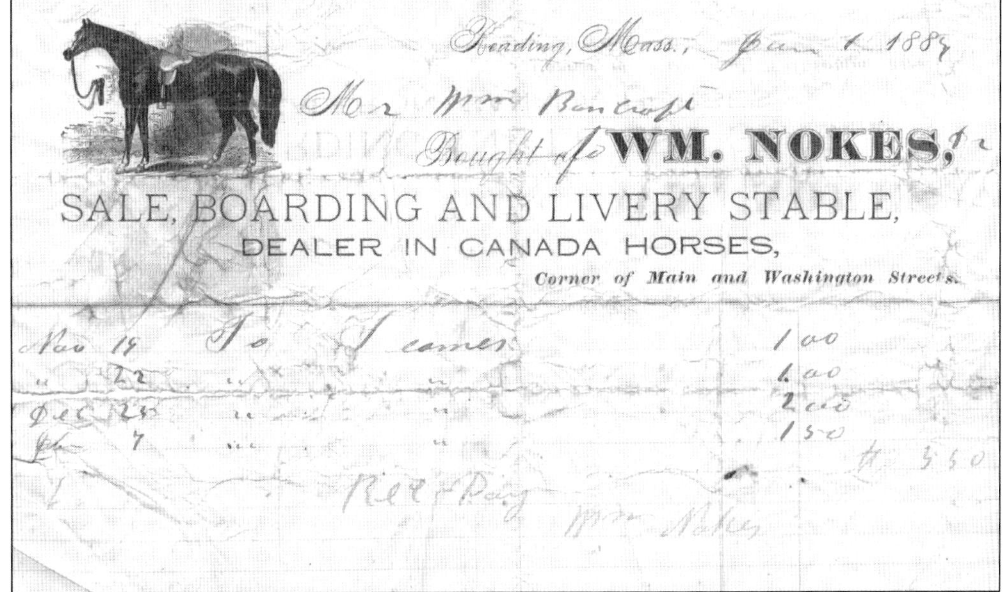

Reading, Mass.,

Mr

Bought of WM. NOKES,

SALE, BOARDING AND LIVERY STABLE,

DEALER IN CANADA HORSES,

Corner of Main and Washington Streets.

The 1870 *List of the Polls and Estates in the Town of Reading* shows Hiram Litchfield owning a barn, four horses, and five carriages on Main Street; the 1875 map shows the location as the northwest corner of Main and Washington Streets. By 1880, William Nokes owned the livery stable at that location. Jimbo's Roast Beef and Dunkin' Donuts are currently located there.

Reading, Mass., 188

BOUGHT OF E. M. RICHARDSON,

MANUFACTURER OF

Infants' Fancy Colored Boots and Shoes.

FACTORY, WOBURN STREET.

Everett B. Richardson was a well-known shoemaker in Reading and had a factory on Woburn Street. In 1886, he built a large factory on Berkeley Street and greatly expanded it shortly after. This receipt is a mystery, because it reads "E.M. Richardson." According to the 1880 census, Emma M. Richardson was Everett's wife—could this be the answer?

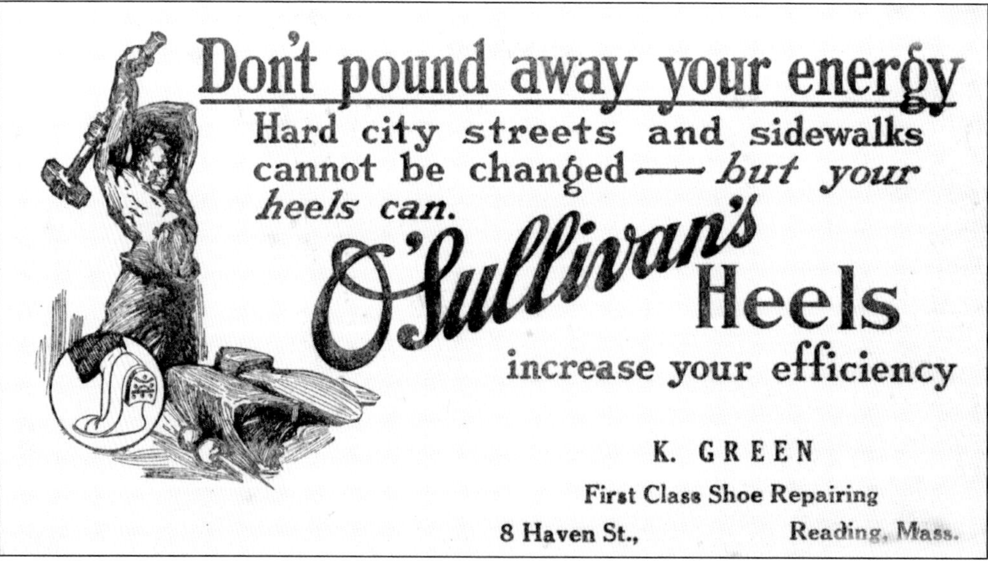

This advertising card is for O'Sullivan's shoe repair, which was located on the north side of lower Haven Street, near the depot. Several businesses in Reading manufactured shoes, especially women's and children's shoes, which were shipped worldwide. But even after the decline of the industry, shoe repair was still carried on by several local cobblers.

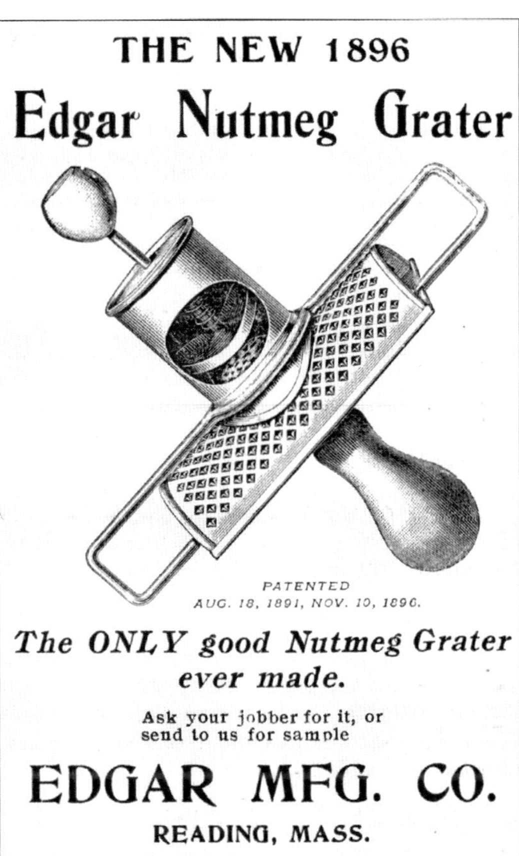

George H. Thomas of Chicopee, Massachusetts, invented a mechanical nutmeg grater and received a patent on August 18, 1891. He died less than four months later. The Edgar Nutmeg Manufacturing Company was organized in early 1892 by Charles, Albert, and Arthur Damon, who were already well known for their involvement in the necktie business in Reading. The Edgar Nutmeg Manufacturing Company was located at 11 Harrison Street and was named for their father, Edgar Damon. The advertisement at right announces the improved grater and its 1896 patent. The grater was carried in the 1901 Sears, Roebuck and Company catalog. As profits declined, the business was sold, but the graters continued to be produced under the name Wm. J. Bride Company until the business closed in 1918.

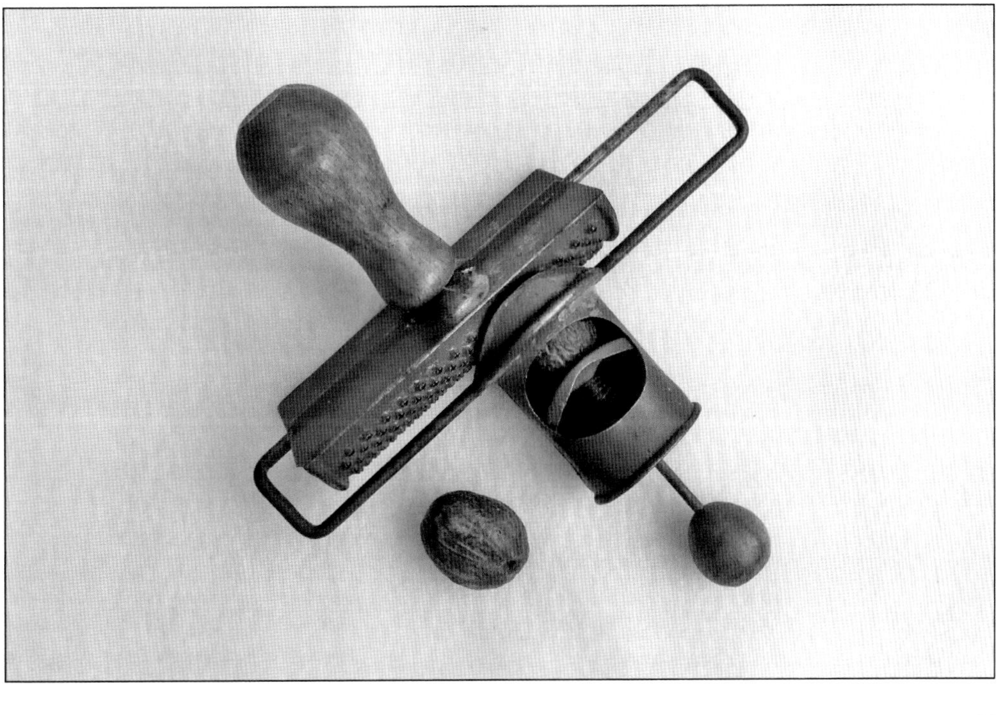

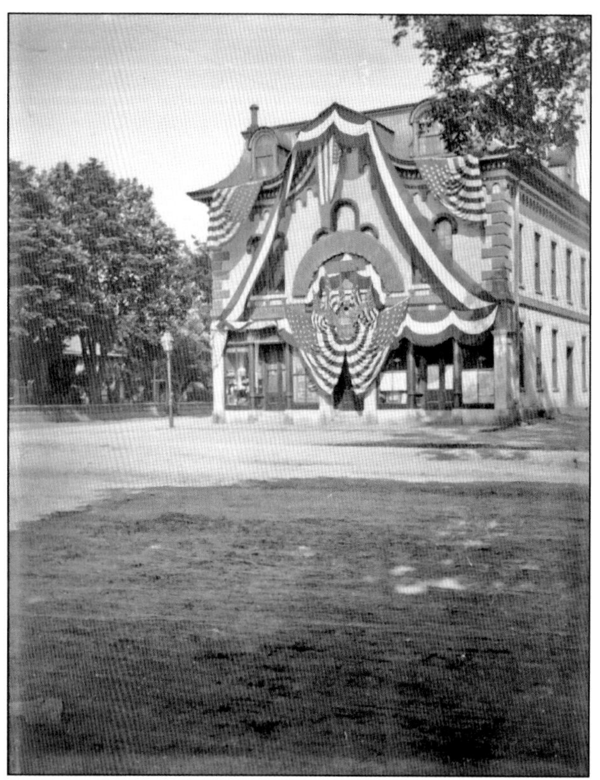

The Bank Building, at the southeast corner of Main and Pleasant Streets, was built in 1860 in the Second Empire or Mansard style. The space on the third floor was named Ellsworth Hall after Elmer Ellsworth, the first Union officer killed in the Civil War. At one time, the library was located on the third floor. Pranksters once took a horse to the third floor, and the dilemma became how to get it down.

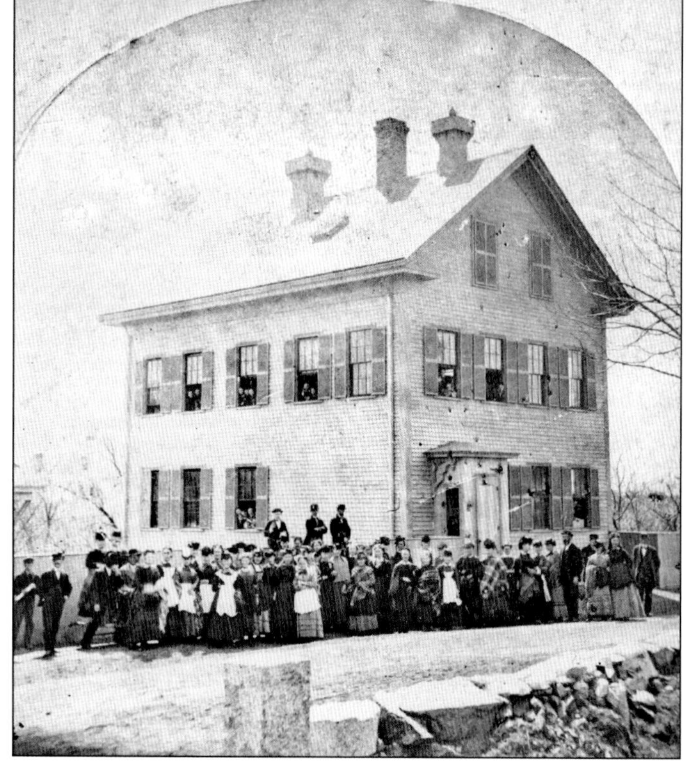

In 1866, the necktie business began here in Reading. Damon & Temple Company opened at the corner of Main and Pleasant Streets in the Bank Building and moved in 1869 to Woburn Street, the present site of the Wright building at 22 Woburn Street. This stereoview shows workers at the Woburn Street building before the 1874 construction of the Presbyterian church to its west.

J. S. TEMPLE,

To PREVENT ANY MISUNDERSTANDING, please notify me at once if this bill is not correct in all respects, as no change of terms, prices, or shortage will be allowed at time of settlement.

MANUFACTURER OF

Men's Fine Neckwear,

Reading, Mass., Sept. 9. 1906

Terms:
10 Days, Less 6 Per Cent.
30 " " 5 " "

Sold to J. K. Ames

2	doz.	4 in H.	4.12½	8 25	
1½	"	"	2.15	3 23	
½	"	Hazelhurst	2.15	1 08	
2	"	4 in H.	1.75	3 50	
1	"	"		2	
1½	"	Hazelhurst	1.75	2 63	20 69

In the 1880s, the original Damon, Temple & Company neckwear manufacturers restructured to become the J.S. Temple Company and served a national market. This billhead is dated September 1906 and must have been for an order from a merchant, since the items were ordered by the dozen. The company continued to operate until 1955.

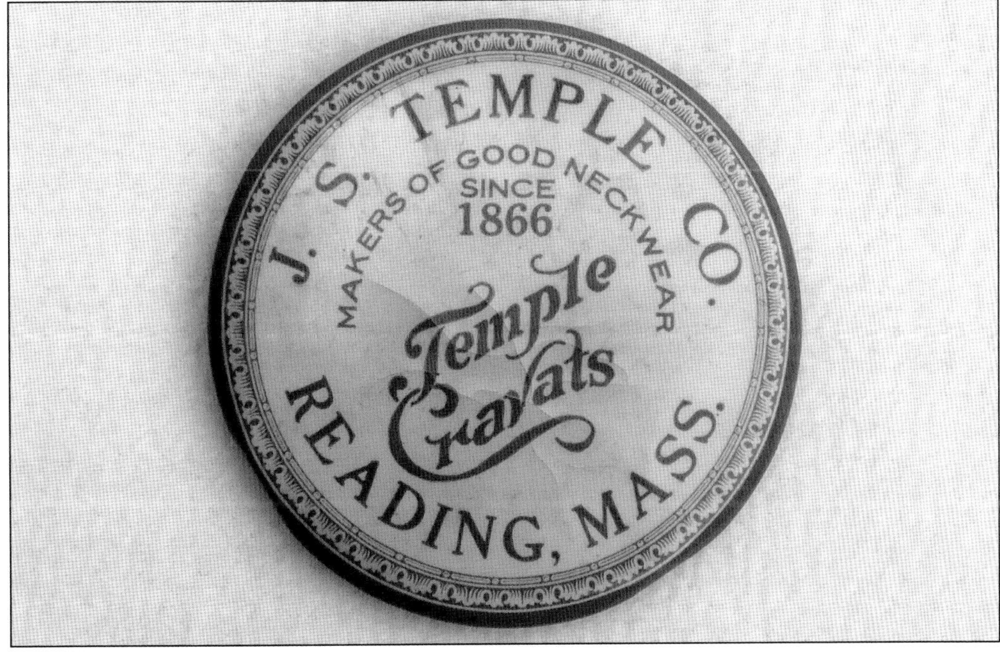

This unique advertising piece measures over three inches in diameter. The opposite side is a mirror that could be used to make sure your cravat was tied correctly. At one time, the company was located in Black's Block at the southeast corner of Haven and High Streets and eventually moved to the lower floor of the Perkins building, now the site of the VFW building on Main Street.

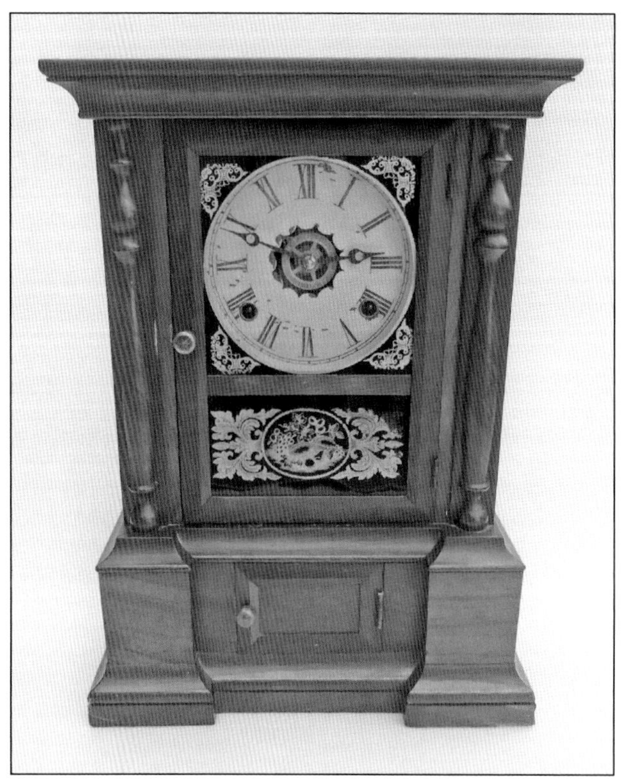

Daniel Pratt Jr. began his clock-making business in Reading in 1832. From 1846 until his death in 1871, he had a storefront at 49 Union Street in Boston, on the same block as the Union Oyster House. By 1849, Pratt included his son Daniel Ford Pratt and his son-in-law Benjamin Boyce in the business, then known as Daniel Pratt and Sons. After Daniel Pratt Jr.'s death, the firm continued until 1880 under the name Daniel Pratt's Sons. The mantle clock shown here has a label inside confirming that it was made during that period. Pratt clocks were shipped all over the world. The advertising piece below shows Daniel Pratt Jr.'s grandson Frank, who continued the business from 1895 to 1916, then located at 53 Franklin Street in Boston.

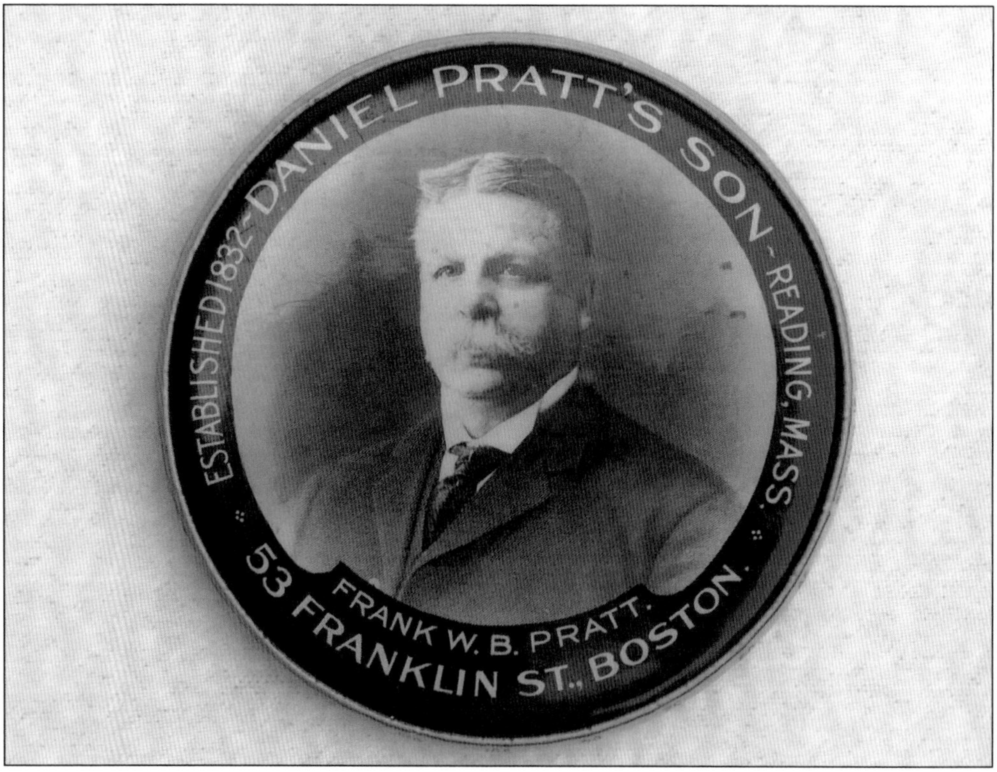

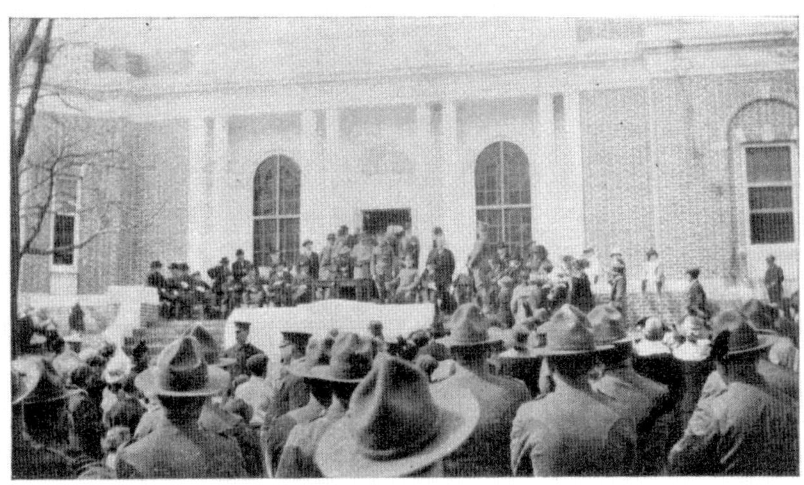

New Federal Post Office Building, Reading, Massachusetts 1918

This postcard captures the September 27, 1918, dedication of the Reading Post Office on the corner of Haven and Sanborn Streets. The post office had been in various locations including the Lyceum Building and the Masonic Block. In 2017, postal services moved across the street, and the post office building was sold to a developer.

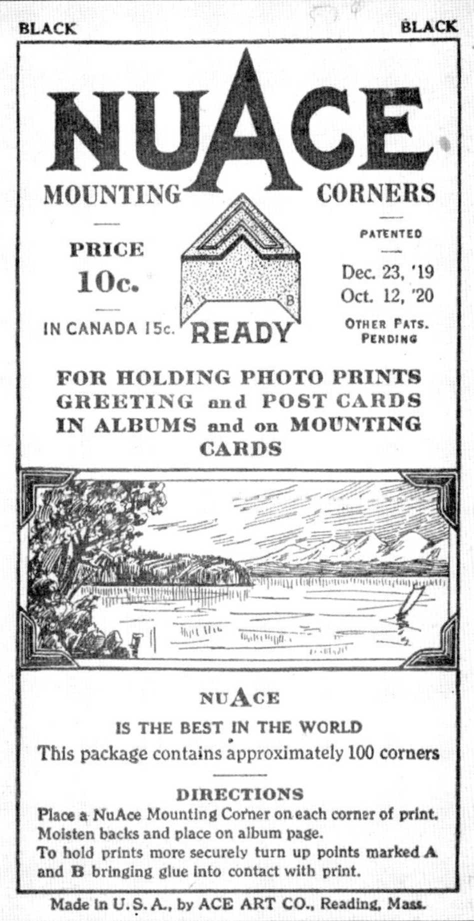

The Ace Art Company was founded by Lester Riley of Reading. He designed NuAce Mounting Corners, which were designed to hold photographs in albums without damaging the photographs. This envelope contained 100 corners and was sold for 10¢. The company erected the building at 24 Gould Street in 1924, which was recently sold for mixed-use development.

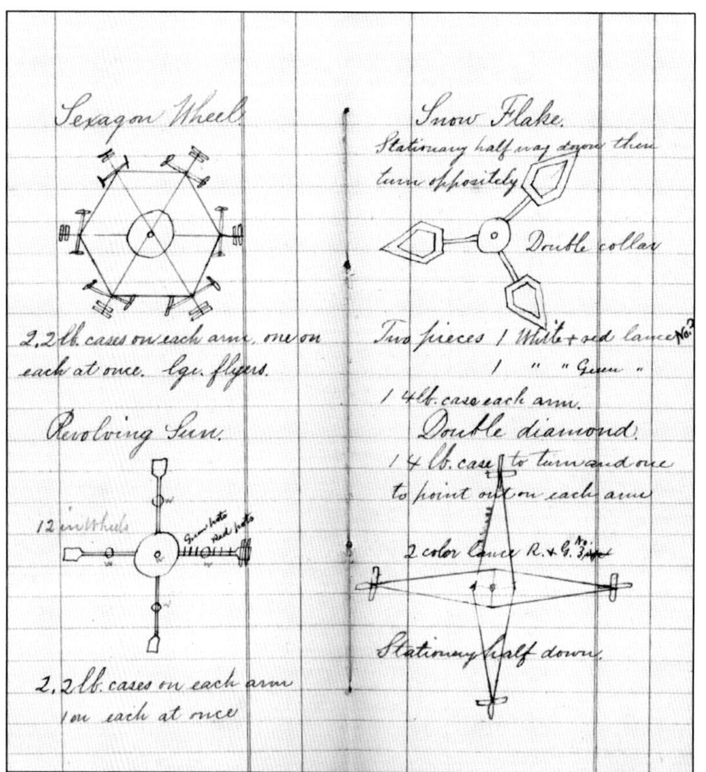

The pages at left are from Walter M. Scott's leather-bound logbook. He worked at the Etna Fireworks Factory off Lowell Street, an area known as "Firecracker Alley." The logbook includes lists of the different chemicals needed, their cost per pound, and as shown here, diagrams for different types of fireworks. Below, a portion of the 1889 map shows the location of the factory. Comparing this map to the present day, on the south side of Lowell Street, Lincoln Street is now Grand Street, and Hinchman Street is now Deering Street

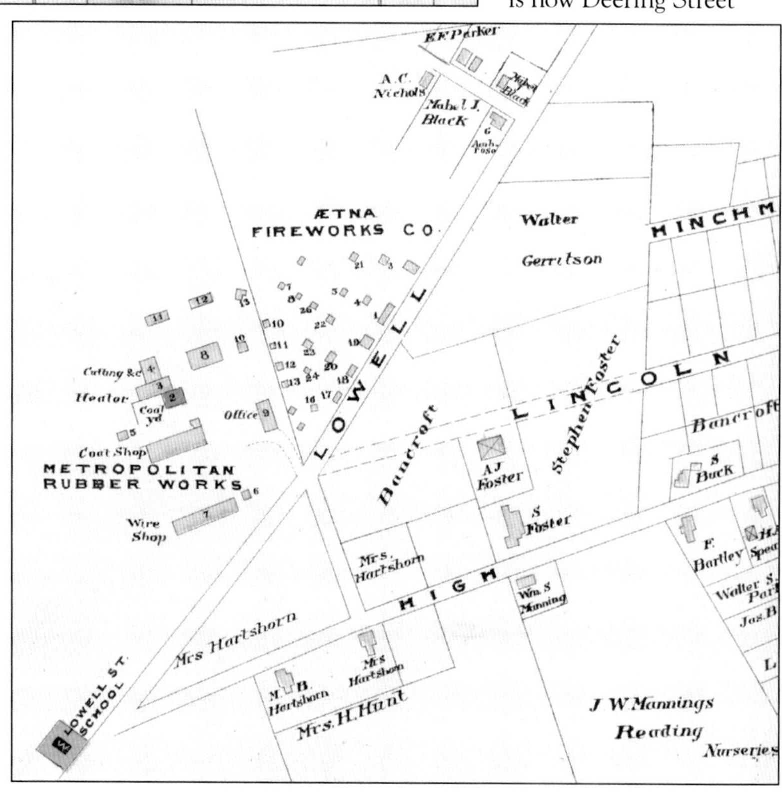

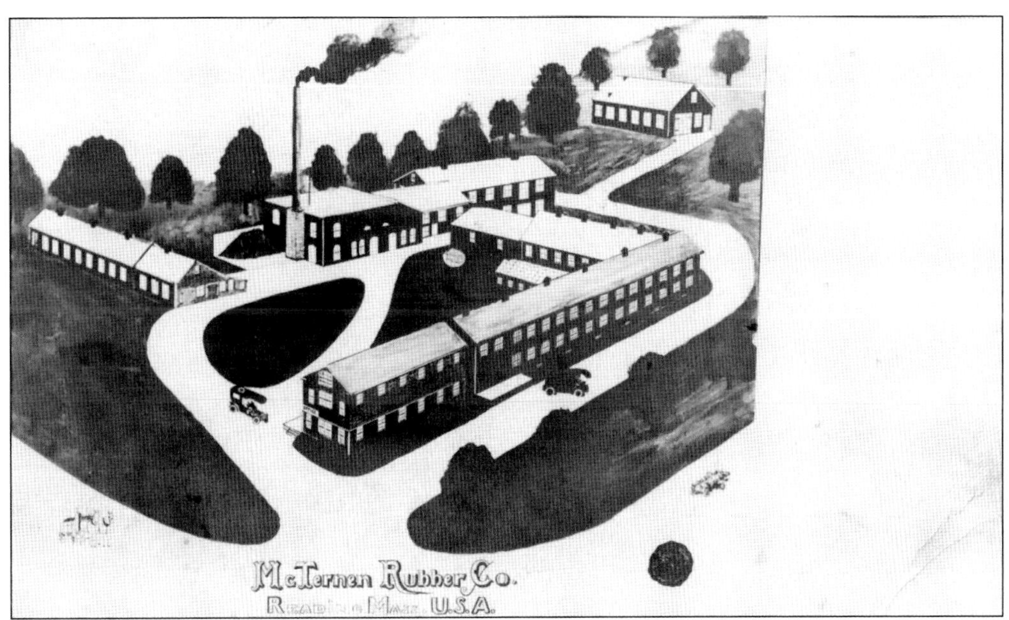

As seen on the map on the previous page, the Metropolitan Rubber Works had several buildings off Lowell Street in 1889. There was a rubber company there as early as 1882 and as late as 1918 but under various names, such as Chauncy (1882), Emerson (1894), Eastern (1900), Commonwealth (1907), McTernan (as seen in this 1915 postcard), and Korker (1917). The postcard also shows that the buildings were of substantial size, and many were two-story. The undated photograph below shows a Selden truck owned by the Cummings Express Company making a delivery to one of those buildings. Selden trucks began production in 1913. Cummings Express, which began in 1821 using horse and wagon, now had motorized trucks and had expanded to include not only its Reading office, but offices at five different Boston locations.

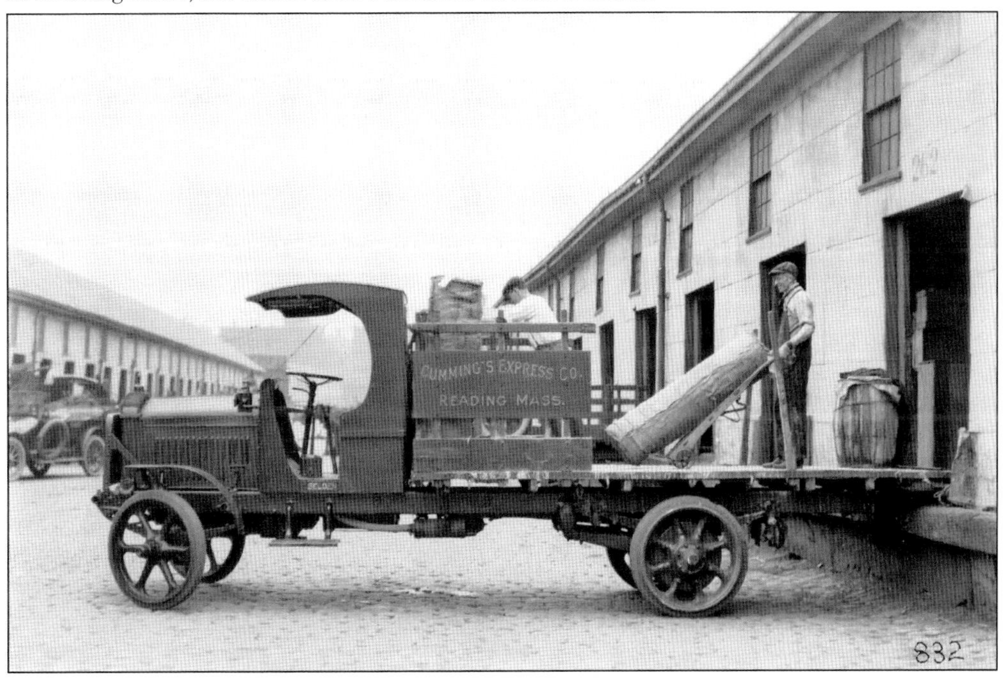

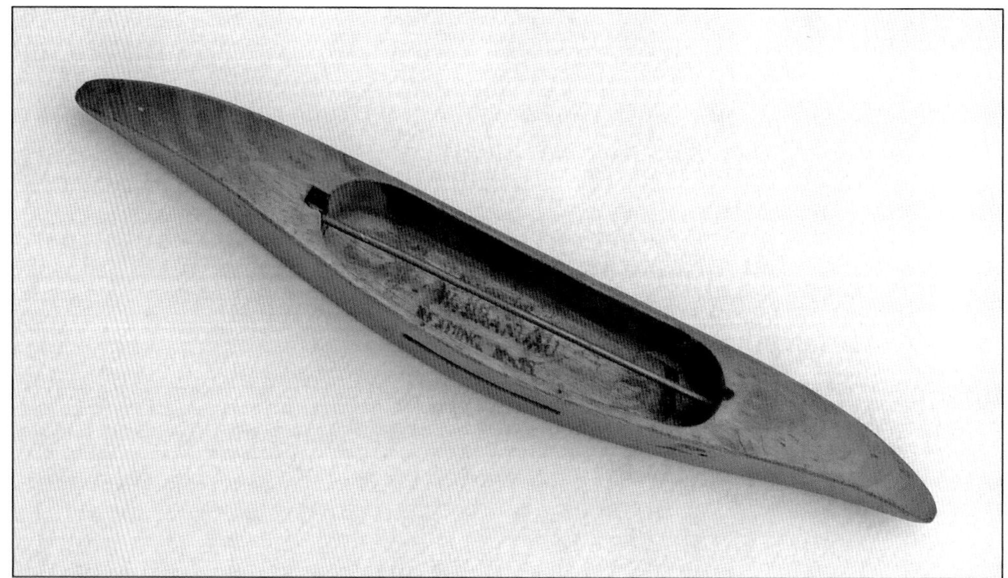

Louis W. Brandau was born in Michigan in 1871, and by 1889, his occupation was listed as carver. He was living in Somerville in 1910, in Wilmington in 1920, and by 1925, at 15 Beacon Street in Reading. The stamp inside this wood shuttle reads, "Reading." Whether this shuttle was created for decorative or practical use is not known.

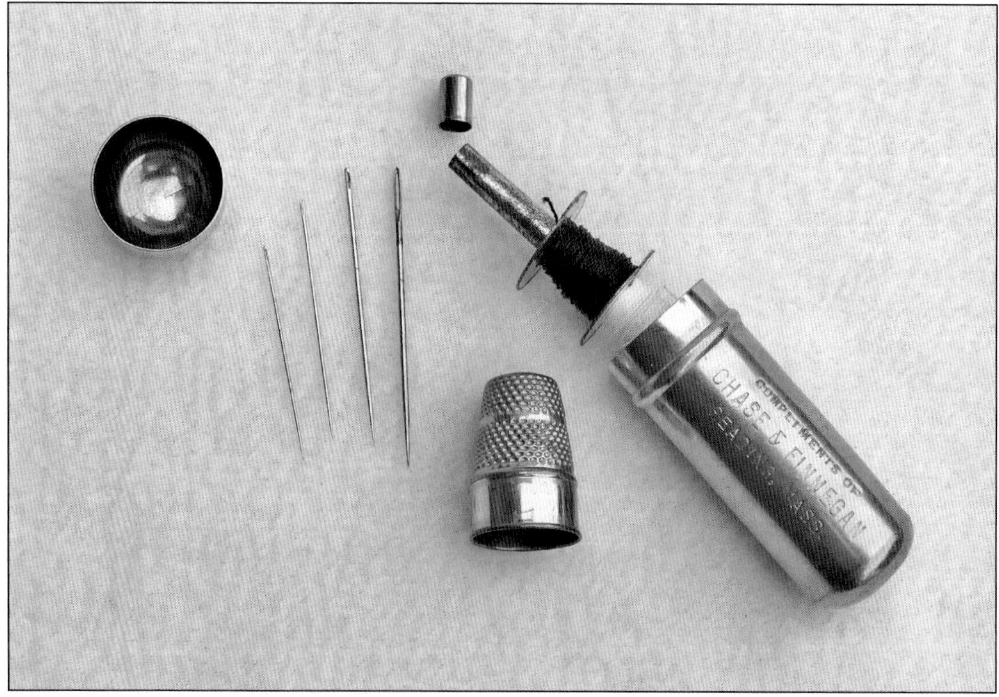

George R. Chase and Thomas J. Finnegan were proprietors of a men's furnishings store that is listed in the 1917–1918 Reading directory at 196 Main Street. Originally the location of the Stephen Foster house, that block was torn down in 1935, and Family Dental occupies the building there now. The needle case shown here contains a thimble, two bobbins, and a space inside the bobbin spindle for the needles.

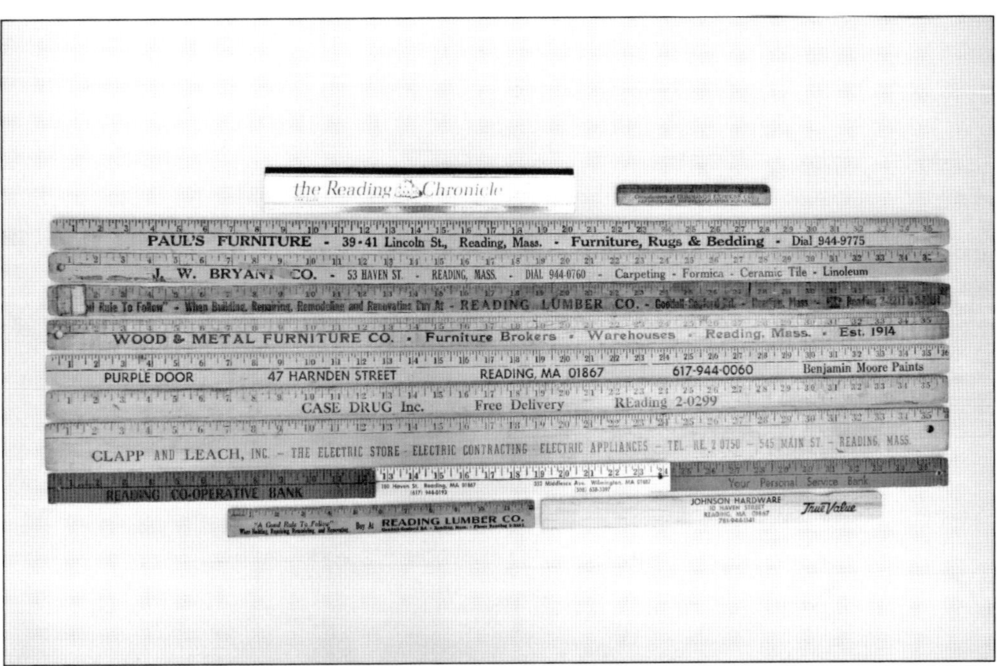

This collection of wood rulers and yardsticks features many Reading businesses, past and present. A look at phone numbers and addresses helps to date them. Probably the oldest one is the small six-inch ruler at the top from Cummings Express. The widest is the one from Clapp and Leach, but its address on Main Street dates it to after the business moved there in the 1940s.

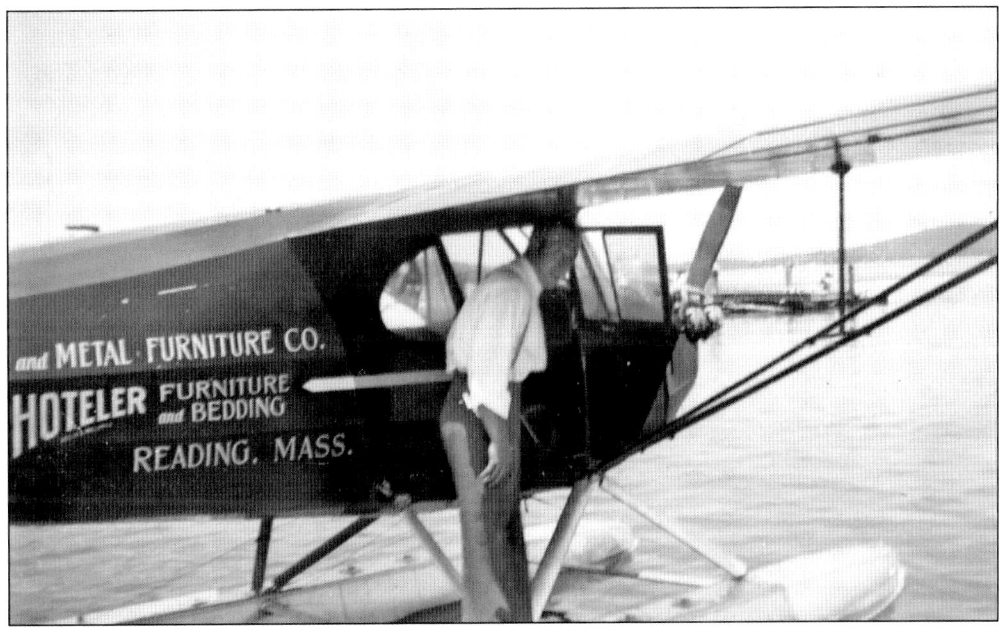

Not much is known of the Wood and Metal Furniture Company. The back of their ruler, in the photograph at the top, reads "Hoteler, Earle G. Steele, Representative." By 1949, Steele and his wife owned several houses in Reading, lived at 84 Prescott Street, and owned businesses at 8–12 Prescott Street (recently torn down) and 525 Main Street. Steele is seen in this undated photograph with his sea plane, with the same company information on the side.

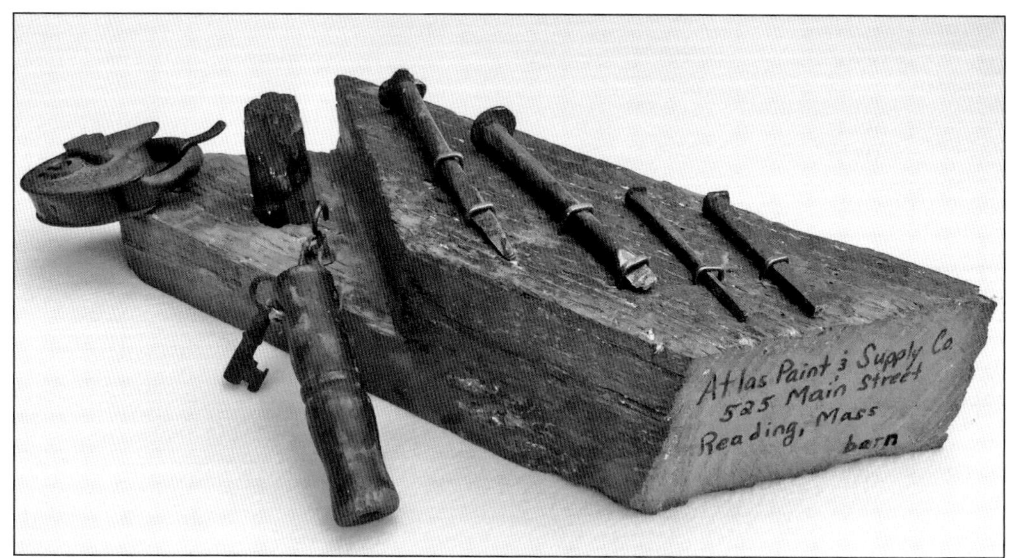

The Atlas Paint & Supply Company was once located at 591 Main Street and later moved to 530 Main Street, with storage in the barn at 525 Main Street. The storefront, probably built in the 1920s, was attached to the much older barn. The photograph above shows a piece of the framing from that barn, with its peg. Also pictured are a variety of early nails and the lock and key for a door at the back of the store, all of which were saved by a former owner of the building. Reading Cleaners and Tailors is currently located in the storefront at 530 Main Street.

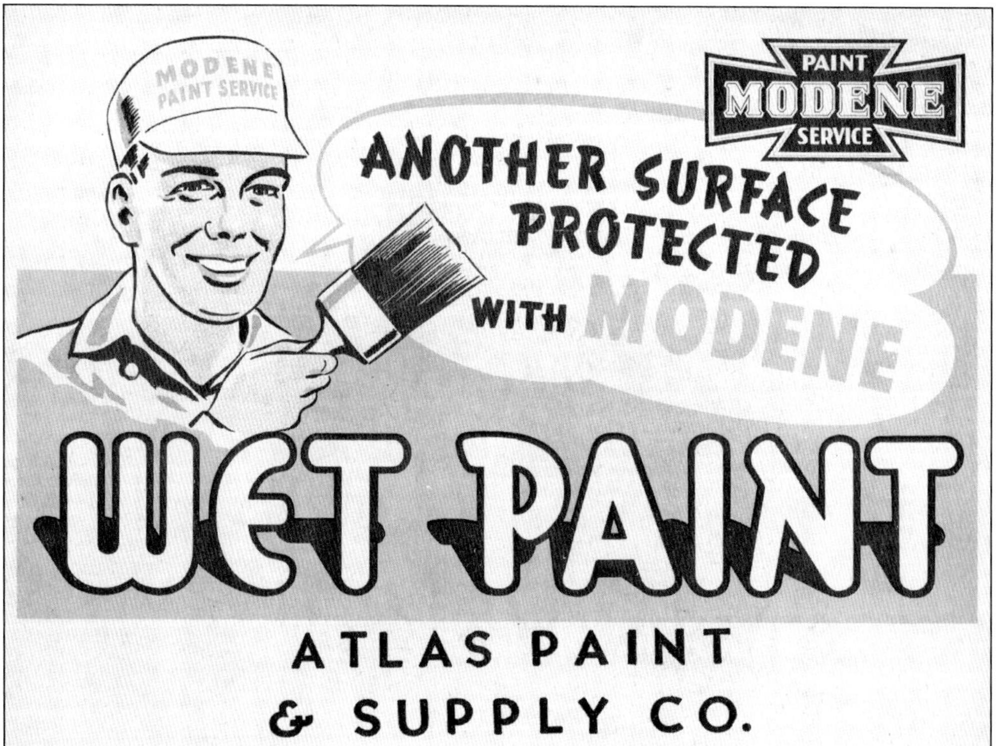

MODENE PAINT SERVICE

PAINT MODENE SERVICE

ANOTHER SURFACE PROTECTED WITH MODENE

WET PAINT

ATLAS PAINT
& SUPPLY CO.

591 MAIN ST., TEL. REA. 1928 READING, MASS.

Harrow's chicken pot pies are well known in Reading and surrounding towns. But Harrow's was known for many years as a restaurant, and even earlier as a place to buy poultry and other meats. Charles and Winnifred Harrow opened at 126 Main Street in the 1930s. They raised chickens just over the town line in Wakefield to supply the restaurant. The double postcard at right shows that not only meats, but also canned goods, fresh fruits, and vegetables were sold there. Below is the cover of one of the restaurant's menus, offering a variety of poultry, seafood, and meat dinners, along with sandwiches and desserts. In 1956, Harrow's was sold to the Arsenault family. A second generation now runs the business, which since the 1990s has been takeout only. It has expanded to include five other smaller storefront locations in eastern Massachusetts.

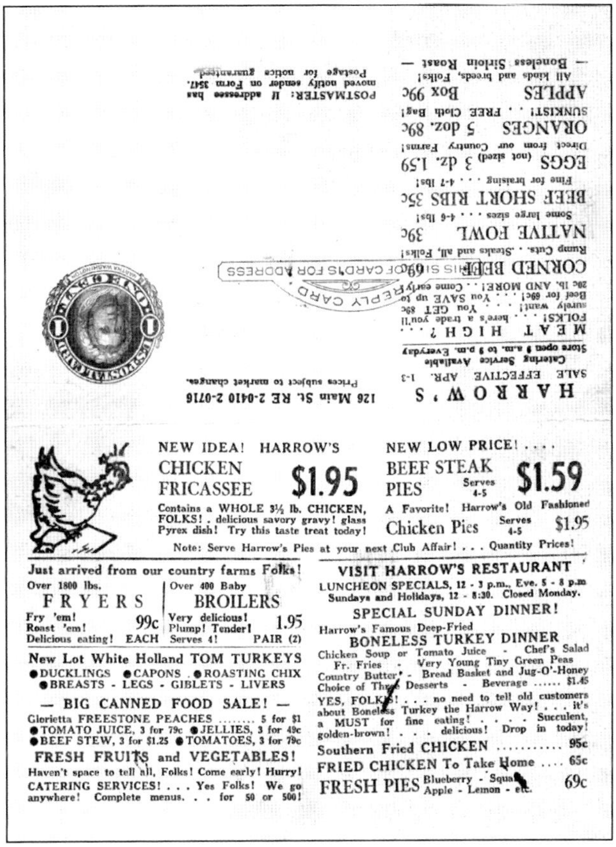

HARROW'S 126 Main St. RE 2-0410 2-0716

SALE EFFECTIVE APR. 1-3 Prices subject to market changes.

Catering Service Available

Store open 8 a.m. to 6 p.m. Everyday

MEAT HIGH? . . .

FOLKS! . . . here's a trade you'll surely want! . . . You GET 85c Beef for 69c! . . . You SAVE up to 20c lb. AND MORE! . . Come early

CORNED BEEF 69c

Rump Cuts . . Steaks and all, Folks!

NATIVE FOWL 39c

Some large sizes . . . 4-6 lbs!

BEEF SHORT RIBS 35c

Fine for braising . . . 4-7 lbs!

EGGS (not sized) 3 dz. 1.59

Direct from our Country Farms!

ORANGES 5 doz. 89c

SUNKIST! . . FREE Cloth Bag!

APPLES Box 99c

All kinds and breeds, Folks!

— Boneless Sirloin Roast —

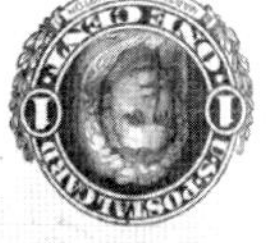

REPLY CARD

THIS SIDE OF CARD IS FOR ADDRESS

POSTMASTER: If addressee has moved notify sender on Form 3547. Postage for notice guaranteed.

NEW IDEA! HARROW'S CHICKEN FRICASSEE $1.95

Contains a WHOLE 3½ lb. CHICKEN, FOLKS! . delicious savory gravy! glass Pyrex dish! Try this taste treat today!

NEW LOW PRICE! . . . . BEEF STEAK PIES Serves 4-5 $1.59

A Favorite! Harrow's Old Fashioned Chicken Pies Serves 4-5 $1.95

Note: Serve Harrow's Pies at your next Club Affair! . . . Quantity Prices!

Just arrived from our country farms Folks!

Over 1800 lbs. FRYERS Fry 'em! Roast 'em! Delicious eating! 99c EACH

Over 400 Baby BROILERS Very delicious! Plump! Tender! Serves 4! 1.95 PAIR (2)

New Lot White Holland TOM TURKEYS

●DUCKLINGS ●CAPONS ●ROASTING CHIX ●BREASTS - LEGS - GIBLETS - LIVERS

— BIG CANNED FOOD SALE! —

Glorietta FREESTONE PEACHES .... 5 for $1

●TOMATO JUICE, 3 for 79c ●JELLIES, 3 for 49c

●BEEF STEW, 3 for $1.25 ●TOMATOES, 3 for 79c

FRESH FRUITS and VEGETABLES!

Haven't space to tell all, Folks! Come early! Hurry!

CATERING SERVICES! . . . Yes Folks! We go anywhere! Complete menus. . . for 50 or 500!

VISIT HARROW'S RESTAURANT

LUNCHEON SPECIALS, 12 - 3 p.m., Eve. 5 - 8 p.m. Sundays and Holidays, 12 - 8:30. Closed Monday.

SPECIAL SUNDAY DINNER!

Harrow's Famous Deep-Fried BONELESS TURKEY DINNER

Chicken Soup or Tomato Juice - Chef's Salad Fr. Fries - Very Young Tiny Green Peas Country Butter - Bread Basket and Jug-O'-Honey Choice of Three Desserts - Beverage $1.45

YES, FOLKS! . . . no need to tell old customers about Boneless Turkey the Harrow Way! . . . it's a MUST for fine eating! . . . . Succulent, golden-brown! . . . delicious! Drop in today!

Southern Fried CHICKEN 95c

FRIED CHICKEN To Take Home 65c

FRESH PIES Blueberry - Squash Apple - Lemon - etc. 69c

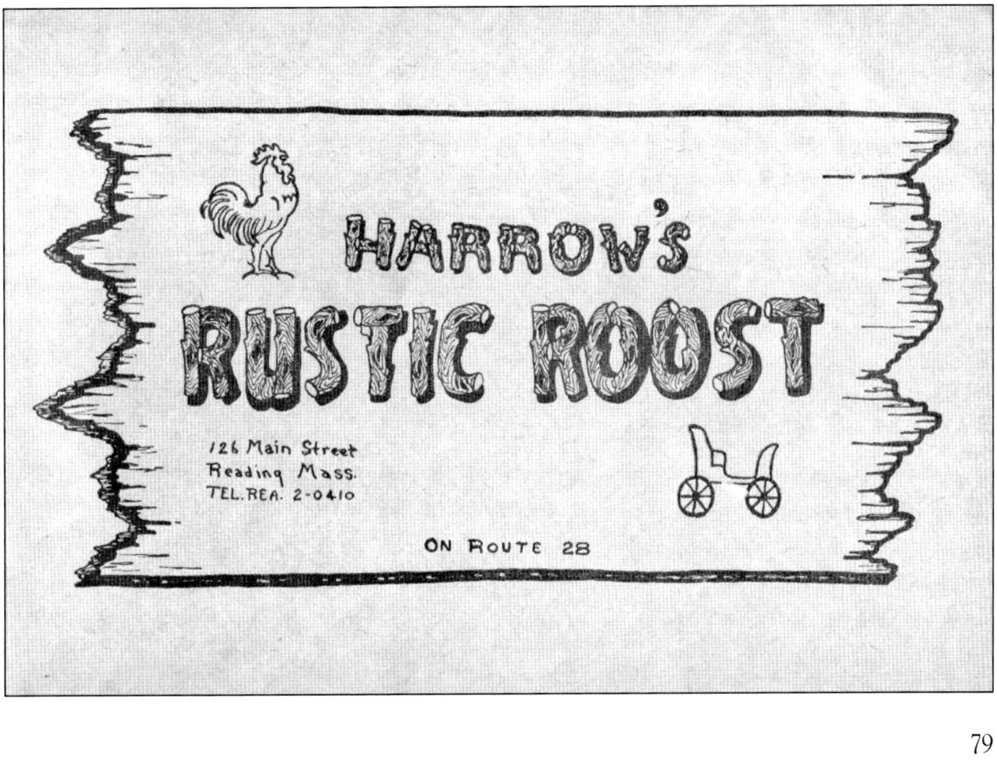

HARROW'S RUSTIC ROOST

126 Main Street
Reading Mass.
TEL. REA. 2-0410

ON ROUTE 28

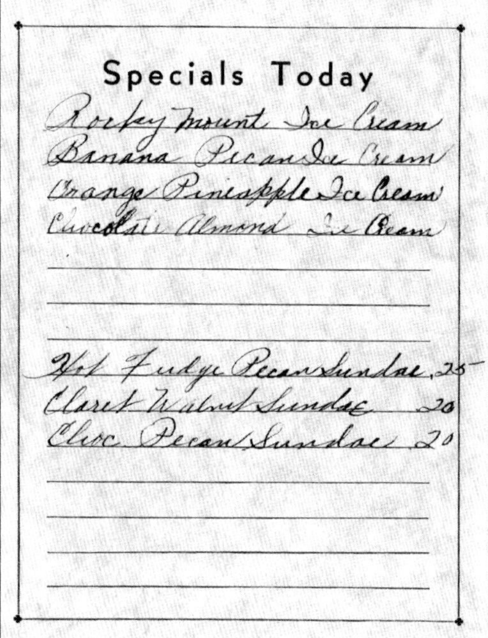

Specials Today

Rocky mount Ice Cream
Banana Pecan Ice Cream
Orange Pineapple Ice Cream
Chocolate Almond Ice Cream

Hot Fudge Pecan Sundae .25
Claret Walnut Sundae .20
Choc Pecan Sundae .20

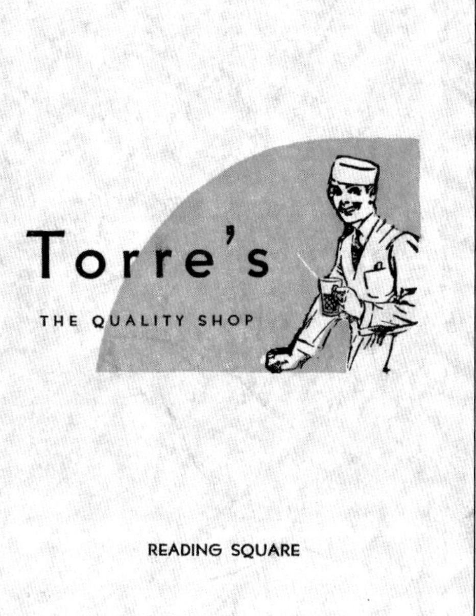

In 1914, Frank and Tillie Torre bought the Reading Spa, a confectionery and ice-cream store on Main Street in the Richmond Block. They changed the name to Torre's sometime after 1931. In the summer, they also had an ice-cream stand on Salem Street near the current location of Planet Fitness. They sold the downtown business in 1954, but it continued to be an ice-cream shop through the 1960s. Their menu shows the variety of items available and some delicious daily specials. Note that the price of a soda depended on whether you sat at the fountain or were in a booth. The Golden Dragon restaurant is currently in this location.

SUNDAES

Chocolate Walnut	15c	Chocolate Nut Marshmallow	20c
Chocolate Almond	15c		
Maraschino Cherry	15c	Pineapple Nut Marshmallow	20c
Hawaiian Pineapple	15c		
Raspberry Fruit	15c	Strawberry Nut Marshmallow	20c
Strawberry Fruit	15c		
Chocolate Shott	15c	Hot Fudge	20c
Chocolate Dusty	15c	Butterscotch Nut	20c
Canton Ginger	15c	Banana Royal	25c
Hot Butterscotch	15c	Hot Fudge Nut	25c
Coffee Spanish	15c	Jiggers (all flavors)	20c

EGG AND MILK DRINKS

Malted Milk and Egg	25c	Frappes	15c
Egg and Milk	20c	Floats	15c
Malted Milk	15c	Milk Shake	10c

FREEZES OR SHERBET SODAS

Orange	15c		15c

SODAS

Plain Cream Sodas ..... 10c Ice Cream Sodas 15c

Chocolate	Strawberry	Mocha
Coffee	Raspberry	Cherry
Vanilla	Pineapple	Claret
Ginger	Lemon	Sarsaparilla

Fresh Fruit Orangeade .. 15c Fresh Fruit Lemonade ... 15c
With Sherbet 20c

ICE CREAM

Vanilla	Chocolate	Frozen Pudding
Strawberry	Maple Pecan	Butter Crunch
Coffee	Ginger	

MISCELLANEOUS

Welch's Grape Juice 15c
Ginger Ale Float ...... 15c Ginger Ale Fizz 15c

Coca-Cola	Root Beer	Moxie
Lemon and Lime	Ginger Ale	Cherry Smash

At Fountain 5c — At Booth 10c

Though undated, this flyer for Batchelder's Yankee Trading Post must have been from shortly after the completion of the Route 128 "super highway" in November 1951. The Trading Post stood on the east side of Main Street just north of the intersection with Franklin Street across from Sailor Tom's (see page 82). It was owned by Elmer and Lillian Batchelder, who lived just around the corner at 125 Franklin Street.

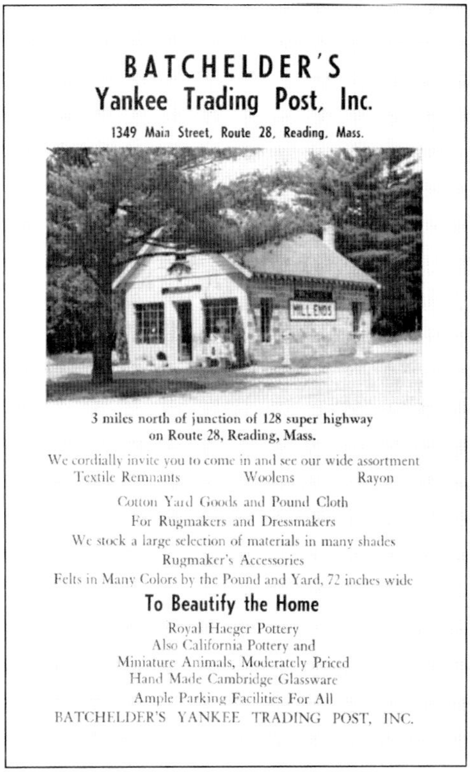

BATCHELDER'S

Yankee Trading Post, Inc.

1349 Main Street, Route 28, Reading, Mass.

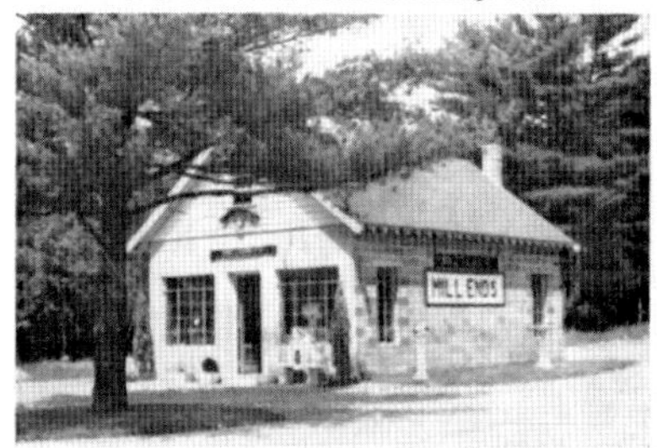

3 miles north of junction of 128 super highway on Route 28, Reading, Mass.

We cordially invite you to come in and see our wide assortment
Textile Remnants Woolens Rayon
Cotton Yard Goods and Pound Cloth
For Rugmakers and Dressmakers
We stock a large selection of materials in many shades
Rugmaker's Accessories
Felts in Many Colors by the Pound and Yard, 72 inches wide

To Beautify the Home

Royal Haeger Pottery
Also California Pottery and
Miniature Animals, Moderately Priced
Hand Made Cambridge Glassware
Ample Parking Facilities For All
BATCHELDER'S YANKEE TRADING POST, INC.

Few folks carry matches anymore, but this collection of matchbook covers shows how Reading businesses used to be able to reach their customers. Thorpe's Service Station was located at the end of Lowell Street just before the Wilmington town line. Banks, restaurants, and car dealerships also advertised on matchbooks, and the impressive large set of matches at center certainly would make an impression about Newman's flower shop.

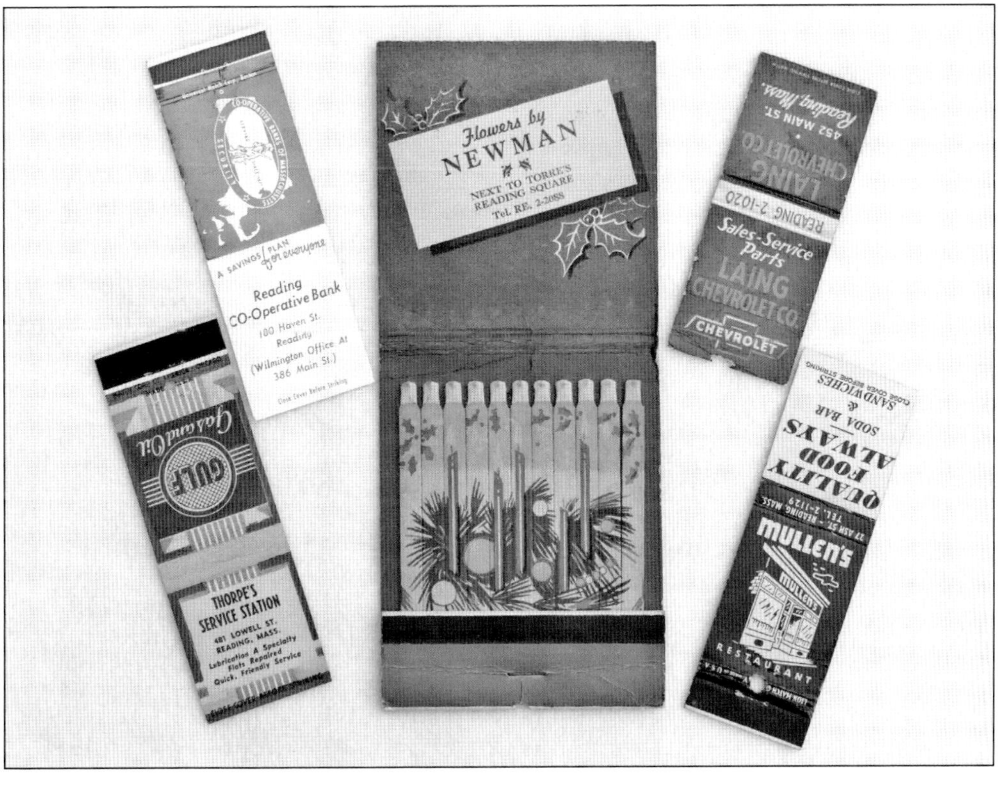

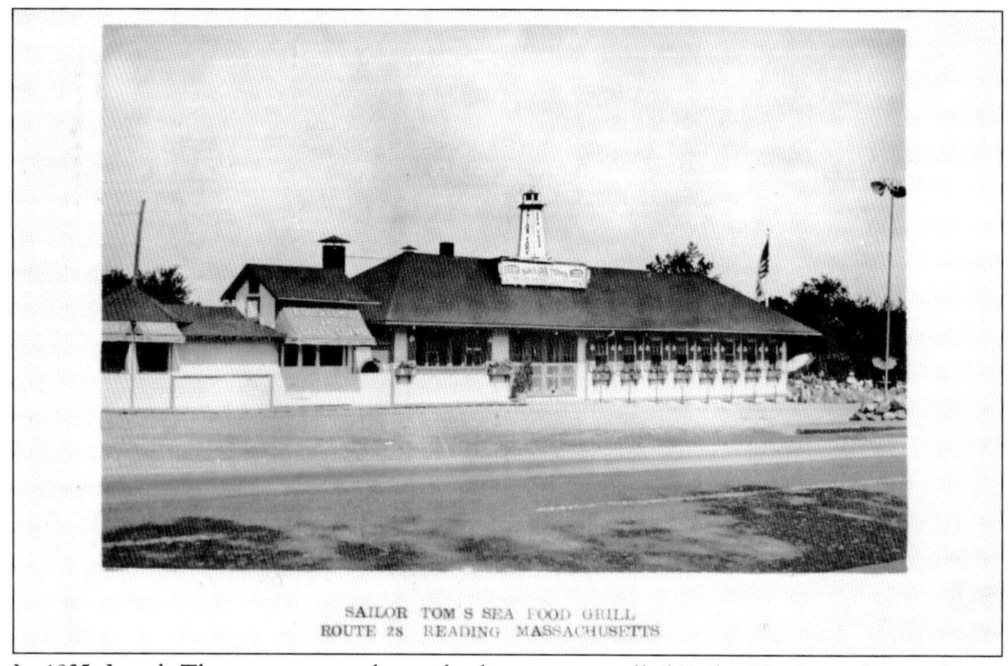

In 1935, Joseph Thompson opened a seafood restaurant called Sailor Tom's on the northwest corner of Main and Franklin Streets. By the 1940s, the property had expanded to 36 acres and included gardens, a miniature fishing village, and a trout pond where folks could catch their own dinner. Later, Thompson opened other restaurant locations in Saugus and Cambridge.

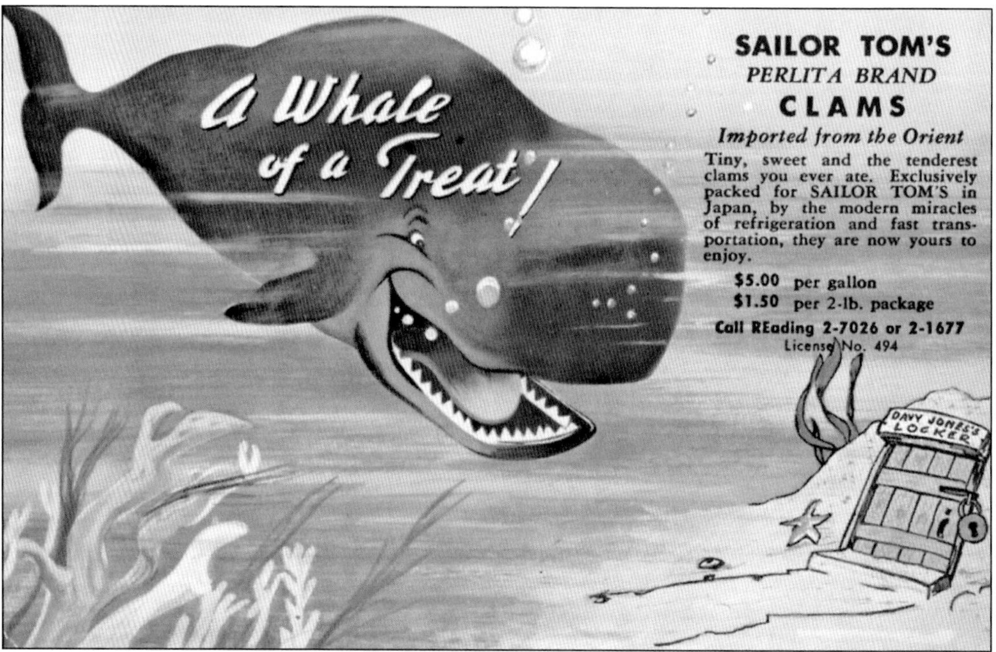

This playful postcard shows that Sailor Tom's imported fish "from the Orient" to serve to diners. In 1941, Thompson built a home for himself on the property, an 85-foot replica of a ship, and gave tours of it for 50¢. The restaurant and amusement area were sold and razed in 1955 to make way for a supermarket, now the location of Home Goods.

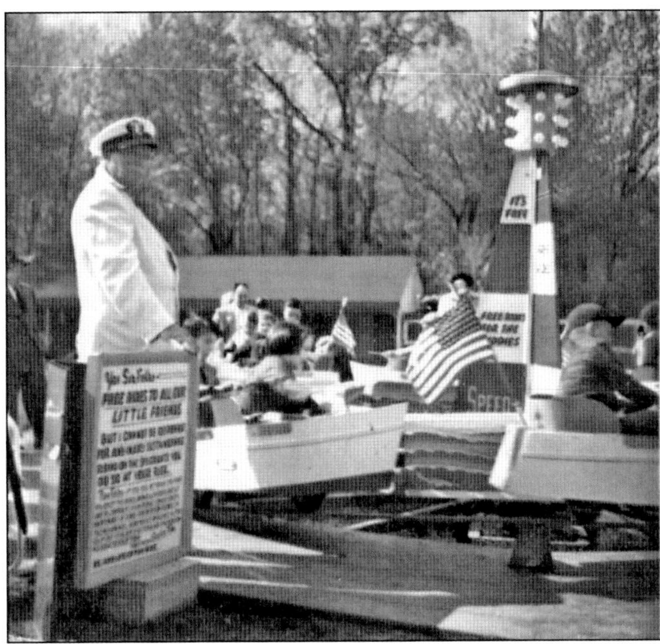

1. Seafood at its best.
2. Bountiful flowers for your enjoyment.
3. Wondrous P.T. Boat full of unusual gifts at reasonable prices.
4. Fortune Teller's Booth for your entertainment.
5. Trout Pool — catch your own trout.
6. Wishing Pool — make your wishes come true.
7. Nautical Home where you may browse around and enjoy the most beautiful flowers.
8. Exotic birds from many lands on exhibition.
9. Free rides on our speed boats for all the kiddies.
10. Refreshment stand — soft drinks, candy and ice cream.
11. Wheel of Fortune — you can't lose — valuable gifts.

Here, Sailor Tom can be seen watching over the young riders in their boats. The list of attractions is impressive. Sailor Tom's ship remained after the rest of the property was sold, and there is a series of postcards that show the interior. It was torn down in 2012, and three new houses were built on the street, fittingly named Sailor Tom's Way.

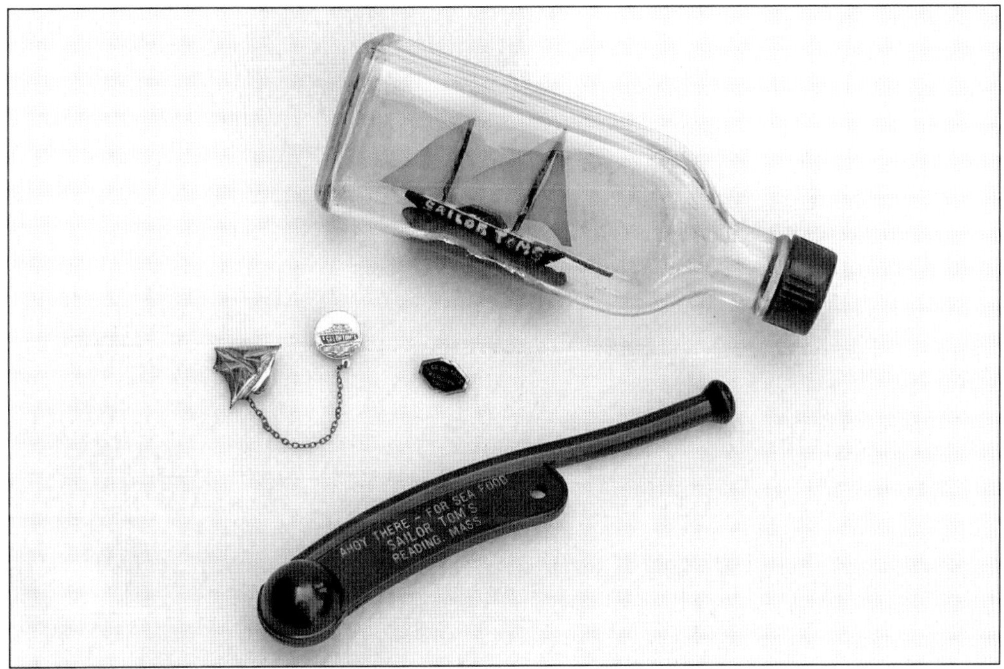

An old PT boat was turned into a gift shop on the property, and this photograph shows some of the memorabilia that would have been sold there, including the ship in a bottle and two different lapel pins. Thompson spent 14 years in the Navy, which probably influenced his choices, especially the bosun's whistle, which reads "Ahoy There – For Sea Food."

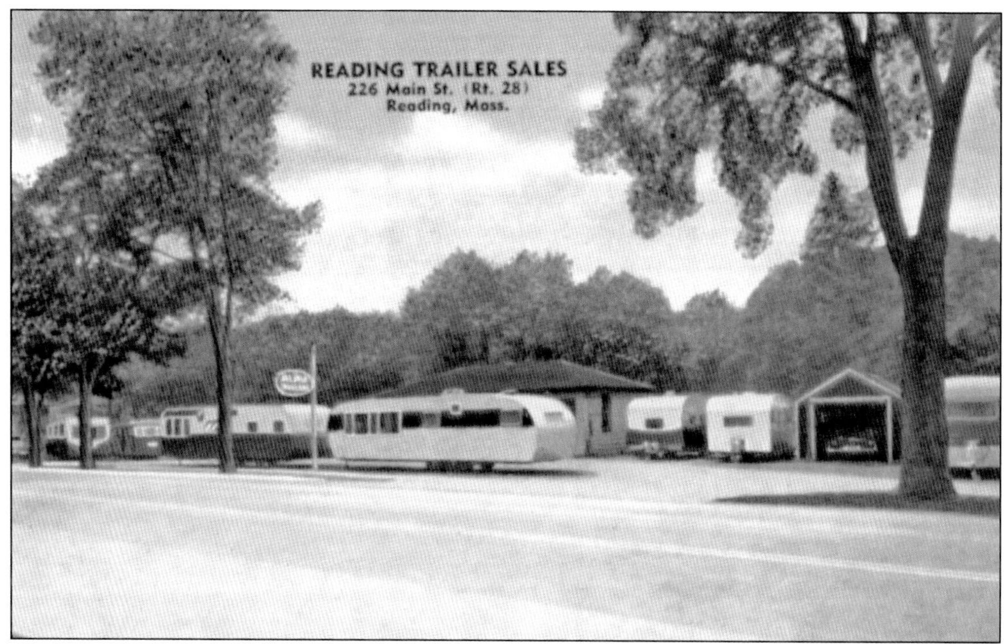

At the turn of the 20th century, the horse and buggy was replaced by the automobile, and a change in lifestyle brought time for leisure travel. Reading Trailer Sales was located on South Main Street at the southwest corner with Knollwood Road. There has been a succession of businesses at that location. A Friendly's restaurant was there in the 1970s, and now the same building is occupied by Santander Bank.

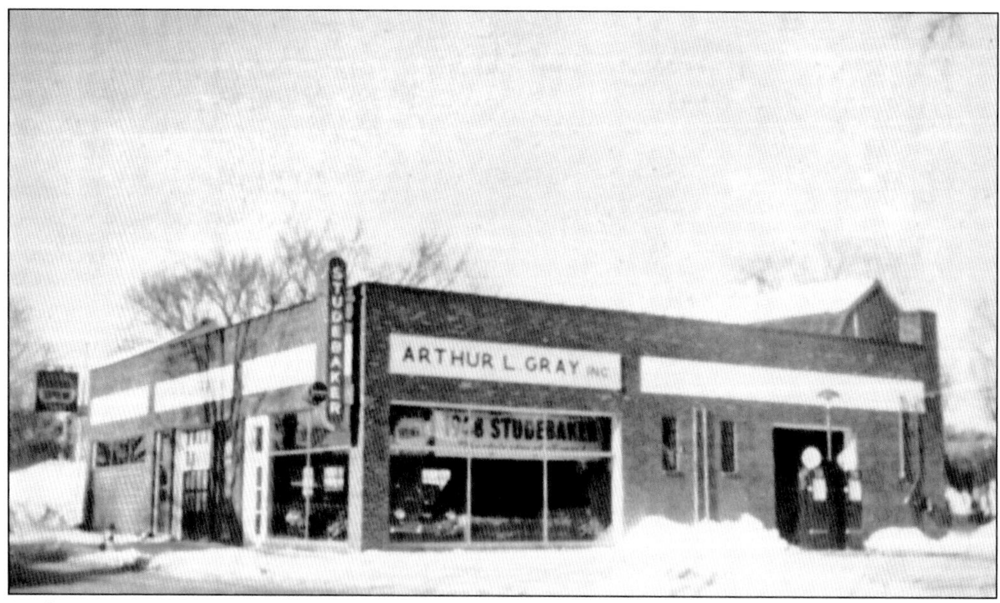

Arthur L. Gray's Studebaker dealership was on the northwest corner of Washington and Ash Streets. It offered sales and service of cars and trucks. There are several apartment buildings located there today. At one time, several different automobile dealerships, including Ford, Dodge, Chevrolet, and Chrysler-Plymouth were in business south of downtown on either Washington or Main Street.

Four

IN TIMES OF CONFLICT

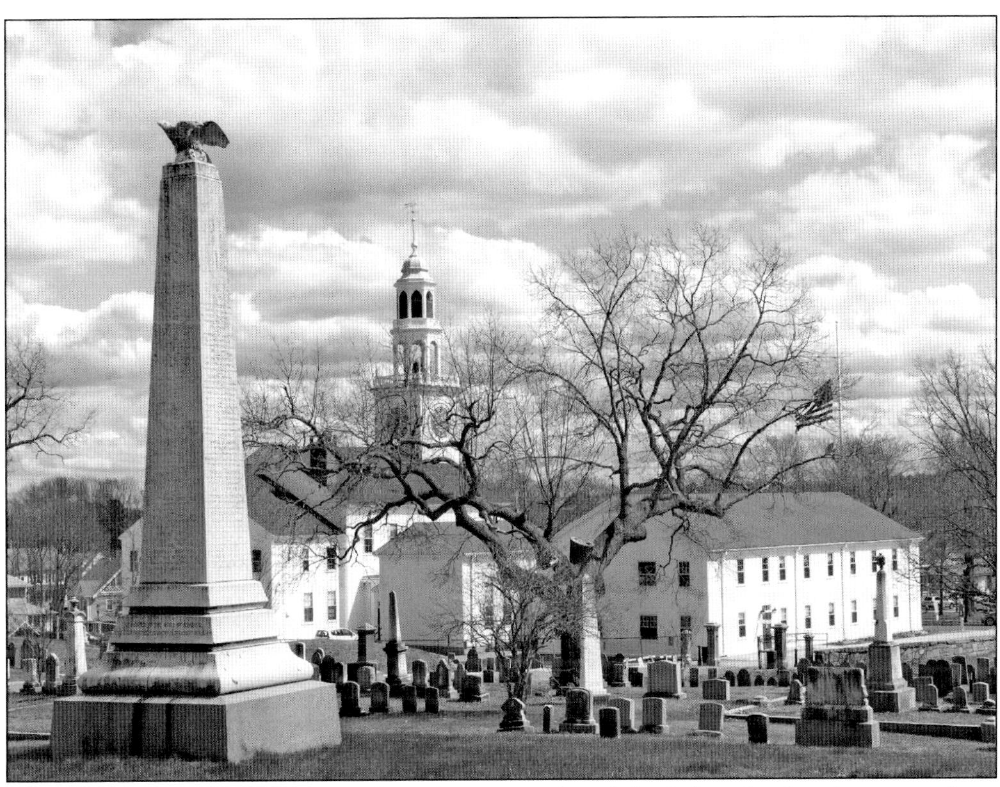

Since Reading's founding, its residents have served to defend their land and property from aggression and to fight for the rights of others. This chapter will tell of individuals whose stories give a glimpse into not only the times, but the impact that those conflicts had on the town. Pictured from Laurel Hill Cemetery and overlooking downtown is the Civil War Monument dedicated in 1865.

[illegible] June 1711, mony Received upon the impressing of men for cannada Expadition for ye incoragment of men & for ye hiering of men for yt expadition	£	s	d
of Deakn Bancroft	10	00	00
of Joseph Daman	10	00	00
of Josias Hodgman	09	19	06
of Ensign Wesson	05	00	00
of Corporal Richard temple	03	00	00
of Corporal nath Parker	02	10	00
of John Harnden	02	00	00
of Joseph Hartrigs	01	10	00
Kendal Briant	02	10	00
Left. Swayne	02	10	00
of Clark Bouttal	02	00	00
of Thomas Tayler	02	00	00
Sar. Kendal Parker	02	10	00
	55	09	06

John Poole, one of original Reading's earliest settlers, owned and operated the first gristmill and fulling mill near where the Mill River goes under Water Street in Wakefield. The family kept an account book that was predominately used to chronicle day-to-day business at the mill. They also owned a sawmill and many acres near the north end of the "Great Pond," Lake Quannapowitt. The earliest date in this book is June 22, 1706, and entries continued through the 18th century, recorded by three generations of the Poole family including Jonathan, grandson of the original settler; Jonathan's son Benjamin; and Jonathan's grandson William. Some births, marriages, and deaths were also recorded, along with occasional comments about the weather and other events. Also included are accounts of money paid to men from Reading who went to Casco Bay Fort and Canada between 1710 and 1712 to fight in Queen Anne's War between Britain and France for control of North America. The excerpt shown here is for an expedition to Canada in June 1711.

To all People Before whom this Deed of Sale Shall Com
Now Know ye that that I Samuel Morow of Reading in the County
of Middx in this his Majst Province of the Masachu Bay in New England
(Doctor) For and in Consideration of the full and Just Summ of
Twenty one Pounds Sixteen Shillings and Six Pence in money already
Paid to me in hand by Josiah Hodgman of Said Reading Husbandman
in the Receipt whereof I doe by these presents acknolodg and my
Self thereunto fully Satisfyd paid and Contented for Every part &
Parcell of the Same forever: have given granted Bargined
and Sold and Doe hereby Further give grant Bargin Sell Setover
Alinate Enfeofe and Conform unto the Said Josiah Hodgman his
heirs Exectr adminr and asignes a Certaine Peice or parcel of
land Containing one acre and one hundred and thirty one Poles: it
being Cituate in the towne Ship of Reading afore Said: lying by a little
Bridg near Said Hodgmans hous: as it is Butted and bounded viz South
westerly By Said Hodgman land about Sixteen Pole: South Easterly by
the land of Nathll Nickols thirty one Pole: at the East Corner by
a black oak tree marked: northerly by the high way about twenty
Six Pole: Norwesterly by the land I Sold to Thomas Eatton: about Eight
Pole: with all the Rights Titles profits priviledges apirtenances
profits and advantages thereunto belonging or in any wise aper-
taing to the Same to him the Said Josiah Hodgman his heirs Exectr
adminr or asignes forever to have and to hold the above
bargined premises with all the Rights above Said for a good time In
defeasable Title of Inheritance forever: And further I the Said
Samuel Morow doe for my Self my heirs Exectr adminr & asignes
Grant unto and Covenant with the Said Josiah Hodgman his heirs Exectr
adminr and asignes that I have good Right full Power and Lawfull
authority to make this Conveiance at this time and that the Said Josi
-ah Hodgman his heirs Exectr adminr and asignes Shall or
may have hold Injoy occupie and possess the Said premises and
every part thereof without the lawfull let Suite hinderance Contradi
ction or molestation of any Parson whatsoever: and I the Said Saml
Morow doe hereby bind and oblige my Self My heirs Exectr
and adminr forever to warrant and defend the Said premises &
Every part thereof from all former gifts grants Sales leases alien
-ations Joyntors Dowries titles of Dowry Will or Intails Bonds or for
-feturs Morgages attachments Judgments or Executions or any
Such like Trouble or troble had made or done at any time by any
Parson lawfully: and in witness of the Same I the Said Saml
Morow and also Mary my now marryed wife as manifesting
her free Consent to the Same have hereunto set our hands and affix
-ed our Seals this fourteenth day of Aprill in the year of our lord
god one thousand Seven hundred and twenty one and in the Seventh year
of the Reigne of our Soveraigne lord Georg King of great Britton &

Signed Sealed and Delivered in the presence of us witnesses
Raham Bancroft
Josiah Temple

Samuell Morrey
Mary Morow her X mark

This deed, dated April 14, 1721, is for the sale of land in present-day Reading by Samuel Morow to Josiah Hodgman. Hodgman was part of the expedition to Canada that took place 10 years earlier, shown on the previous page. The deed gives the names of the abutters, Nathaniel Nichols and Thomas Eaton, and the signatures of witnesses Raham Bancroft and Josiah Temple. The last line reads "in the seventh year of the Reigne of our Soveraigne lord George King of Great Britton," a reminder that the colonies did not seek independence until more than 50 years later. The "X" next to the words "her mark" after the name of Mary Morow, wife of Samuel, indicates that she was probably unable to write.

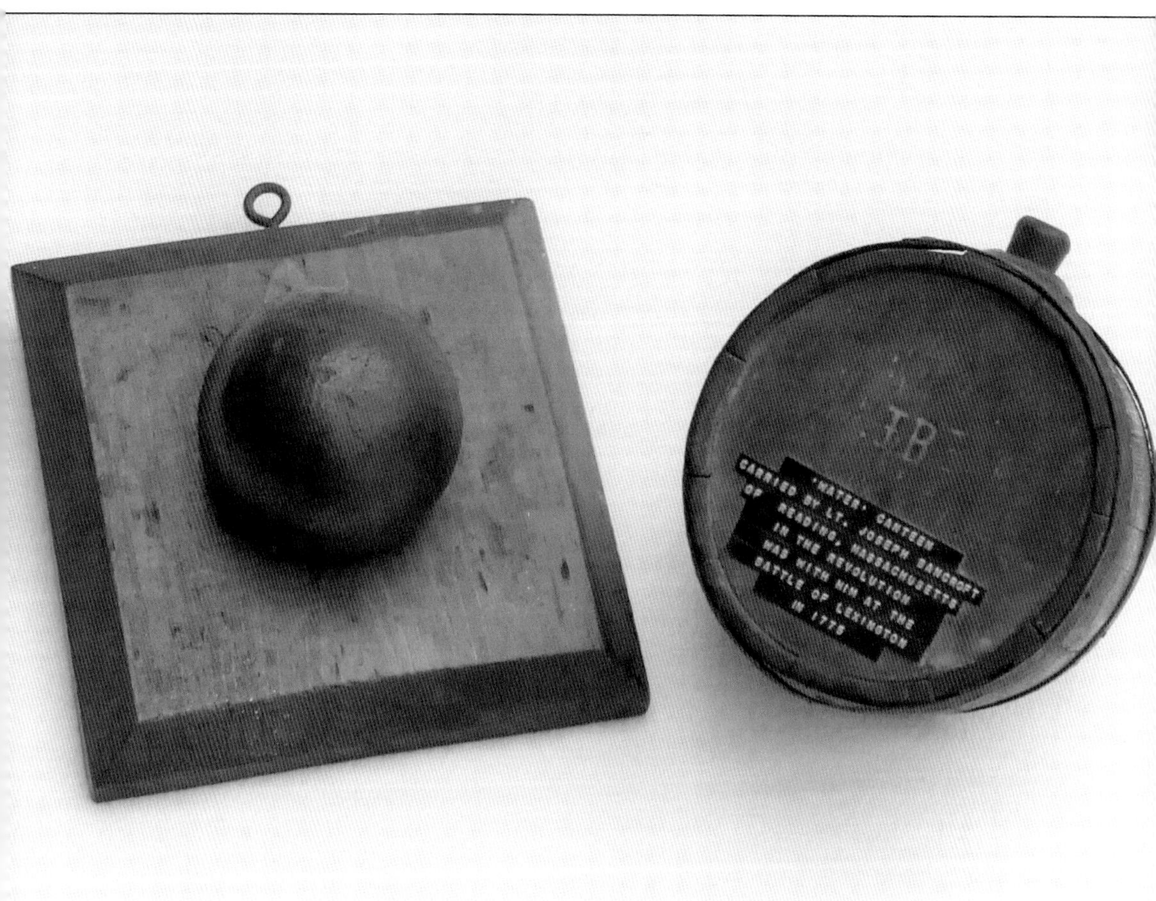

On April 19, 1775, Sgt. Joseph Bancroft (see page 14) and Reading's Third Parish Company responded to the news that the British were marching to Concord. At 12:30 p.m., after marching for six hours, they encountered the retreating British at Meriam's Corner in Concord. Along with colonists from other communities, the Reading militia skirmished with the British as they retreated toward Charlestown. Lord Percy and British reinforcements arrived in Lexington at 2:30 p.m. with two cannons and 48 cannonballs. He fired at the colonists, allowing the fleeing British to reach safety behind his lines. This was the first use of artillery in the American Revolution. Clinton L. Bancroft recorded and signed the family legend on the back of the plaque seen here at left, which reads, "This Cannon Ball was fired at the Reading Minutemen's Company by one of Percy's guns in the battle of Lexington, and was located by Joseph Bancroft who afterwards found it and brought it to Reading and it has been in his family ever since." The canteen at right was carried by Joseph Bancroft on that day.

By His Excellency

Samuel Adams, Esquire,

Governor and Commander in Chief of the

COMMONWEALTH OF MASSACHUSETTS.

Samuel Adams

To Joseph Bancroft jun. Gentleman Greeting.

YOU being appointed Lieutenant of a company in the second Regiment (First Brigade) Third Division of the Militia of this Commonwealth.

BY Virtue of the Power vested in me, I do by these Presents, (reposing special Trust and Confidence in your Ability, Courage and good Conduct) COMMISSION you accordingly :— You are, therefore, carefully and diligently to discharge the Duty of Lieutenant in Leading, Ordering and Exercising said Company in Arms, both inferior Officers and Soldiers ; and to keep them in good Order and Discipline : And they are hereby commanded to obey your as their Lieutenant And you are yourself to observe and follow such Orders and Instructions, as you shall from Time to Time receive from me, or your superior Officers.

GIVEN under my Hand, and the Seal of the said Commonwealth, the Thirtieth *Day of* May *in the Year of our* LORD, 1796 *and in the* Twentieth *Year of the* Independence *of the* United States *of AMERICA.*

BY THE GOVERNOR.

John Avery Secy.

Above is the commissioning paper of Lt. Joseph Bancroft Jr., son of the Revolutionary War soldier. Joseph Jr. was born in 1762 and was too young to serve in the war, but the newly formed United States of America still needed a militia. This document is dated May 30, 1796, and is signed by Massachusetts governor Samuel Adams near the top left corner. The items shown on these two pages were passed down through the Bancroft family. Clinton L. Bancroft, shown at right, was a direct descendant of Sgt. Joseph Bancroft, a well-respected Reading historian, secretary of the Reading Antiquarian Society, and member of the board of directors of the Bay State League, and lived in Reading until shortly before his death in 1949.

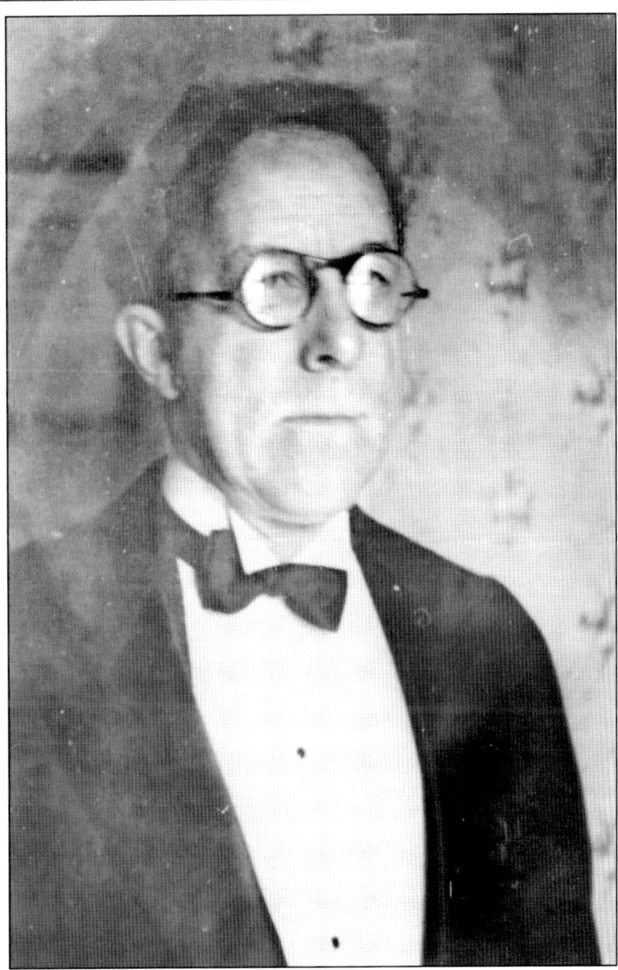

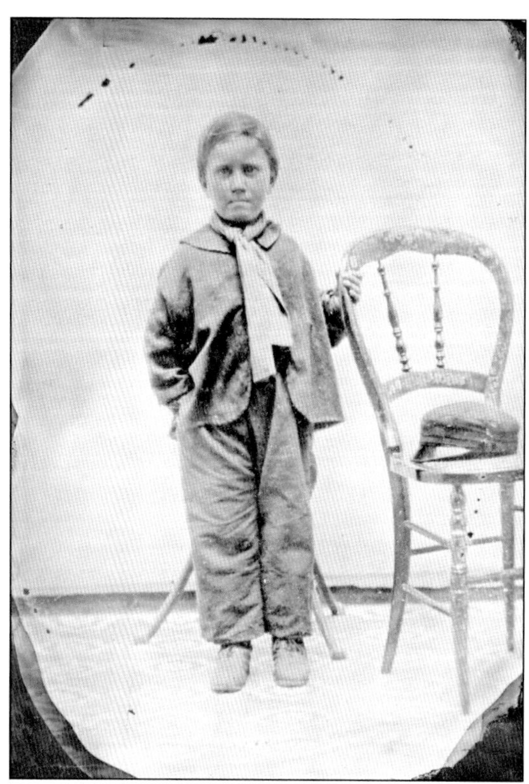

Henry Francis Wardwell was born in Cambridge, Massachusetts, on December 25, 1844. He was the first child born to Samuel and Fidelia Jane (Flint) Wardwell. The 1855 and 1860 censuses show him living with his mother and younger sister Isabella at the home of his grandparents Amos and Selina Flint on Forest Street (see page 21).

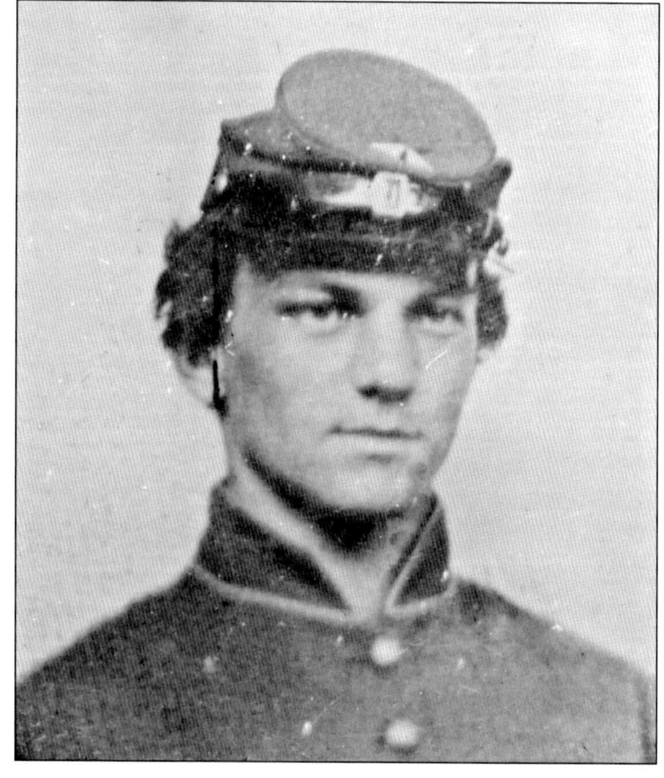

On April 12, 1861, shots were fired by Confederates on Fort Sumter in South Carolina. Three days later, Pres. Abraham Lincoln put out a call for troops to suppress the rebellion. Henry Wardwell was a member of the Richardson Light Guard, a local militia unit. On April 19, they received orders to report for duty. By that evening, they were on trains bound for Boston and, from there, by rail, boat, and on foot to Washington, DC. Henry was 16.

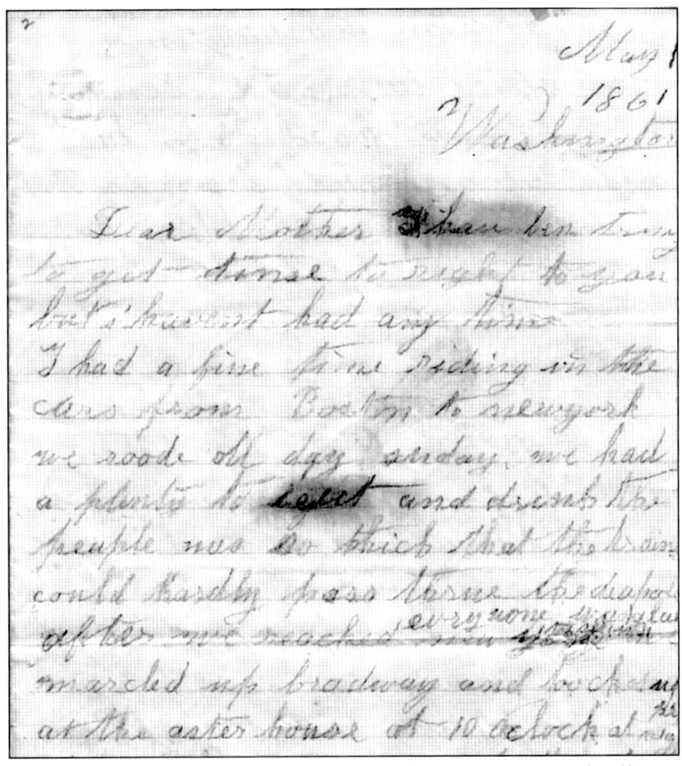
May 1
1861
Washington

Dear Mother I have ben trying to get time to right to you but i havent had any time
I had a fine time riding in the cars from Boston to newyork we roode all day sunday we had a plenty to eat and drink the peuple was so thick that the train could hardly pass throu the depot
~~after we reached new york~~ every one ... marched up bradway and locked up at the aster house at 10 oclock at ...

On May 1, 1861, less than two weeks after leaving Reading, Henry Wardwell wrote to his mother from the roof of the Treasury Building in Washington, DC, where his regiment was quartered. Later that day, the regiment was mustered into service as Company B, 5th Massachusetts Regiment, and passed in review before President Lincoln. In July, they were one of three Massachusetts regiments fighting at the Battle of Manassas. Reading's first Civil War casualty, Thomas Hetler, died at Manassas at age 20. Shortly thereafter, the regiment returned to Reading, having completed their three-month enlistment. A total of 411 men served from or for Reading in the Civil War, nearly 60 percent of those eligible. Even though they did not all serve at the same time, the impact on families, farms, and businesses must have been great.

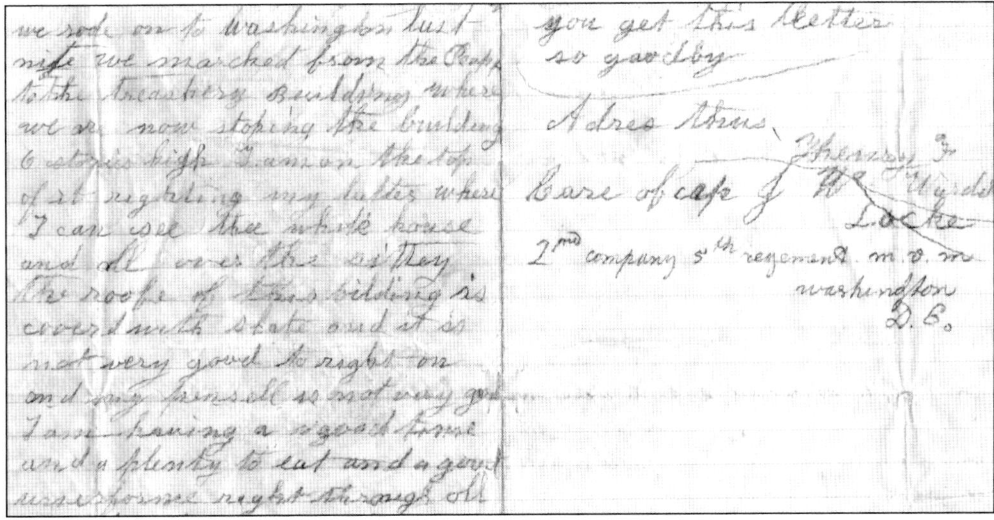
we rode on to washington last nite we marched from the depo to the treasury Building where we are now stoping the building 6 stories high I am on the top of it righting my letter where I can see the white house and all over the sitty the roofe of this bilding is coverd with slate and it is not very good to right on and my pensill is not very good I am having a good time and a plenty to eat and a good ... right through all

you get this letter so goodby

Adres thus
Henry F Wardwell
Care of capt J W Locke
2nd company 5th regiment M.V.M
washington
D.C.

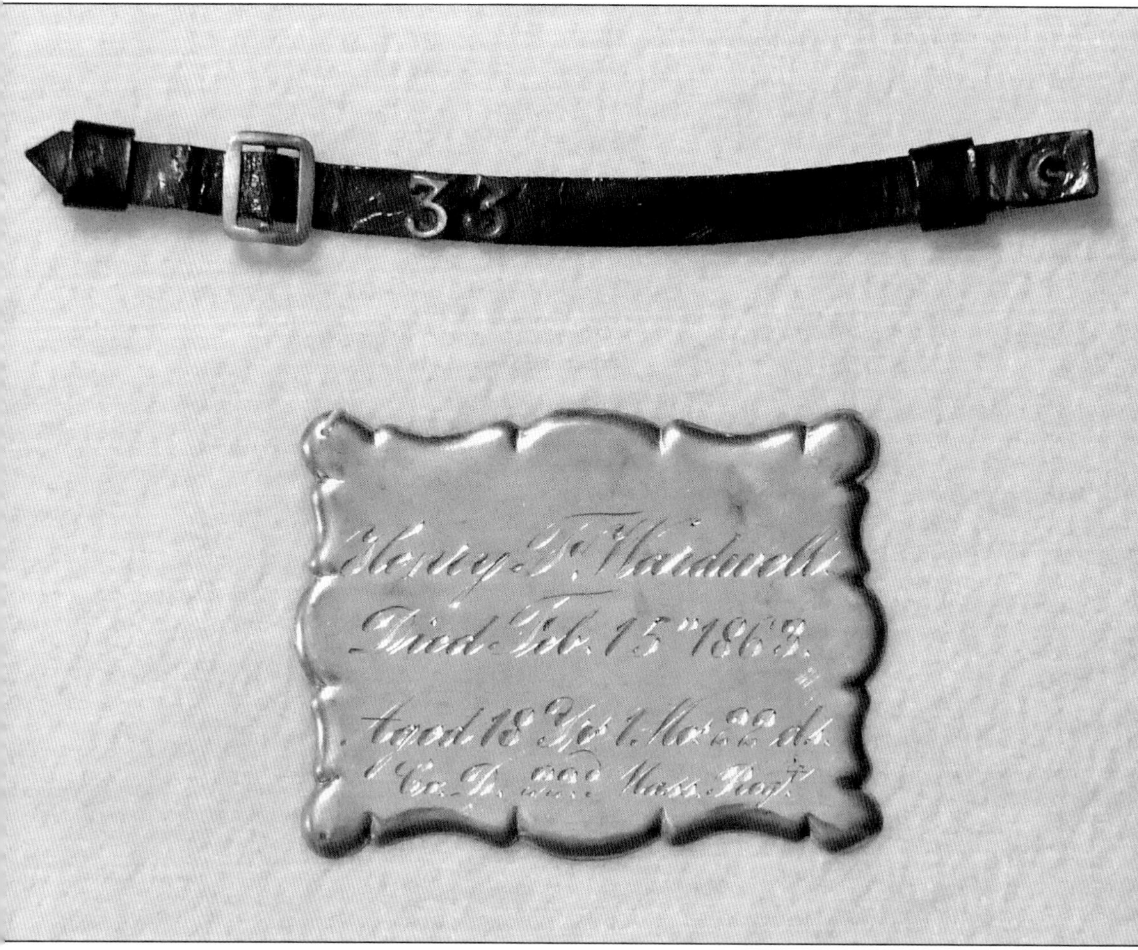

Henry Wardwell re-enlisted in August 1862 in Company D, 33rd Massachusetts Regiment. The regiment left the state on August 14, 1862, for Washington, DC, where it remained until October 10. After several short marches, due to rumors of the enemy's presence, they started for Fredericksburg, Virginia, on December 10. They participated in the "Mud March" and made winter quarters near Stafford Court House. Wardwell fell ill in early February 1863 and was eventually transferred to the Mount Pleasant General Hospital in Washington, DC. He died on February 15 of typhoid fever just two months after his 18th birthday. His body was sent home for burial in Reading. Pictured here is the strap from his hat with the insignia of his regiment, and his casket marker. The marker incorrectly reads "22nd Massachusetts Regiment."

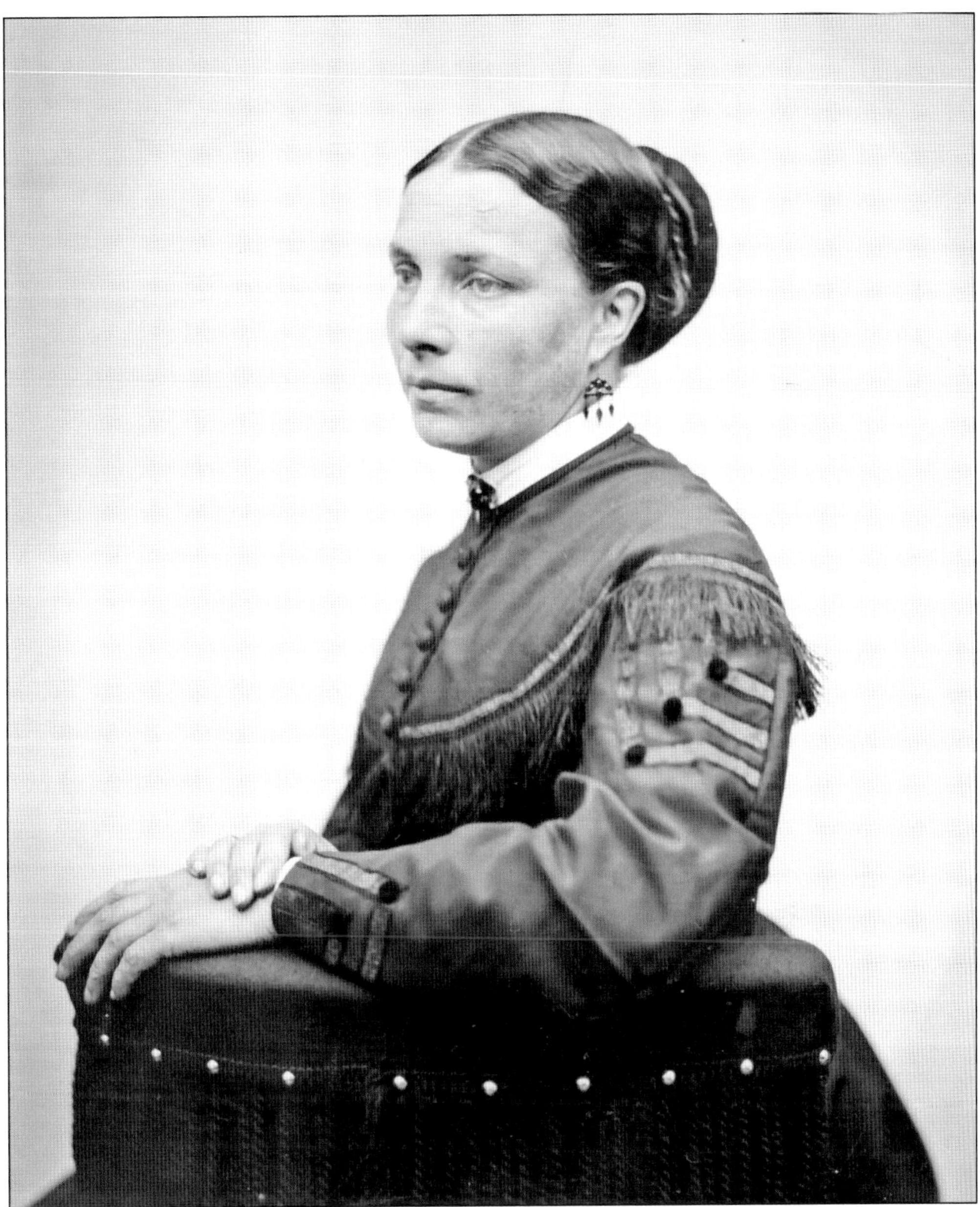

Fidelia Jane (Flint) Wardwell Austin was the mother of Henry Wardwell. This photograph is from a rare half-page tintype and shows her in a military-style dress that pays tribute to her late son. She married Samuel Wardwell in 1842 in Andover, Massachusetts. He was the great-great-great-grandson of the Samuel Wardwell who was convicted and put to death in the Salem witch trials in 1692. In the 1850 census, Fidelia and her children were living with her parents, Amos and Selina Flint, in Reading, but Samuel was not with them. No records have been found to determine what happened to him. In 1858, Fidelia married Harris Austin, a jeweler, and lived in Reading until her death in 1903. Her two granddaughters, Isabella Hartwell's daughters, Addie and Francena, were raised in different families. Addie lived with her paternal grandparents in Amherst, New Hampshire. Francena grew up in Reading and was adopted at a young age by George E. and Susan Smith, who lived next door to the Austins.

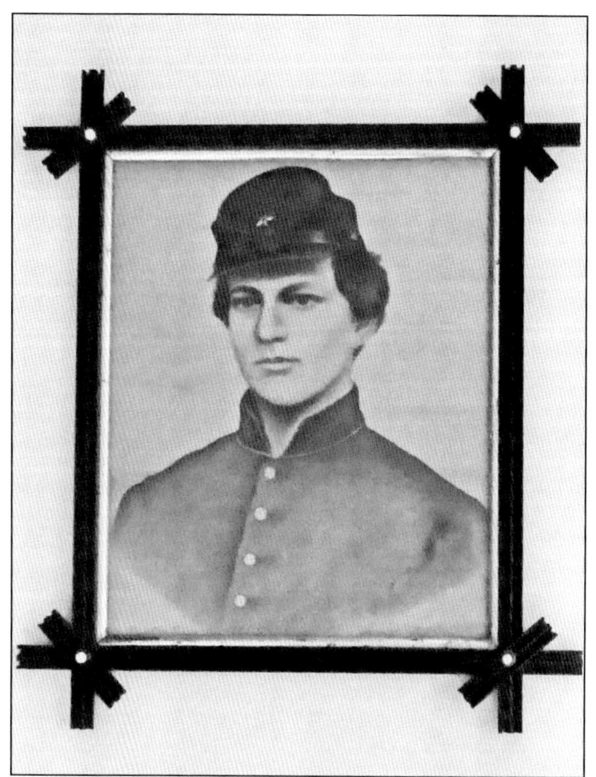

These large pastel portraits of Henry Francis Wardwell and Isabella Francena (Wardwell) Hartwell, brother and sister, were done from their thumbnail tintypes presumably shortly after their deaths. They are framed in 16-by-19-inch "bowtie" wooden frames with ceramic buttons that were popular in the 1860s. Henry, 18 years old, died on February 15, 1863, while serving in the Civil War.

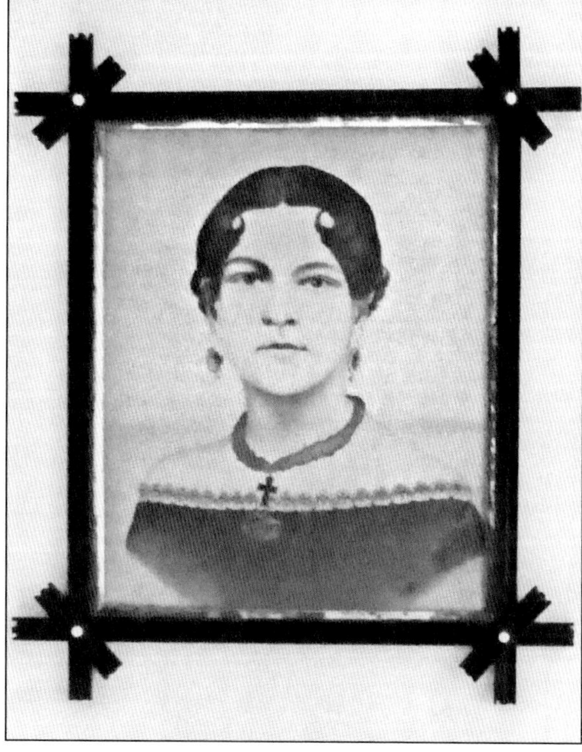

Henry and Isabella were Fidelia and Samuel Wardwell's only children. Isabella died a year after Henry, on March 10, 1864, just two months before her 18th birthday and shortly after giving birth to her daughter Francena ("Sis"), her second child. Both Henry and Isabella are buried at Laurel Hill Cemetery with their mother, stepfather Harris Austin, and other family members.

March 14th 1863
Stafford Va.
I received your letter last night so you see I hasten to answer it.
With regard to Henry, it will please me to give you all the information I am able. His watch he sold last fall or early winter, his dress coat he had on the last time I saw him, and also his overcoat and Blouse.

I think you have nothing at all to regret on your part, He was tired of the war, like a thousand others, but I do not know as that had anything to do with his sickness, I told him to put on all the under clothes he could and he said he would, the last he said to me,

Duncan Harriman of Stoneham married Fidelia Jane (Flint) Wardwell's sister Selina, and therefore was an uncle of Henry Wardwell. Harriman was a corporal in Company D of the 33rd Regiment with Wardwell. After Wardwell's death, Harriman wrote a four-page letter to Wardwell's mother, Fidelia, in response to several questions she had about Henry's death. Excerpts from his letter are shown at right. In another section of his letter (not shown), Harriman asked if "Henry had a ring on his finger, I made it out of a Beeff Bone for him." That bone ring, shown below, was passed down through the family. Six other Reading soldiers in Company D died during the war: Henry Damon II, Jules Allen, and Leonard Peterson died of wounds, and Otis Sanborn, Mathias Gambell (see page 99), and George Winn died of disease.

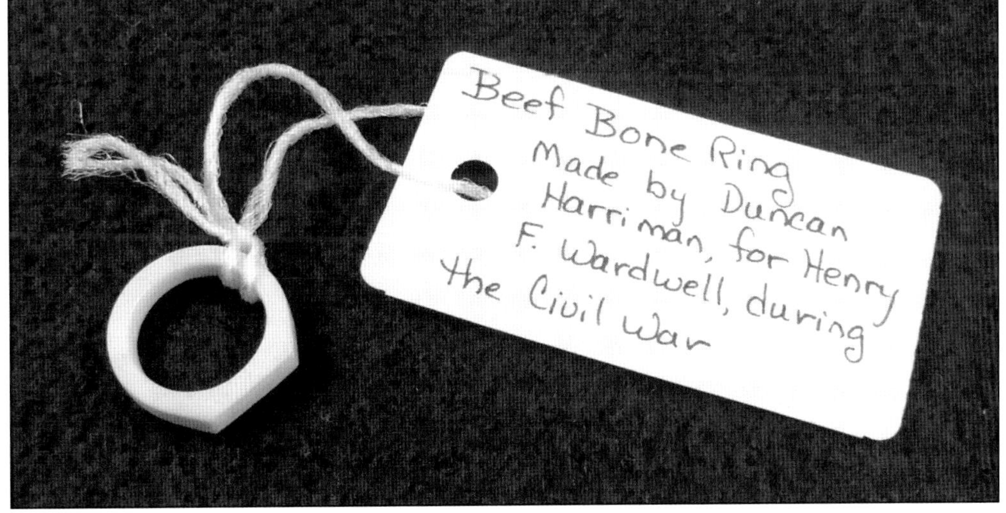

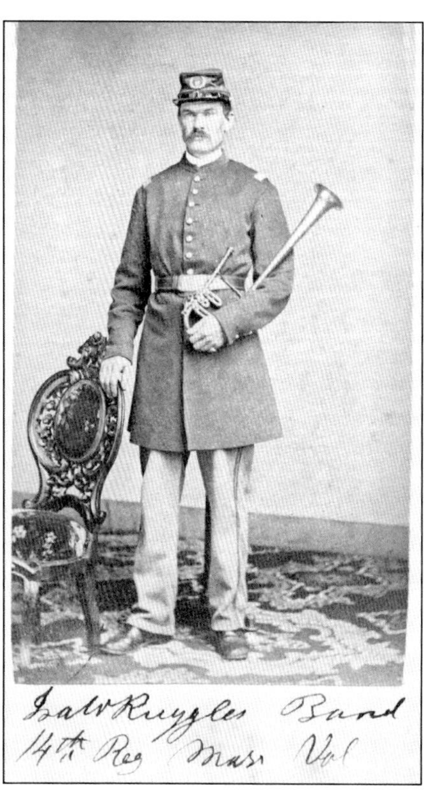

Several Reading men served as musicians in the Civil War. Ira White Ruggles enlisted early in the war and was discharged in 1862 when all bands were discharged because men were needed as soldiers. Ira's sister Emily Ruggles (see page 66) felt so strongly about wanting to serve that she paid $125 to the Commonwealth of Massachusetts for Matt Briggs, of the 5th US Colored Heavy Artillery, to serve as her representative recruit.

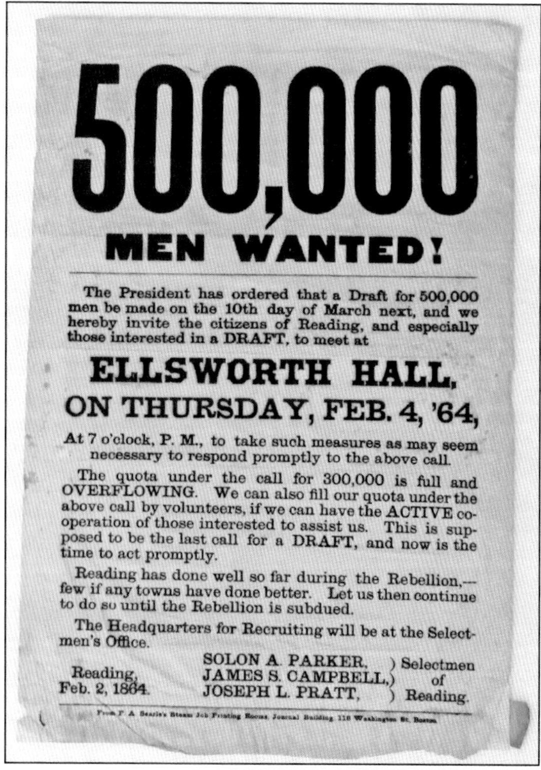

500,000

MEN WANTED!

The President has ordered that a Draft for 500,000 men be made on the 10th day of March next, and we hereby invite the citizens of Reading, and especially those interested in a DRAFT, to meet at

ELLSWORTH HALL,

ON THURSDAY, FEB. 4, '64,

At 7 o'clock, P. M., to take such measures as may seem necessary to respond promptly to the above call.

The quota under the call for 300,000 is full and OVERFLOWING. We can also fill our quota under the above call by volunteers, if we can have the ACTIVE co-operation of those interested to assist us. This is supposed to be the last call for a DRAFT, and now is the time to act promptly.

Reading has done well so far during the Rebellion,—few if any towns have done better. Let us then continue to do so until the Rebellion is subdued.

The Headquarters for Recruiting will be at the Selectmen's Office.

Reading, Feb. 2, 1864.

SOLON A. PARKER,
JAMES S. CAMPBELL,
JOSEPH L. PRATT,
Selectmen of Reading.

By 1864, President Lincoln put out another call for volunteers. This 12-by-18-inch broadside was posted in Reading announcing an informational meeting to encourage men to sign up to fill Reading's quota before the draft took effect. Over the course of the Civil War, many men signed up in towns other than their own in order to take advantage of bonuses being offered in order to fill quotas.

Charles Everett Flint was born in Reading in 1838 to Amos and Selina Flint. Mary Jane Hayden was born in Hollis, New Hampshire, in the same year. Shortly after their marriage in 1860, they moved to Milford, New Hampshire. He was a shoemaker when he enlisted in Company B, 1st New Hampshire Heavy Artillery in September 1864. The 1870 and 1880 censuses show them still residing in Milford, but by 1900, they were living in Reading at 83 King Street (new No. 105). Below are his belt buckles. He would have worn the US buckle in the Civil War. The Grand Army of the Republic (GAR) was a fraternal organization founded in 1866 for Union veterans of the Civil War. Flint belonged to a New Hampshire GAR post and later to Reading's GAR Post 194 after moving back to Reading.

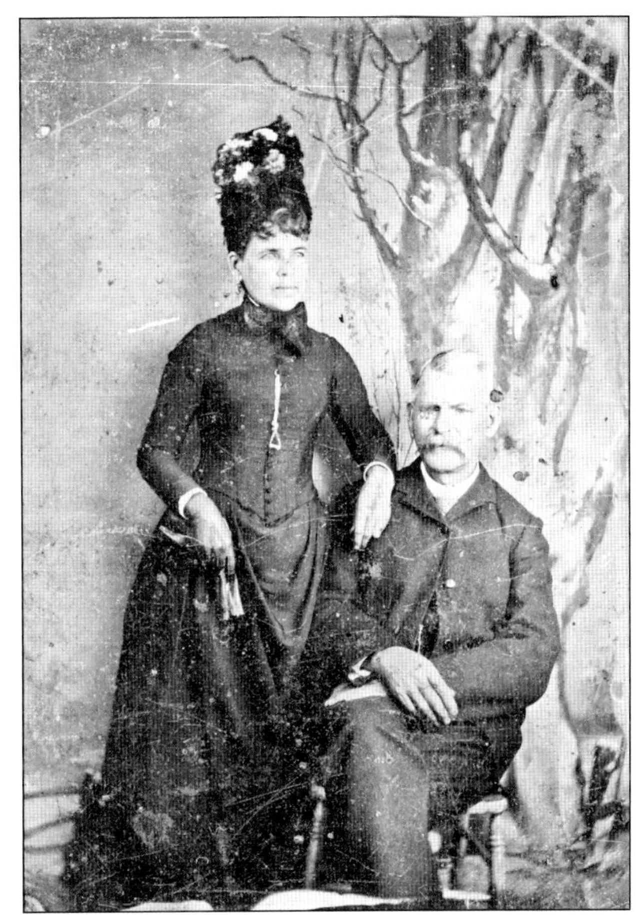

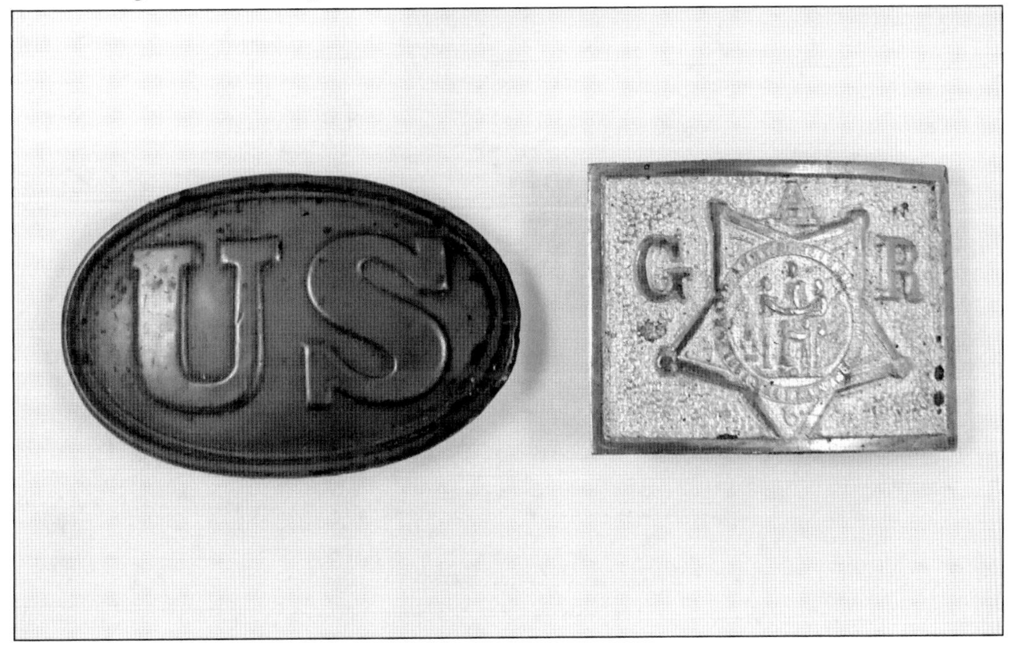

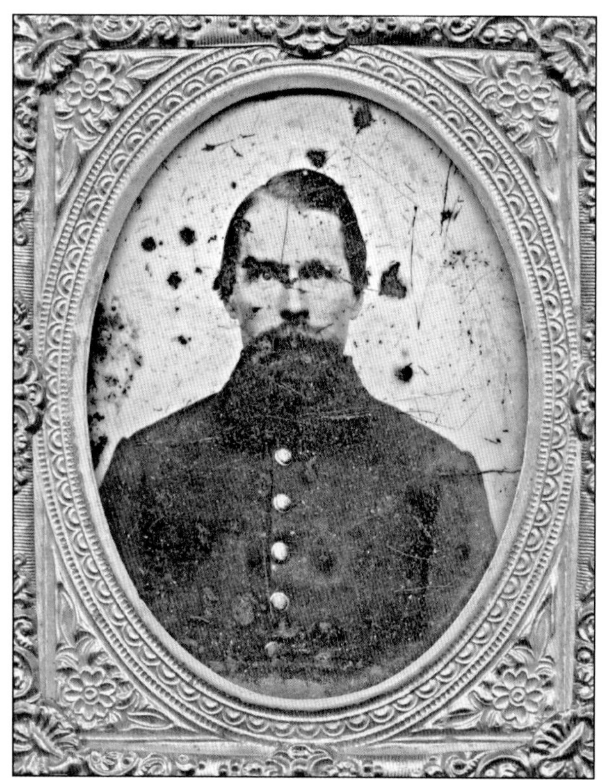

Seth Bessey enlisted in the Civil War at the age of 36, gave his occupation as butcher, and served in the 13th Massachusetts Regiment. He was discharged for disability at Antietam in October 1862. In December 1863, he re-enlisted in the 59th Massachusetts Regiment and was mustered out at the end of the war. In 1882, he owned a boardinghouse in Weston's Block on Haven Street.

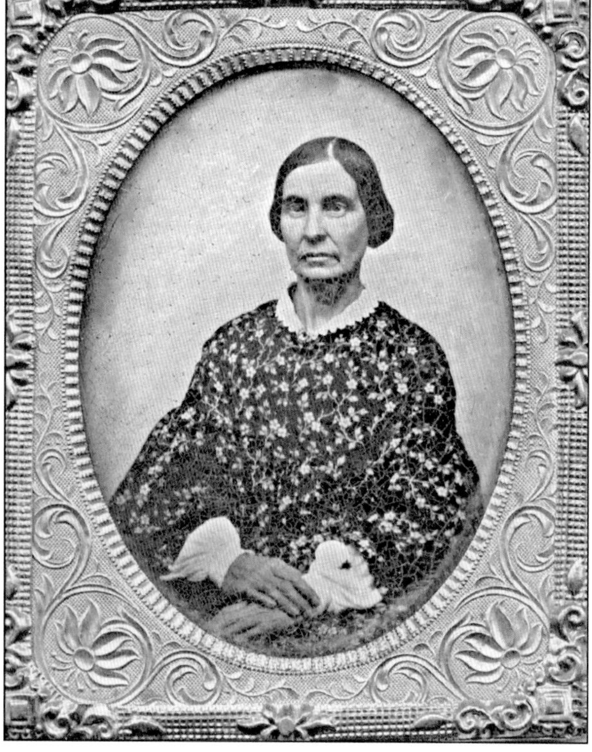

Martha (Nichols) Bessey and her husband, Seth, were living at what is now 1243 Main Street in Reading in 1855. She was born in Reading in 1822 to Edmund and Bethiah Nichols. Both Martha's and Seth's photographs are rare ambrotypes—negatives on glass. Seth is pictured in his Civil War uniform. Their son George and nephew Charles (see page 101) also served in the war.

The house shown at right, currently at 273 Pearl Street, appears on the 1795 map and was then occupied by James Nichols. Pearl Street was one of Reading's major roads before the Andover-Medford Turnpike, now Route 28, was built in 1806. In 1851, Mathias and Huldah Gambell moved to this house from Stoneham. He enlisted in Company D, 33rd Massachusetts Regiment in August 1862 when he was 42 years old. He was a farmer. He died less than two months later at a hospital in Alexandria, Virginia. Pictured below is his grave at the Alexandria National Cemetery. Another Reading soldier, David O'Keefe, is also buried there.

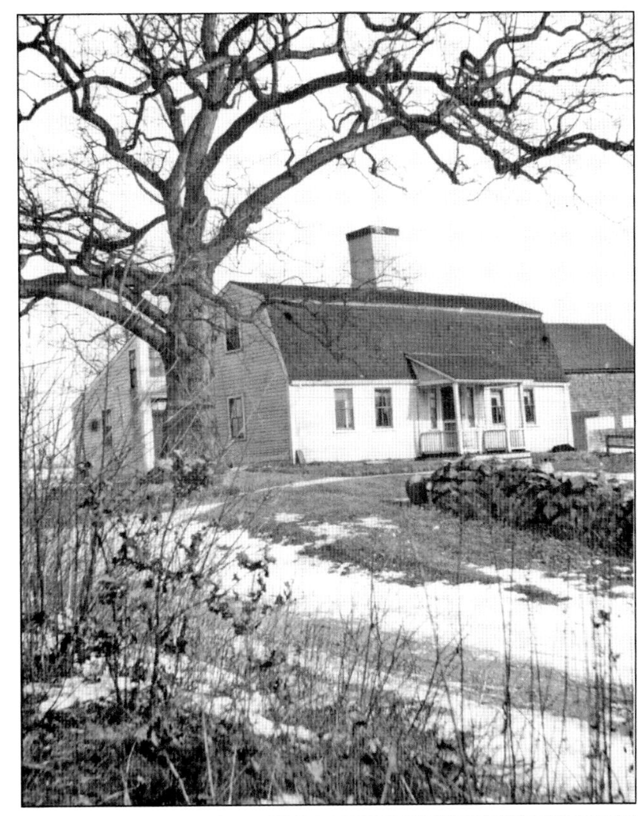

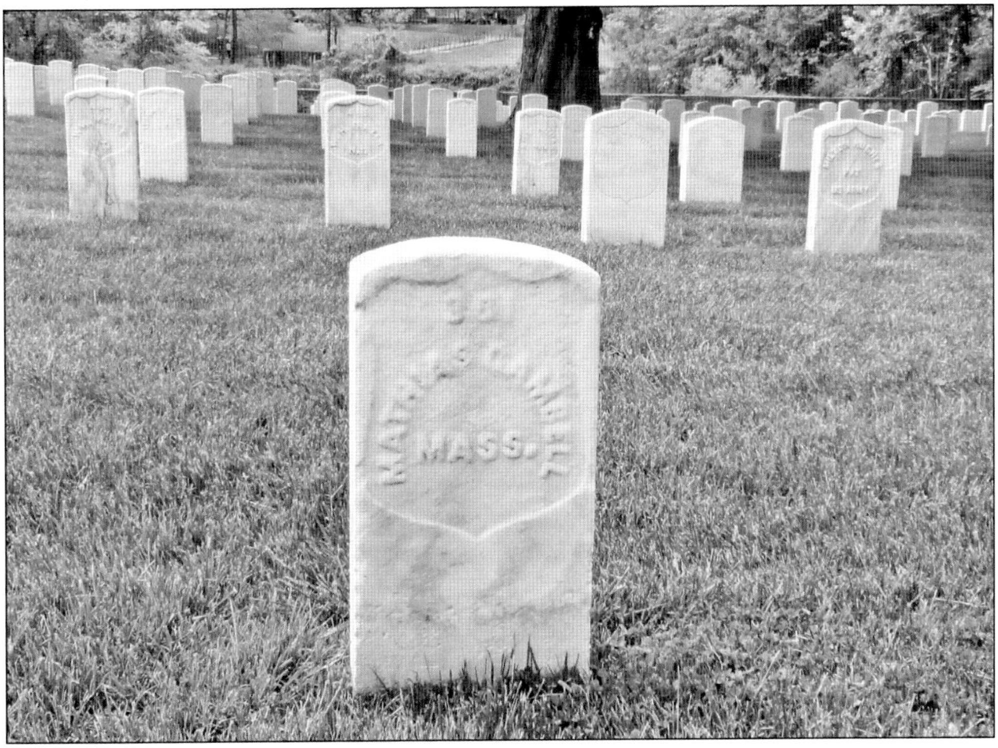

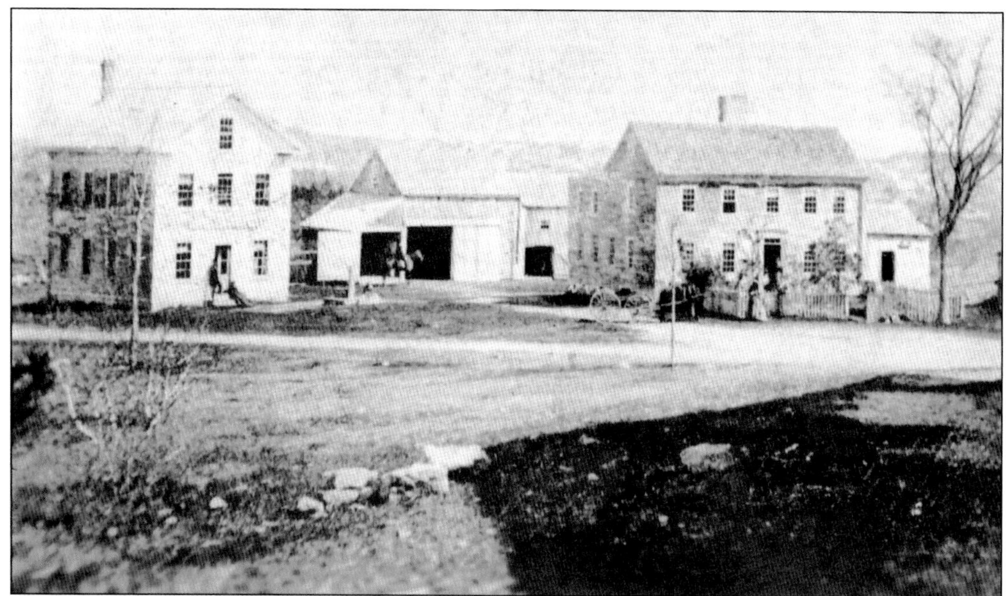

The photograph below of Thomas Pickett Sweetser, born in Reading in 1850, is from a thumbnail tintype. The family home, shown above on the right, was on the east side of Summer Avenue near Leach Park. It was moved around 1871 and was torn down for the building of the Joshua Eaton School. In September 1875, Sweetser enlisted in the US Army. Two days earlier, another young man from Reading, George Emerson Smith, whose father and brother served in the Civil War, also enlisted. In October, Sweetser and Smith reported for duty at Fort Lincoln, Dakota Territory, as members of the 7th Cavalry. Sweetser was in Company A and Smith in Company M. On June 25, 1876, both were killed in the valley fight at the Battle of Little Bighorn in Montana, known as Custer's Last Stand. Their names are listed on the monument on Last Stand Hill.

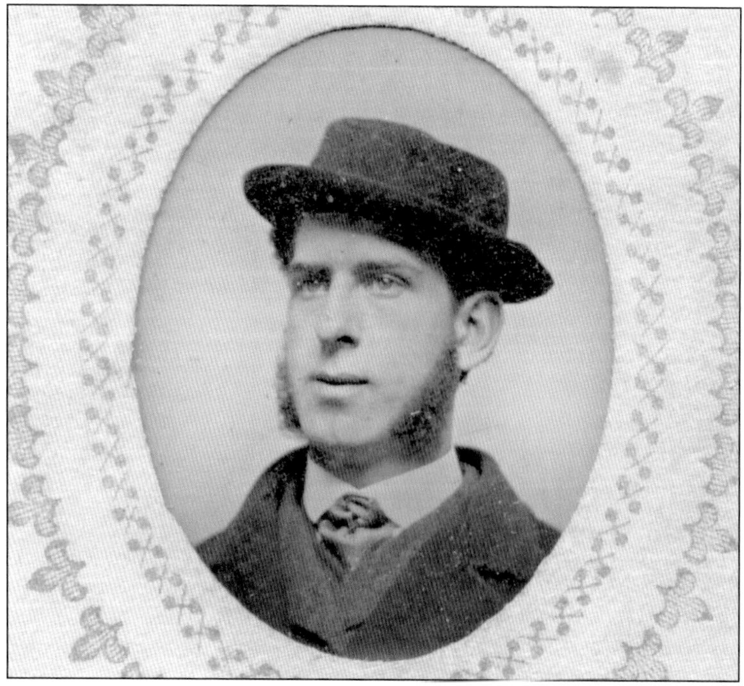

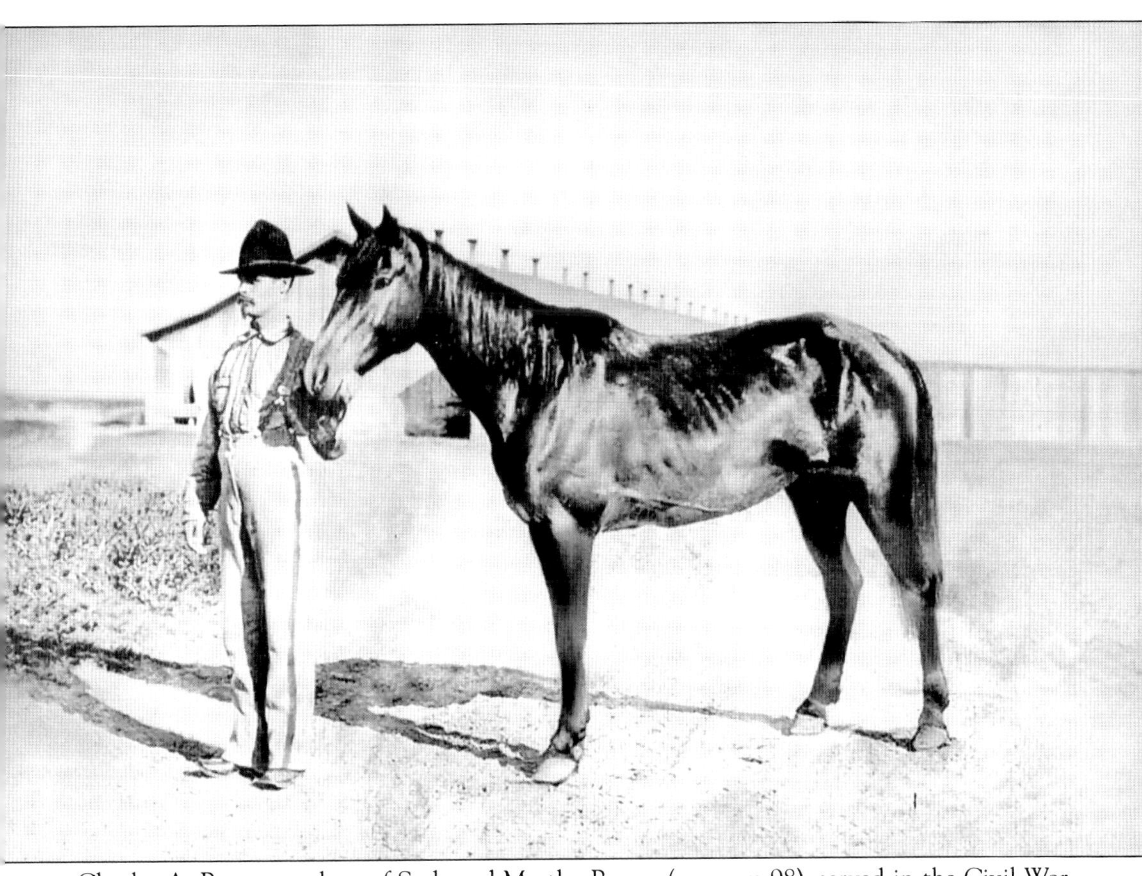

Charles A. Bessey, nephew of Seth and Martha Bessey (see page 98), served in the Civil War in two different regiments, the 8th Massachusetts for a three-month enlistment, and the 1st Massachusetts Battalion Cavalry, known as the Frontier Cavalry. The Frontier Cavalry was created late in 1864 to patrol the border between Canada and the United States in response to a group of Confederate soldiers and sympathizers who crossed the border and robbed three banks in St. Albans, Vermont. After the war, Bessey continued to serve. He enlisted in the cavalry in 1870 and served on the western frontier. For his bravery on January 13, 1877, he received the Congressional Medal of Honor in 1890. His citation reads, "while scouting with four men and attacked in ambush by 14 Indians, held his ground, 2 of his men being wounded, and kept up the fight until himself wounded in the side, and then went to the assistance of his wounded comrades." Bessey is the only known Reading resident to receive the Medal of Honor. This photograph was taken at Fort Laramie, Wyoming. (Courtesy of James Moniot.)

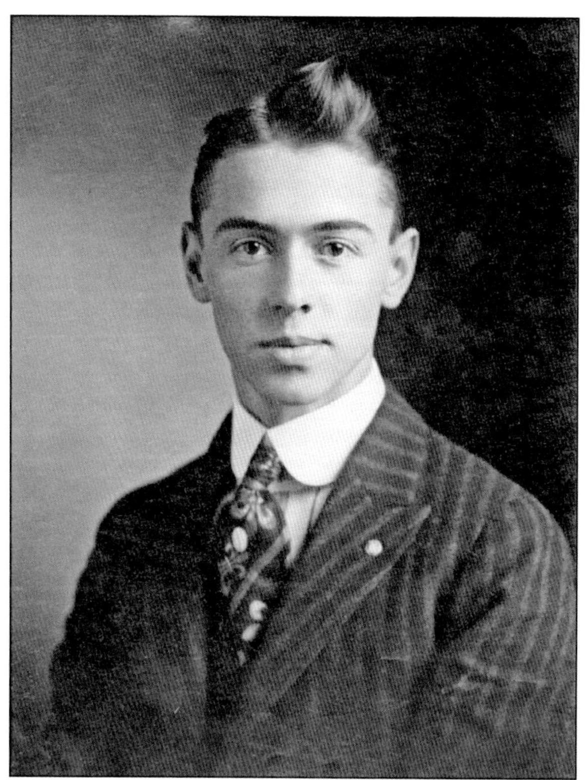

Ernest Hunnewell Leach was born in Hanson, Massachusetts, in November 1895. He attended Reading schools, worked for the First National Bank of Reading as a clerk, and in 1910 was living at 12 Pratt Street with his parents, Rev. A. Judson and Mary (Lewis) Leach and siblings William, Josephine, and Edwin. He was granted a passport on March 30, 1917, to go to France to serve as an ambulance driver with the American Field Service.

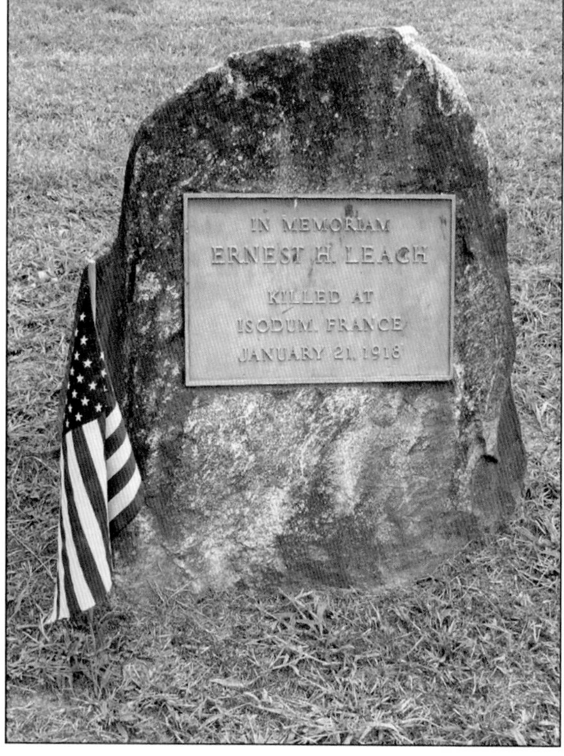

When the ambulance service was disbanded in October 1917, Ernest Hunnewell Leach enlisted in the American Aviation Service. He was killed in an airplane accident on January 21, 1918, and was the first of 14 Reading residents to die in World War I. Leach Park, at the intersection of Summer Avenue, Hopkins Street, and Walnut Street, was named in his honor.

Five

READING PASTIMES

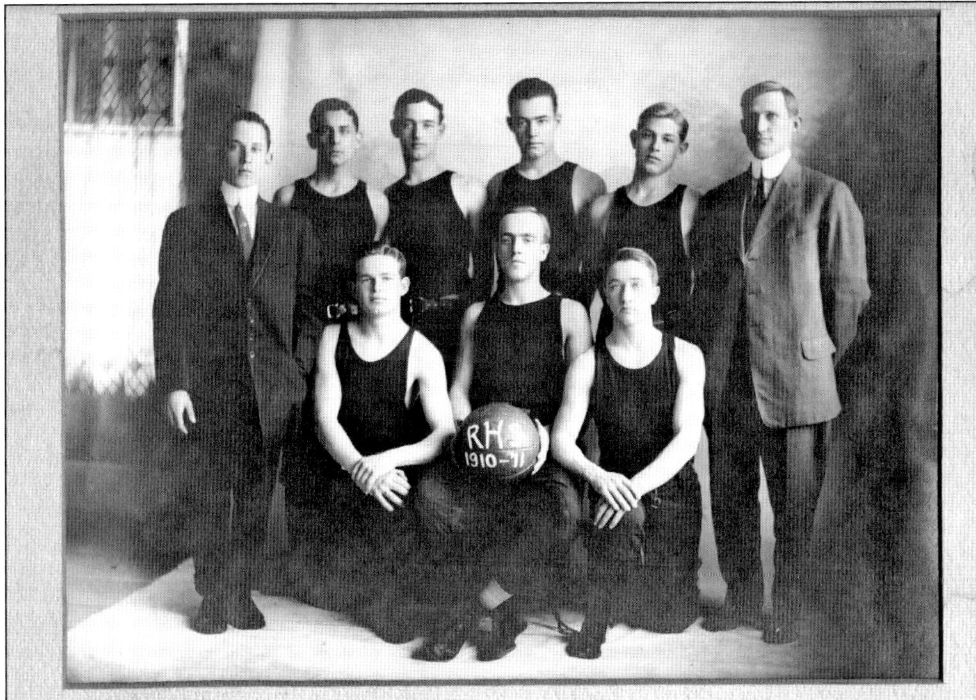

It is the authors' hope that this chapter will provide a glimpse into organizations, sports, and activities enjoyed by residents of Reading through the years. This photograph shows the 1910–1911 Reading High School basketball team. The name of the player at center in the second row was omitted, but is believed to be Romeo Michelini.

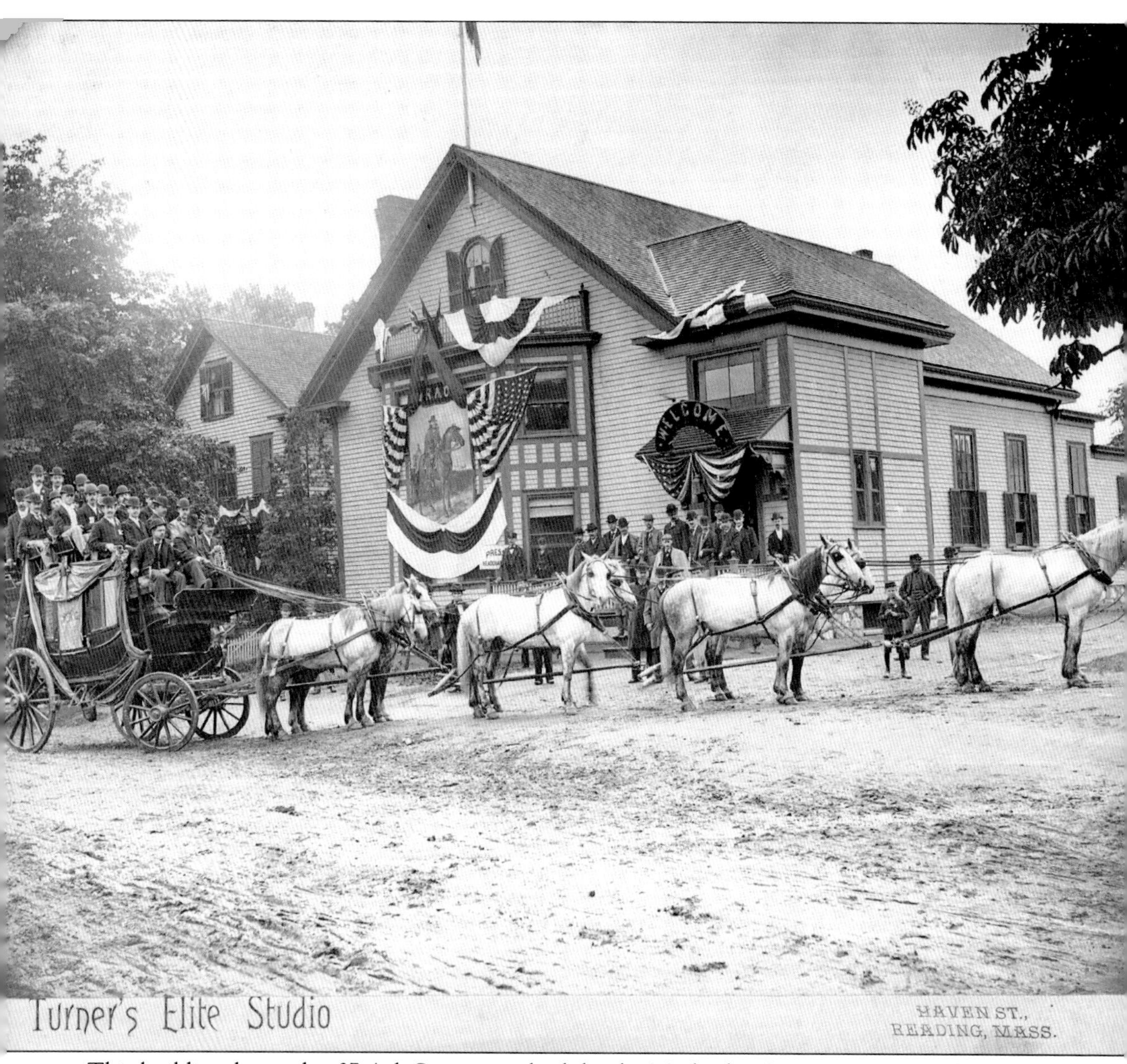

This building, located at 37 Ash Street, was built by the Methodist Society in 1869 and was used as a chapel until the society bought the Old South building at the head of the common from the Congregationalists in 1887. The Reading Athletic Club, formed in the winter of 1886–1887, was the next occupant. This photograph shows the building decorated for the 250th anniversary of Reading in 1894. The Reading Athletic Club's purpose was to encourage athletic sports and fellowship. In less than 10 years, it had grown to include over 150 members. Its facility contained a gymnasium, dance hall, parlor, whist room, bowling alley, and shooting gallery. Its baseball team competed in a league of area towns. In 1919, the building was renovated by architects Adden and Parker, and Victory House officially opened on November 11, 1919. It has been home to American Legion Post 62 since then.

The Reading Athletic Club Wheelmen had their first meeting April 1, 1893. Their purpose was to promote "athletic exercise by the use of riding bicycles." Annual dues were 50¢, payable in advance. The bylaws contained road rules for the use of public ways that included the use of hand signals, no riding on sidewalks, and "especial care exercised about surprising foot passengers, frightening horses and fast or reckless riding." But at a meeting two years later, on April 17, 1895, they voted to disband the club "due to lack of interest." Certainly, the sport of bicycling did not die out, and the number of bicycles eventually led to the issuing of bicycle license plates, like the one shown below. The 1943 town report states that 1,508 plates had been issued in 1942 and 1943.

—By-Laws—

We whose names are appended associate ourselves under the name of Reading Athletic Club Wheelmen for the purpose of promoting athletic exercise by the use of Bicycles and for social purposes and for the government of our body we adopt the following By Laws

Art 1 Our Annual Meeting shall be held the second Monday in April of each year

Art 2 Regular business meetings shall be held Saturday evenings fortnightly and shall be called for 9.00 P.M.

Art 3 The Annual dues shall be Fifty (50) cents payable in advance

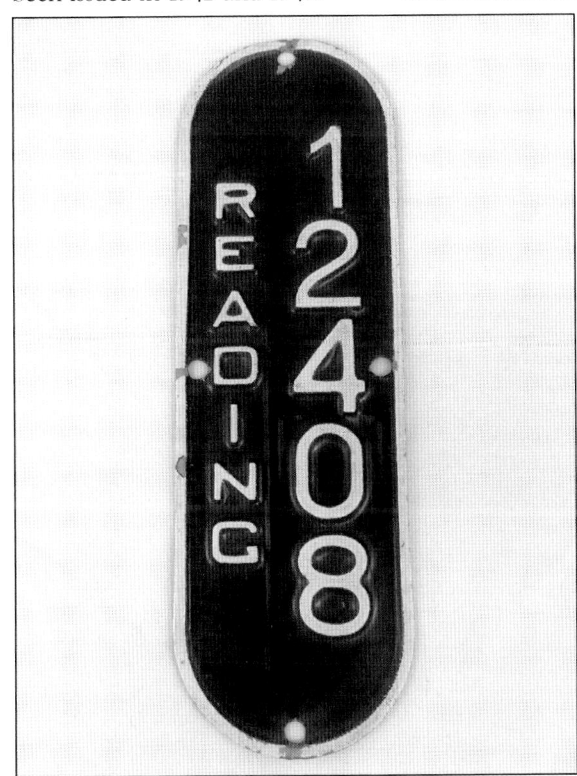

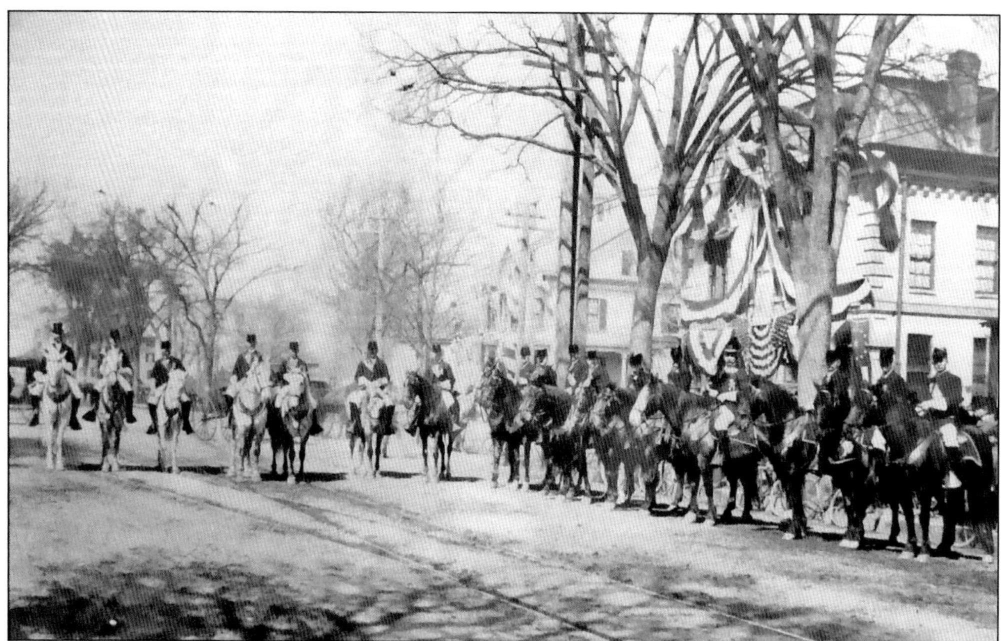

Security Lodge No. 208 of the Order of Odd Fellows was instituted in November 1890. The following year, members formed a Building Association. By December 1891, they had purchased a building at 26–30 Woburn Street, called Security Hall, which was originally built for the Presbyterian Society. The photograph above was taken on April 20, 1900, when Reading hosted the 81st anniversary of the Odd Fellows. The parade was led by chief marshal James W. Grimes, who rode a white charger, and was attended by thousands. Charles D. Wells is seventh from the left. A banquet for 800 guests followed in Black's Block. The Rebekahs had their banquet for 100 members at Security Hall. The certificate below was issued to Charles D. Wells for the purchase of one share and is shown along with his membership pin.

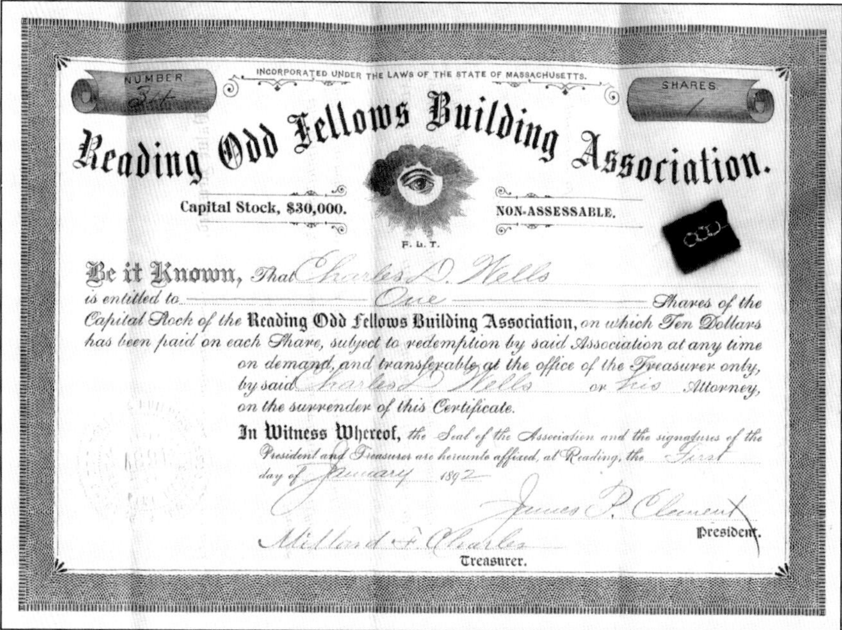

NUMBER [illegible]

INCORPORATED UNDER THE LAWS OF THE STATE OF MASSACHUSETTS.

SHARES 1

Reading Odd Fellows Building Association.

Capital Stock, $30,000.

NON-ASSESSABLE.

F. L. T.

Be it Known, *That* Charles D. Wells *is entitled to* One *Shares of the Capital Stock of the* **Reading Odd Fellows Building Association,** *on which Ten Dollars has been paid on each Share, subject to redemption by said Association at any time on demand, and transferable at the office of the Treasurer only, by said* Charles D. Wells *or* his *Attorney, on the surrender of this Certificate.*

In Witness Whereof, *the Seal of the Association and the signatures of the President and Treasurer are hereunto affixed, at Reading, the* First *day of* January 1892

James P. Clement
President.

Millard F. Charles
Treasurer.

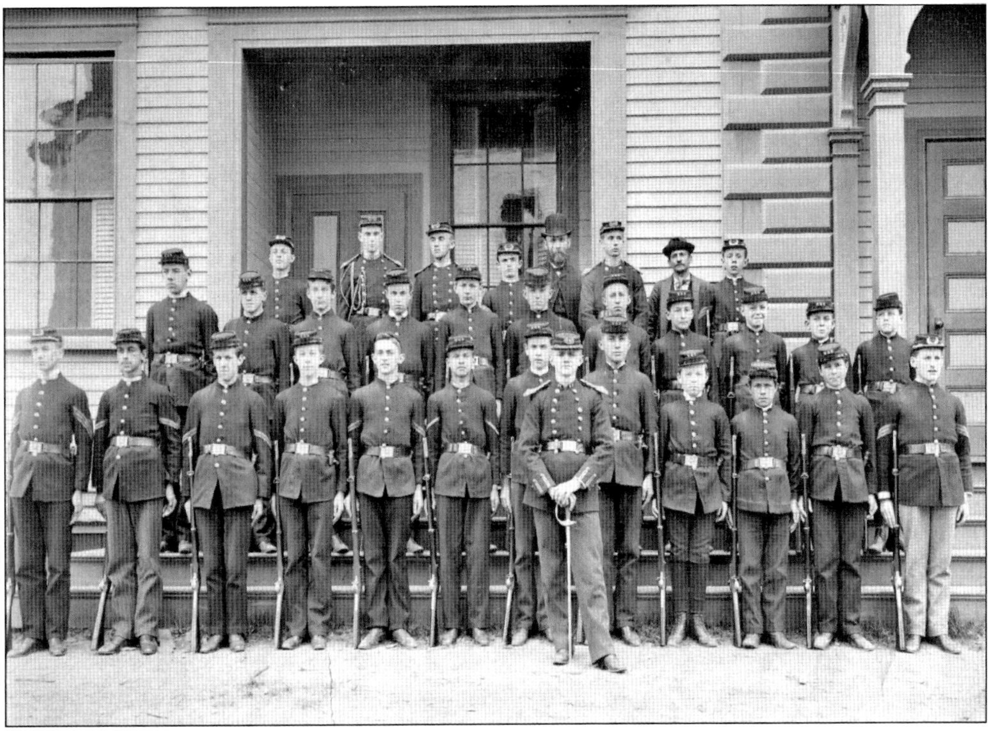

During the 1887–1888 school year, military drill was introduced into the course of study at the high school. The annual report of the school committee states, "It ought to develop a higher type of manhood among the boys, a spirit of loyalty to all authority, a recognition of the principal: 'He only who is willing to obey is fit to command.'" The undated photograph above shows a large group of cadets standing near the side entrance of the Center School. The photograph below shows seven young men with an empty chair. It is believed that the missing cadet is Fred P. Hayden, who died by accidental drowning on July 11, 1891, at Foster Pond in Andover, Massachusetts. He was 16 years old.

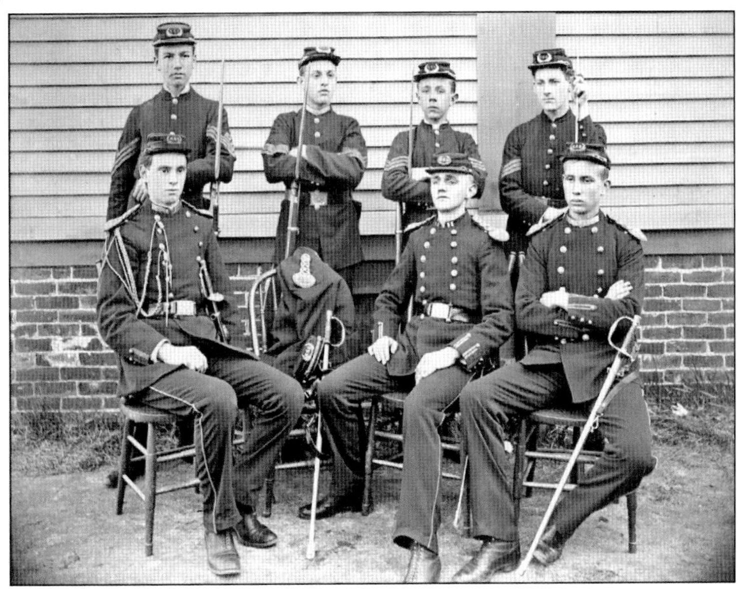

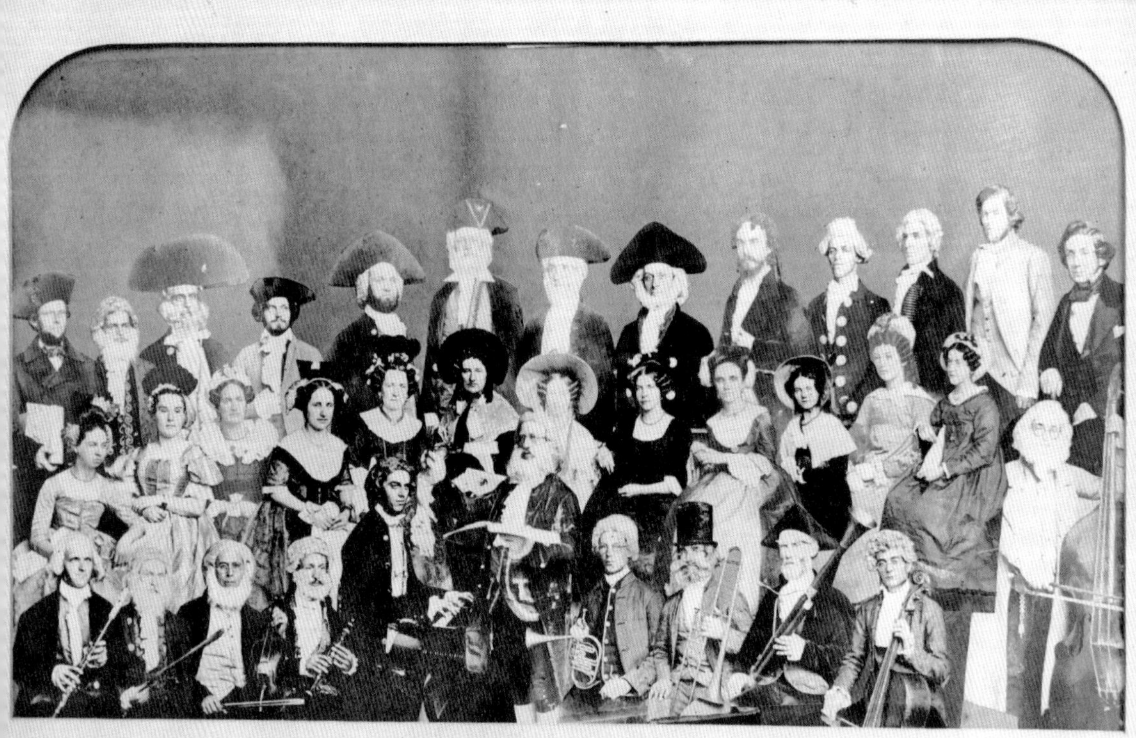

In the mid-1850s, Robert Kemp moved to Reading and bought property at 122 (new No. 186) Summer Avenue. He tried his hand at gentleman farming while still commuting to Boston for work. He formed a singing group made up of neighbors and friends known as "Father Kemp's Olde Folks." They revived old memories by singing "some of the tunes which strengthened the religious faith of our grandparents" and wore costumes appropriate to those times. This photograph was taken in 1858. The members of the group are, from left to right (first row) R.N. Temple, P.E. Bancroft, J.B. Nichols, W. Mansfield, F.J. Bancroft, Robert Kemp, C.J. Patterson, Needham Nichols, J.D. Cook, D. Pratt, and Daniel Foss; (second row) N. Bimblecom, F.J. Bancroft, H. Johnson, A.J. Owen, Elizabeth Jane Kemp, M.H. Robbins, S. Walton, P.E. Bancroft, C.B. Nichols, J.T. Dane, M.A. Robbins, and L. Kemp; (third row) E. Safford, J.F. Wiley, S. Walton, Dr. E. Cutter, M.E. Parker, C.S. Mallette, T.M. Leavitt, H. Johnson, W.L. Peabody, H.M. Brown, W.H. Hartshorn, E.B. Frost, and H.C. Jarrett, agent.

Ye

OLD FOLKES' CONCERTE

Complimentary to ye young man of Reading,

Mr. GEO. C. MEADER,

will be held in the

Towne Halle,

Which is at ye head of Haven Street, in ye Towne of Reading, near bye ye Post Office. Ye common name of thys Halle is

Lyceum Halle,

Ye Concerte is upon

Monday Evening, Dec. ye 17, 1888

At 7.45 by ye new-fangled lyte.

Ye door-tenders are commanded to admit nobodie who do not pay them Two York Shillings (25 cents) for ye common seats and Ten Pennies more for ye best seats.

Ye smart looking lads at ye doors with rosettes on theyr coates will see to it that ye people do obtain good seats.

The first Father Kemp's Olde Folks concert was held in Lyceum Hall on December 6, 1856. They were well received, and after several concerts locally, they performed in front of a packed crowd at the Tremont Temple in Boston. After 10 more concerts in Boston, the troupe went on the road to New York and Washington, DC, where they sang for President Buchannan, his cabinet, and Congress. In 1861, they visited England for an eight-day tour. Father Robert Kemp retired in 1868, but Olde Folks concerts continued to be popular throughout the rest of the 19th century. Twenty years later, the cover of this program shows that every effort was made to recreate the spelling and language of earlier times. And even though tickets were 25¢ for common seats and 35¢ for the best seats, apparently young men were admitted free. Over the years, the songs and entertainment became more patriotic and less religious.

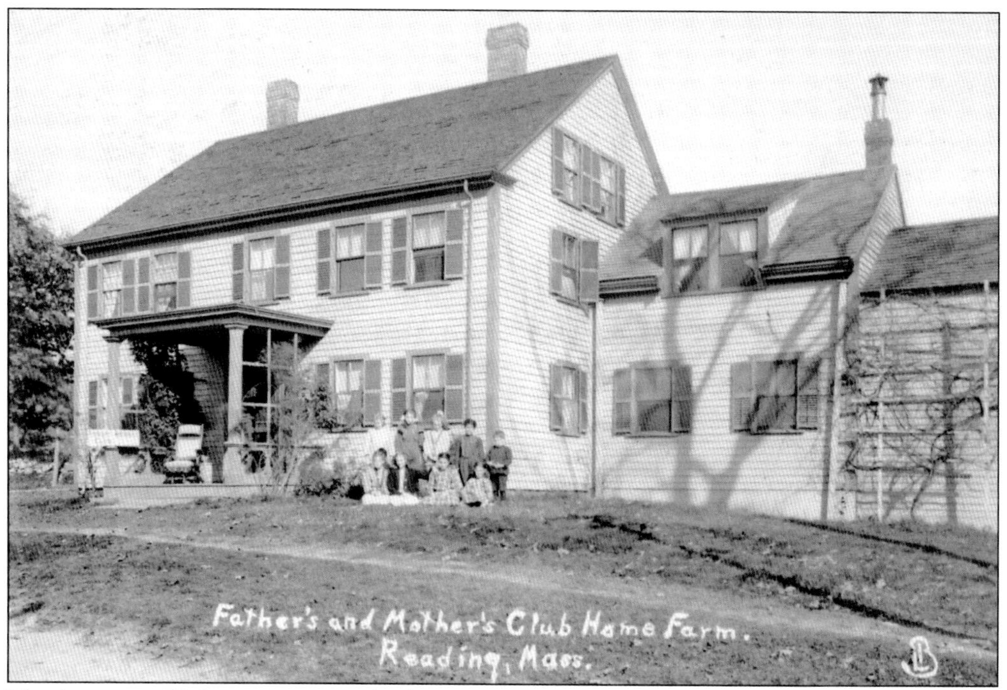

This house at 107 Grove Street was built before 1795. In the late 19th century, F. Howard Gilson, an early Reading photographer, lived there. The early 20th century saw a linking of two new organizations. In 1904, the Fathers' and Mothers' Club was founded by Mary Pamela Rice to bring underprivileged children from the city to Reading, and six years later, she bought the property. The first Girl Scout troops began in Reading in 1918. In 1932, the house was sold, and the Camp Rice bungalow was built on the remainder of the property. In 1946, the club assets were turned over to the Girl Scouts. The undated photograph below, taken on the south side of the old high school on Sanborn Street, shows one of Reading's Girl Scout troops.

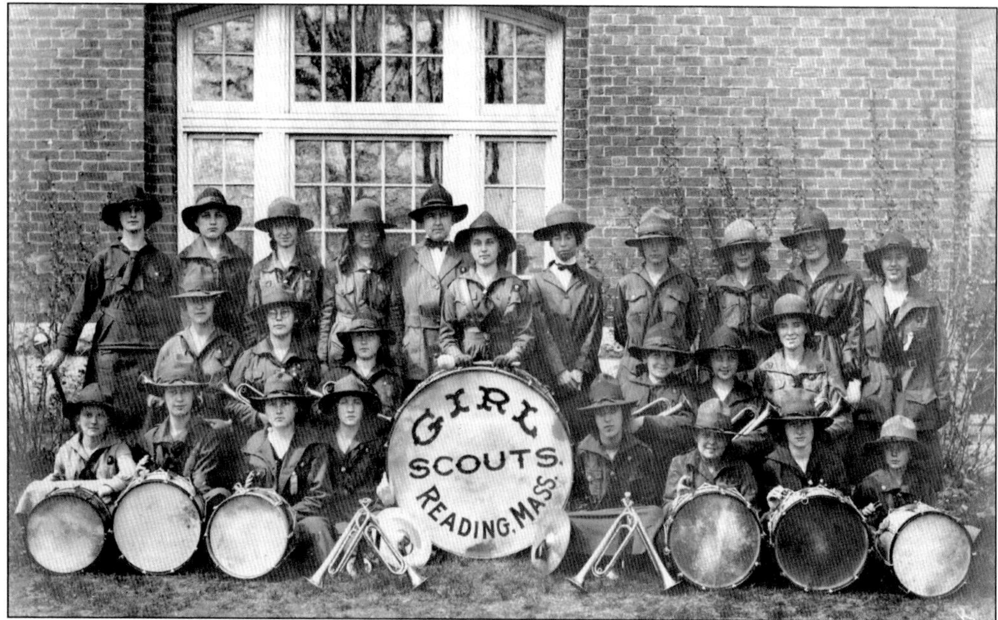

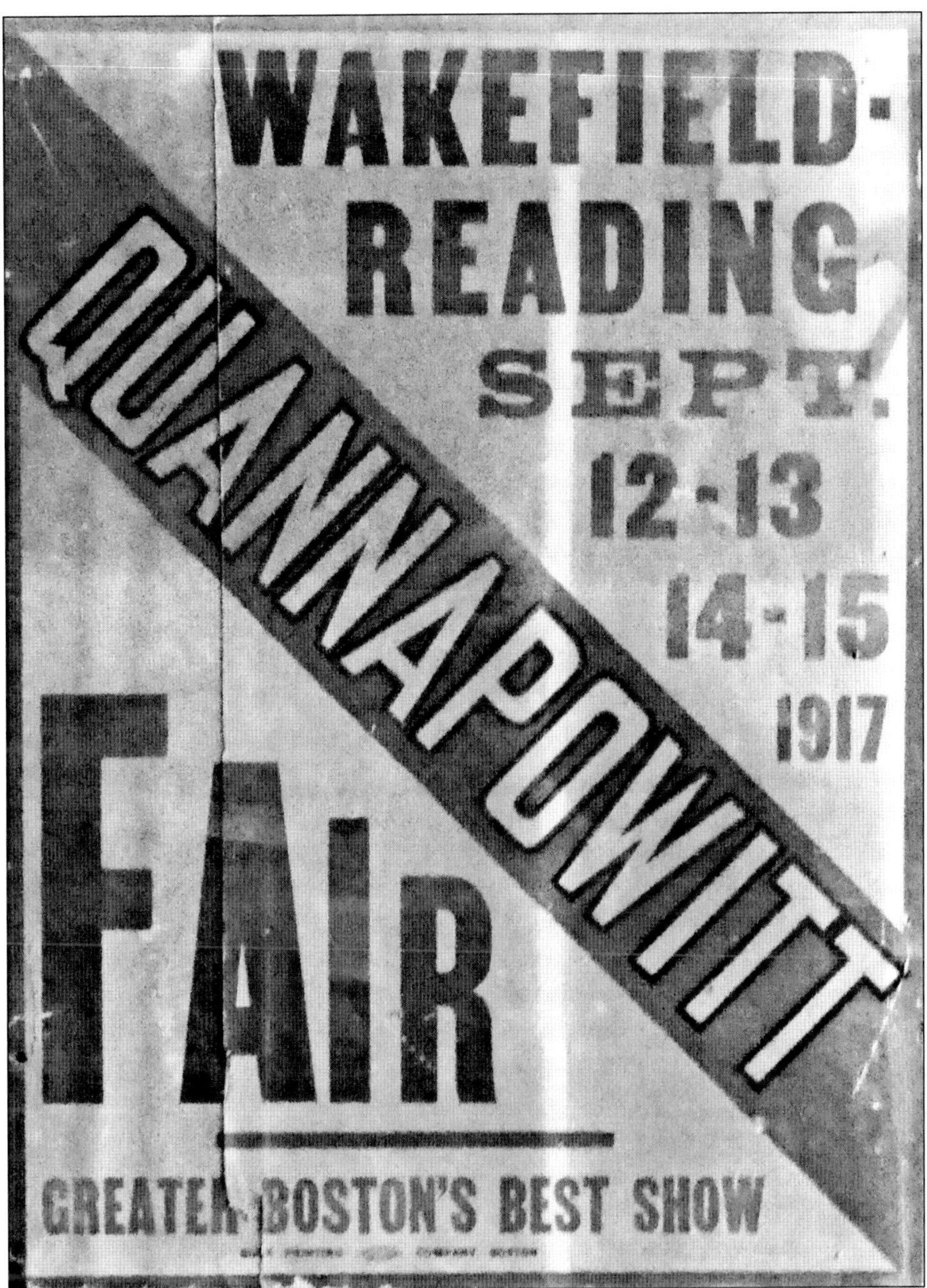

This 28-by-38-inch poster advertising the Quannapowitt Wakefield-Reading Fair in September 1917 was found in the walls of a barn in Reading. It was actually two posters cut to fit between the studs, presumably to act as insulation. But the pieces have been laid together to show what the original poster would have looked like. The fairground was located along the Reading and Wakefield town lines, near Lake Quannapowitt, and its first season was in the fall of 1898. A look at a current map of Reading clearly shows the location of Track Road, which follows the footprint of the Reading half of the original track. In the early 1920s, after the last fair took place, the area was developed into house lots. The lots were in both Wakefield and Reading. Folks could buy just the lot or choose to have a bungalow built on the land.

Third Annual Fair

—OF THE—

Middlesex East Agricultural Associa'n

AT AGRICULTURAL PARK,

READING and WAKEFIELD,

September 26th, 27th, 28th, 29th, 1900.

PROGRAM.

WEDNESDAY, SEPT. 26, 1900.

Grounds open 7 a. m. Close 6 p. m.

9.00 a. m. BAND CONCERT.

9.30 a. m. BOYS' SPORTS AND RACES ON TRACK.

10.30 a. m. DRAWING MATCH—Single and Double Teams—Two Classes.

11.00 a. m. AUTOMOBILE EVENTS ON TRACK—School Children in Motor Carriages.

11.30 a. m. to 1.30 p. m. DINNER IN GRAND STAND.

12.00 m. ENTRIES FOR EXHIBITS in every Department will positively close.

1.00 p. m. JUDGES WILL MAKE AWARDS.

1.00 p. m. **HORSE RACING.**

2.22 Class, pace; . . . . Purse $300.00.
2.40 Class, trot and pace; . . Purse $250.00.

3.00 p. m. EXHIBITION OF AUTOMOBILES.

4.00 p. m. BALLOON ASCENSION AND SHOT FROM CANNON IN MID-AIR.

VAUDEVILLE. ☞ Continuous Stage Show, commencing at 10 o'clock a. m.

This program is from the Middlesex East Agricultural Association's fair in September 1900. Notice that they are calling the location the "Agricultural Park." Inside the program are the details of each day's activities, including automobile events, horse racing, balloon ascension, cannon jump, a ball game between the "nines" from Wakefield and Reading, and of course, dinner in the grandstand for 50¢.

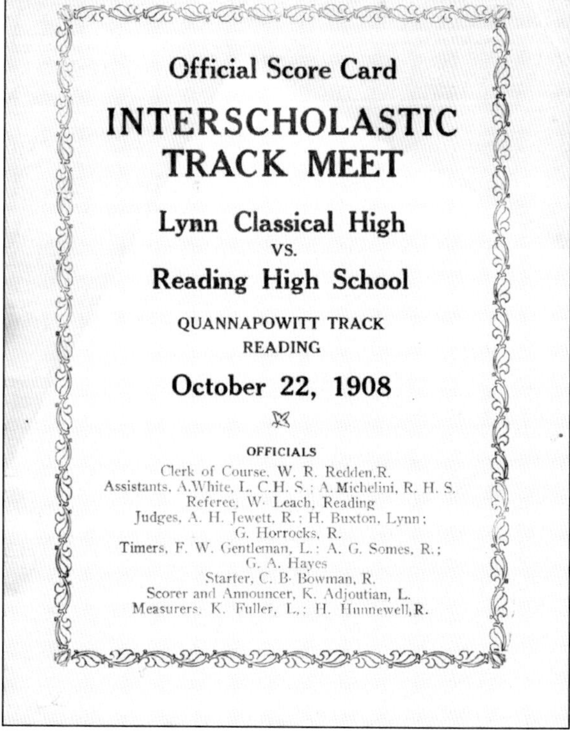

Official Score Card

INTERSCHOLASTIC TRACK MEET

Lynn Classical High
vs.
Reading High School

QUANNAPOWITT TRACK
READING

October 22, 1908

OFFICIALS

Clerk of Course, W. R. Redden,R.
Assistants, A.White, L. C.H. S.; A. Michelini, R. H. S.
Referee, W. Leach, Reading
Judges, A. H. Jewett, R.; H. Buxton, Lynn;
G. Horrocks, R.
Timers, F. W. Gentleman, L.; A. G. Somes, R.;
G. A. Hayes
Starter, C. B. Bowman, R.
Scorer and Announcer, K. Adjoutian, L.
Measurers, K. Fuller, L.; H. Hunnewell,R.

The Reading track was used for more than just automobile and horse racing. Inside this program for an interscholastic track meet is a list of each event and the participants from both schools. The back provided a place to record first, second, and third place, the winning time or distance, and the total team scores. Unfortunately, the program was unused, so it is not known who won.

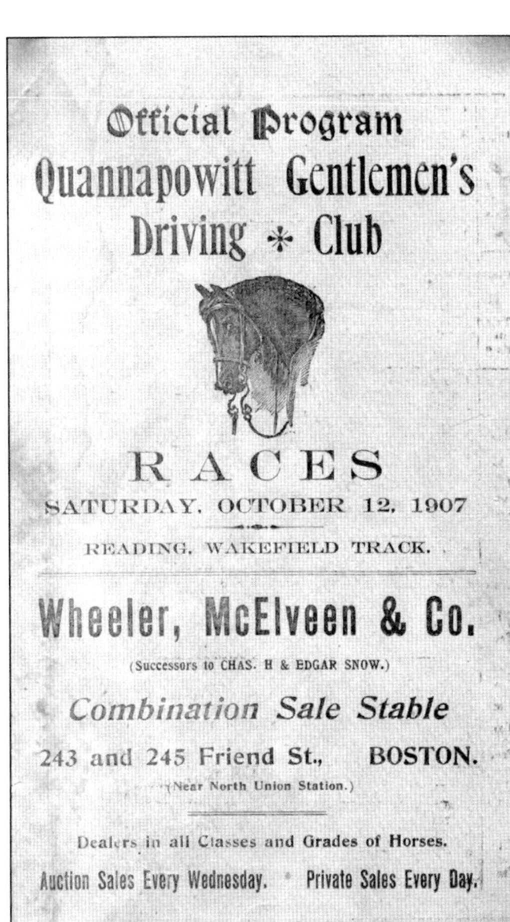

Official Program

Quannapowitt Gentlemen's Driving * Club

RACES

SATURDAY, OCTOBER 12, 1907

READING, WAKEFIELD TRACK.

Wheeler, McElveen & Co.

(Successors to CHAS. H & EDGAR SNOW.)

Combination Sale Stable

243 and 245 Friend St., BOSTON.

(Near North Union Station.)

Dealers in all Classes and Grades of Horses.

Auction Sales Every Wednesday. Private Sales Every Day.

The Quannapowitt Gentlemen's Driving Club was founded in May 1907 and continued through 1914. Meetings were held in Odd Fellows Hall, and the club's first task was to rent the Wakefield-Reading half-mile track. The program at right is from the first season. According to the program, six races were scheduled on this date and races were in two gaits: trot and pace. Charles D. Wells, who moved to Reading from New Brunswick at the age of 18, is shown below on his sulky. He was a charter member of the club and operated a horseshoeing business in Reading. In the second year of club racing, his daughter Myrtle won for most ribbons in the ladies' driving classes.

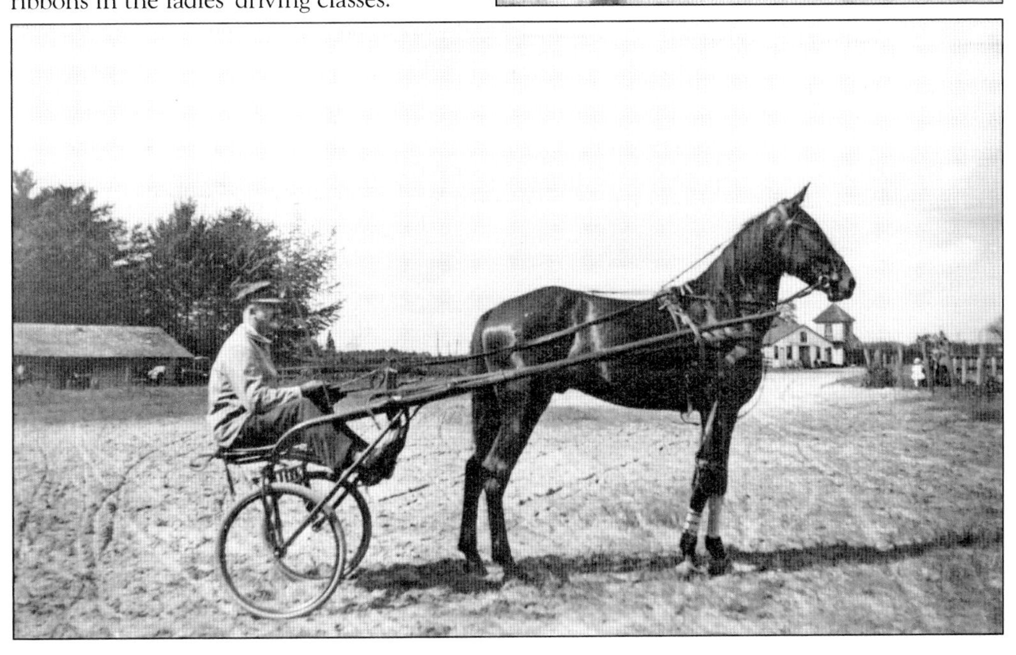

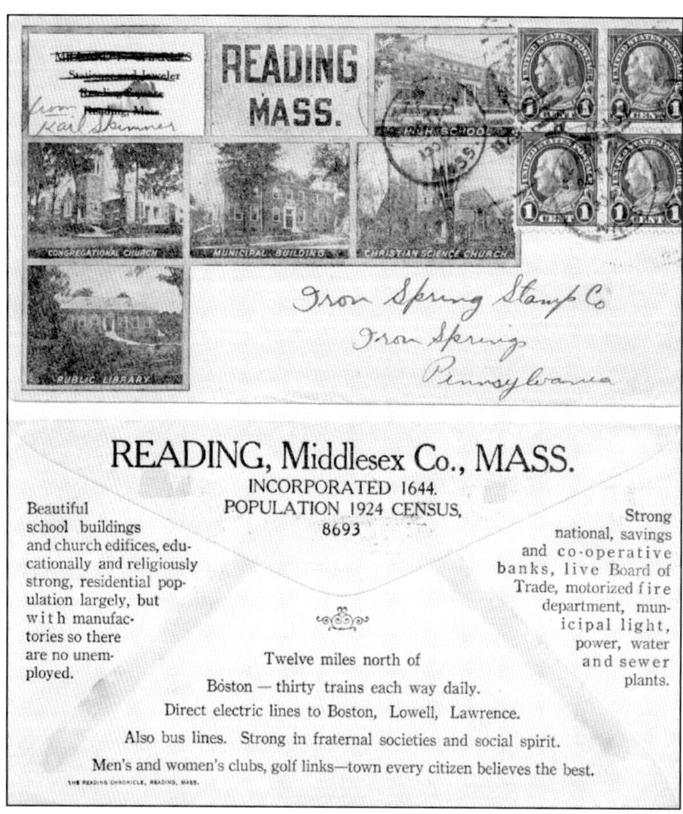

Collecting stamps is a hobby that has been enjoyed by many over the years, but this envelope is interesting because it apparently was created as a way to advertise Reading. The front shows photographs of municipal buildings and churches, and the back is filled with information about why Reading is such a great town. The return address that is crossed out is that of Millard F. Charles, stationer and jeweler.

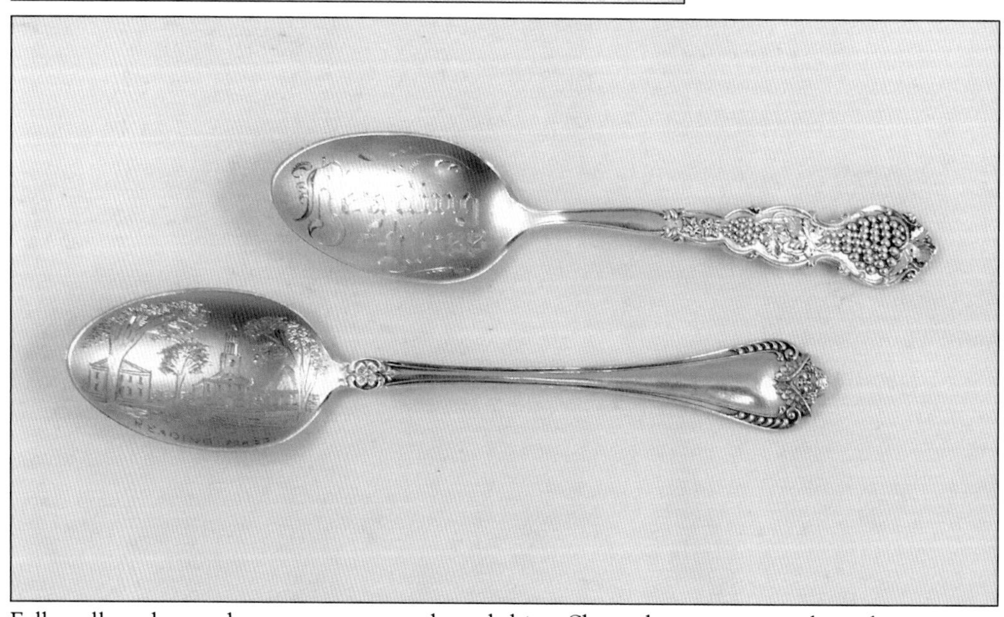

Folks collected more than stamps, postcards, and china. Shown here are two sterling silver souvenir spoons from Reading. Neither of the spoons is marked with a manufacturer. The top spoon's bowl is gold washed and is heavily decorated with a grape and grapevine motif. The second, also gold washed, shows the common with the bandstand, old high school, and the Old South, a similar scene to the cover of this book.

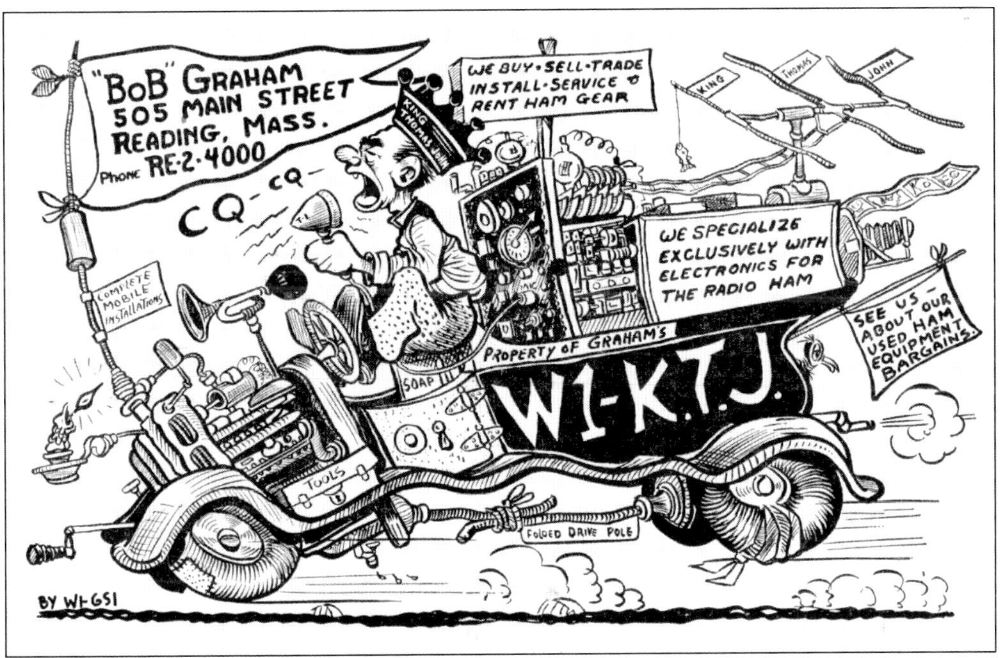

Congress approved the Radio Act of 1912, which required that amateur radio operators be licensed and restricted to the single wavelength of 200 meters. Amateur/ham radio became a popular hobby as a way to communicate with others around the world. This postcard advertises Bob Graham's store at the northeast corner of Main and Green Streets.

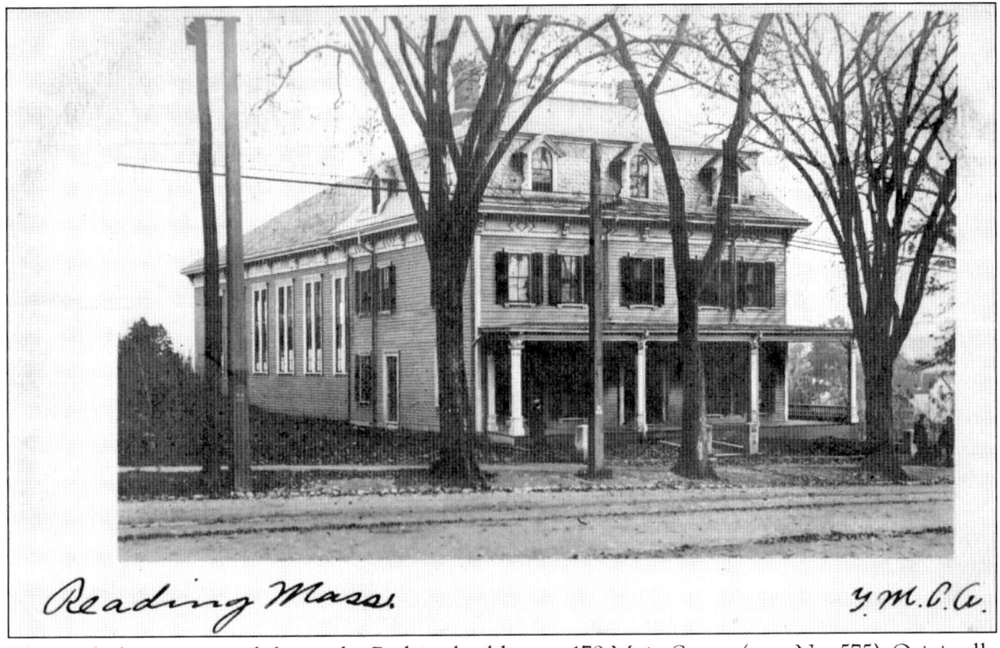

This real-photo postcard shows the Perkins building at 179 Main Street (new No. 575). Originally built as a home about 1825, the third floor was added in the 1860s. In 1904, the YMCA bought the building as its headquarters and added a gymnasium. The building was torn down after a fire in 1975, and the Veterans of Foreign Wars, who owned it at the time, built the current structure.

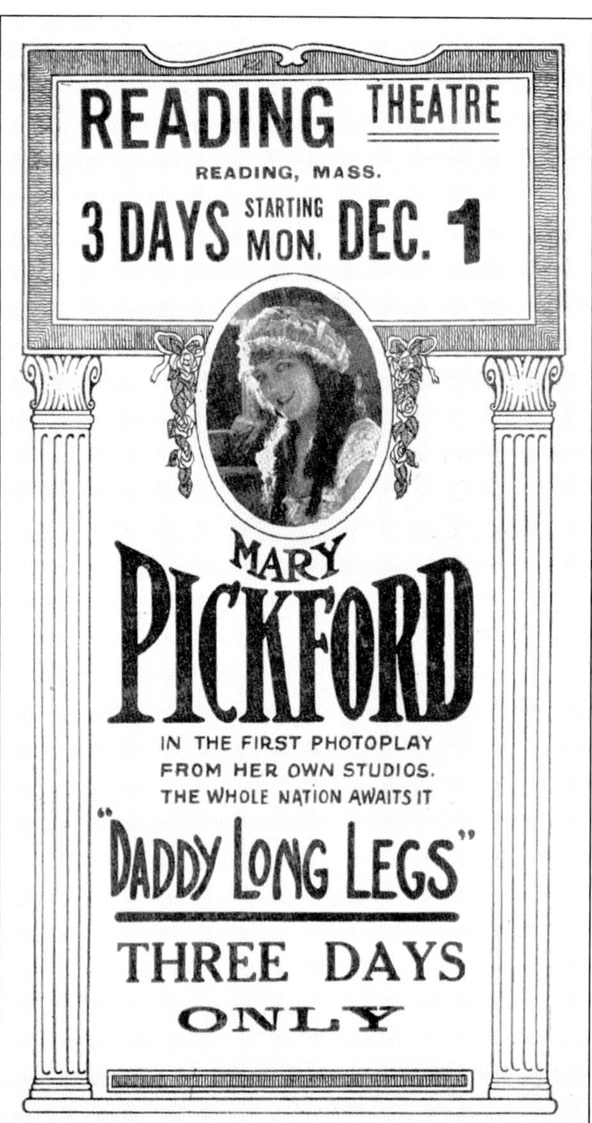

The Reading Theatre opened in February 1914 and was located at the back of the Chamberlain Block, but with its entrance on Main Street. That block was torn down and a new building, which is now the location of CVS Pharmacy, was built on the site. The movie booklet at left for December 1, 1919, folds out to include a letter from Mary Pickford and scenes from the movie. Below are two small booklets showing coming attractions. On the left is the cover for the week of September 1, 1919, and on the right is the inside of a second booklet showing information about the movies, as well as dates and times of shows beginning on October 6, 1919.

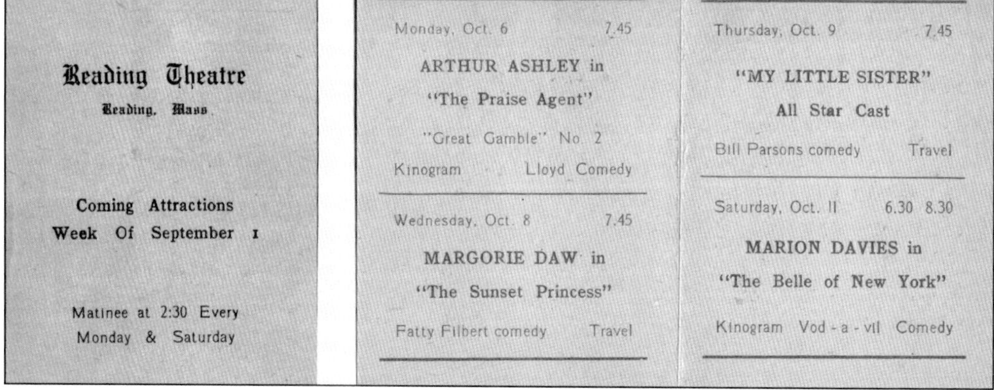

In 1924, the original owners Edward Turnbull and Timothy Rogers opened a new Reading Theatre farther south on Main Street at the current location of RCTV Studios. This undated advertisement for Letner's Dog and Pony Show starring Nellie and Bing reveals that the theater's stages were used for live entertainment as well as movies.

READING
THEATRE

EXTRA ADDED ATTRACTION
WEDNESDAY, JUNE 10th
AFTERNOON AND EVENING

LETNER'S DOG AND PONY SHOW

Nellie—the educated pony, answers all questions, waltzes, plays the piano.

"Bing"—the educated dog, imitating Charlie Chaplin.

"Strawberry Short Cake"
The Real Clown

SPECIAL SHOWING IN THE AFTERNOON
DIRECTLY AFTER SCHOOL
ALSO
SHOWING IN THE EVENING

THEATRE PHOTOGRAPH and REPORT

State: MASS. City: READING
Branch: BOSTON Zone:
Date Photo Taken: 4/41 Theatre Name: READING

Street Address: 555 MAIN STREET
City Population (1940): 10.9
Competing Theatres: NONE

Is Theatre an M-G-M Customer Now? YES
How Long Has It Been Playing M-G-M Product? OVER 10 YEARS
Date Built: OVER 10 YEARS Condition: GOOD
Seats: Main Floor ~~700~~ 834 Balcony
Type of Patronage: GENERAL

Balcony for Colored?

Signed: Branch Manager — Use reverse side for additional information

2M 5-41-U

This inspection card from April 1941 includes a photograph of the new theater building with its marquee advertising the movie *Sea Wolf*, starring Edward G. Robinson. To the right of the marquee were showcases to hold movie posters for upcoming films. The new theater increased both the size of the stage and the seating capacity over the old location.

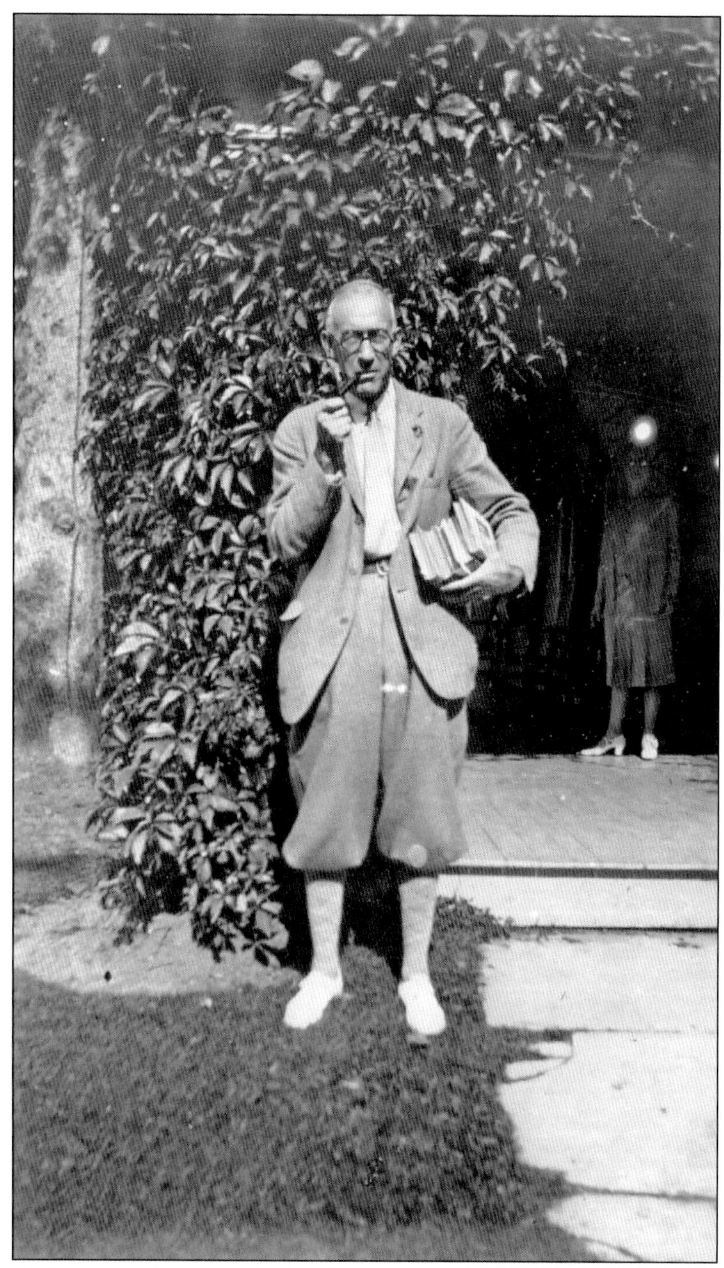

Walter Prichard Eaton was born in Malden, Massachusetts, in 1878, but by 1889, his family was living in the large house at the northwest corner of Main and Locust Streets. The house was torn down in the early 1970s. Eaton graduated from Phillips Academy in Andover and Harvard University. He was a well-known New York theater critic, head of the playwriting department at Yale University, and a prolific author including a series of books about Boy Scouts. Each of the books was set in a different wilderness location, such as Glacier Park, the Dismal Swamp, Katahdin, the White Mountains, and Death Valley. But he also wrote many other books including *The Theatre Guild: The First Ten Years*. Eaton is best known in Reading for his *Lament for Birch Meadow* written in 1953. The Birch Meadow area was about to be developed and he railed against the loss of the pine woods and fields.

Stanley Stembridge, a lifelong resident of Reading, graduated from Reading High School in 1911 and was a sports enthusiast. He played basketball for four years and became captain during his senior year. He also played baseball for three years. The medal shown at the bottom corner of his photograph was given to him by the Reading High School Athletic Association.

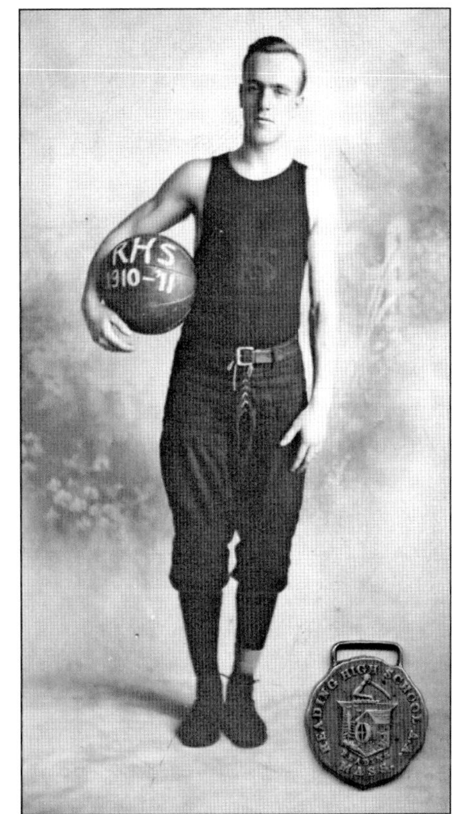

The members of the 1949 Reading High School girls' second basketball team are, from left to right (first row) B. Muise, R. Lehman, J. Cook, C. Nelson, J. Lane, and N. Davis; (second row) R. Silva, L. Williams, J. Farnsworth, J. Bacigalupo, N. Haines, and E. Flater; (third row) D. Brown, S. Putnam, J. Crosby, J. Symonds, and B. Johnson.

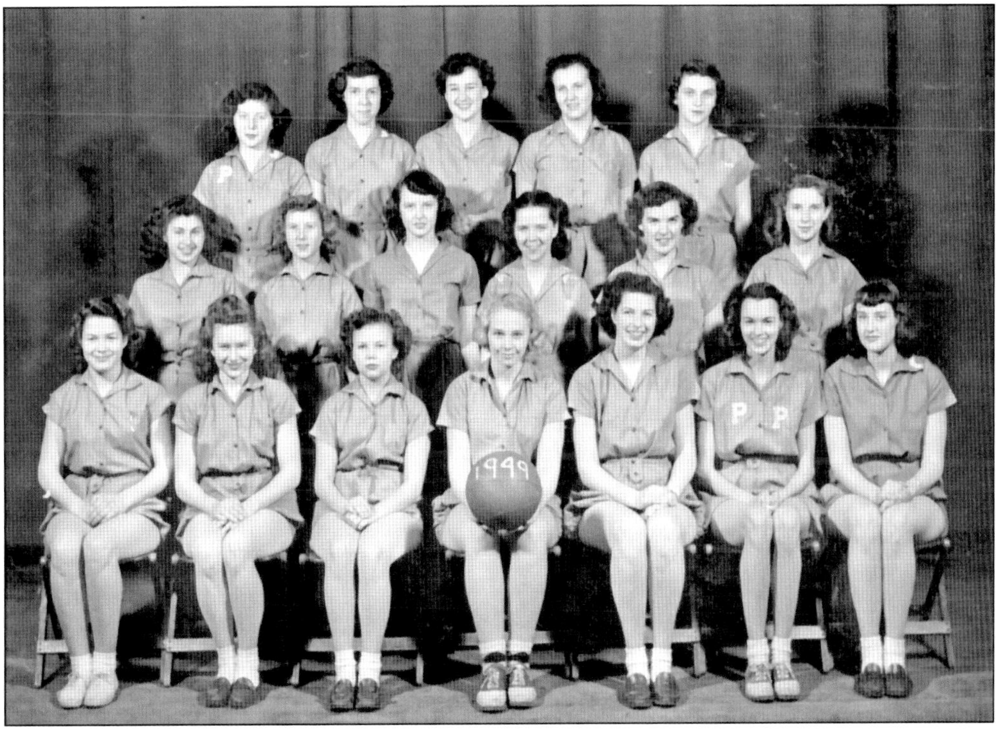

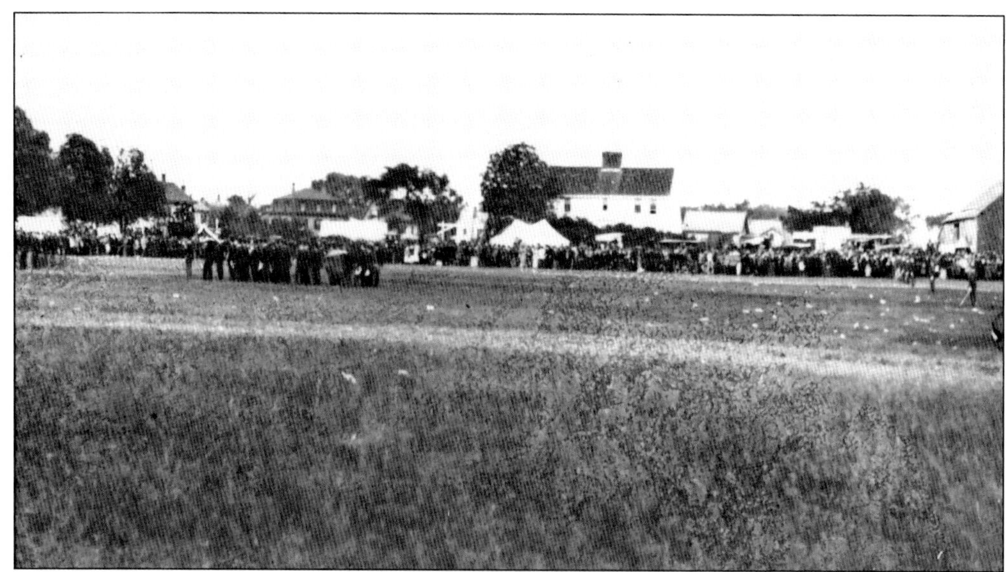

This undated glass plate photograph was taken at Sweetser Field, now known as Washington Park. The land was privately owned by the Sweetser family and often rented by the town for events. The large house with the center chimney in the background is Parker Tavern. Its barn can be seen at far right.

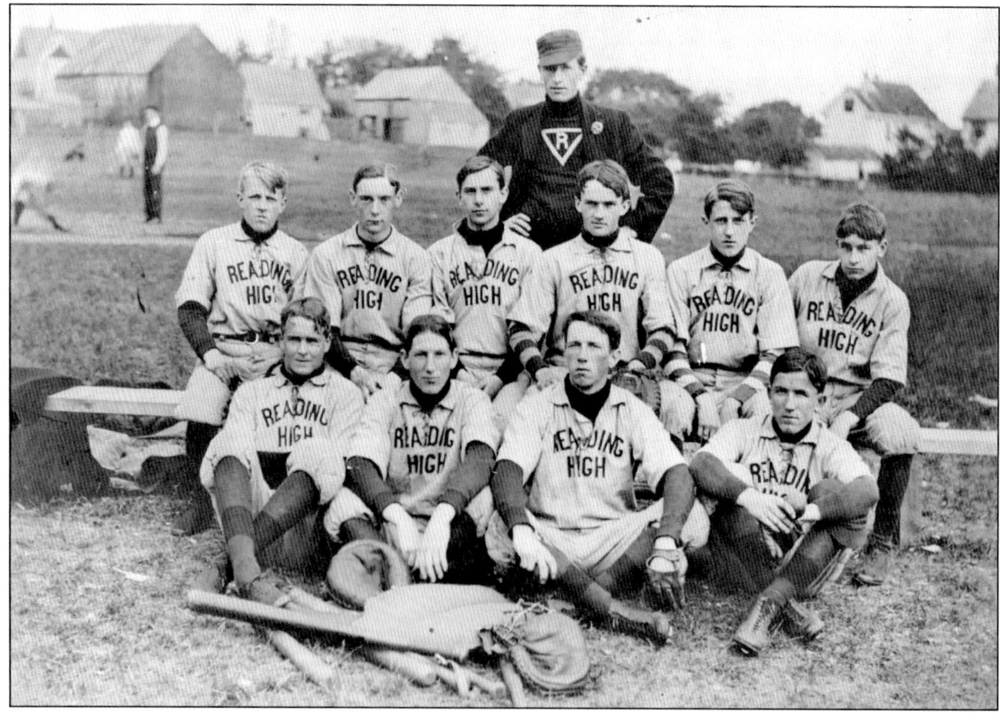

This W.P. Gleason photograph was taken in 1903. The members of the Reading High baseball team are, from left to right (first row) Len Nichols (class of 1904), Carl Sawyer (1904), Homer Morrison (1903), and Lawrence Crafts (1903); (second row) Ed Abbott (1904), Fred Day (1903), Dick Walsh (1903), Moses Parker (1904), Jimmie Fairchild (1904), and Ray Parker (1904); (standing) coach Len Chapman.

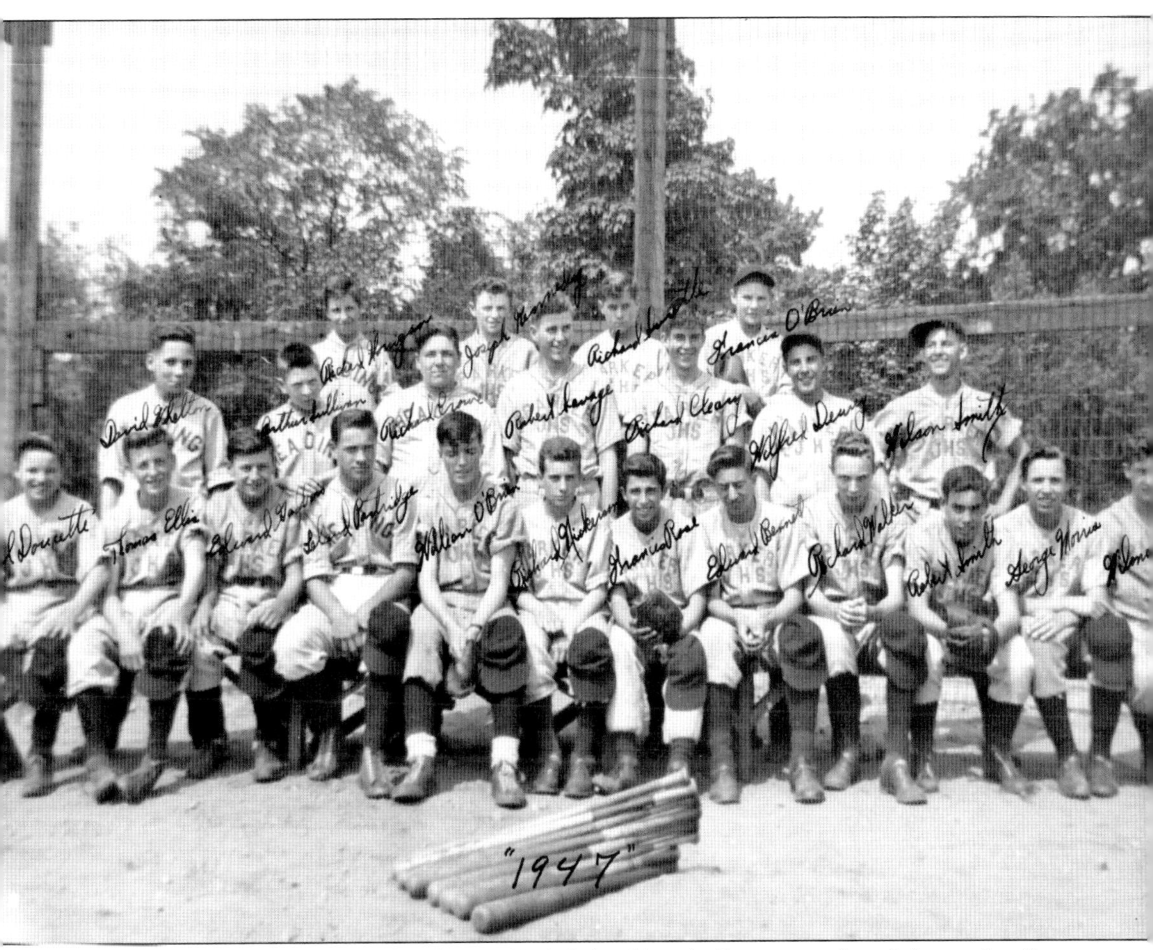

The members of the 1947 Reading Junior High School baseball team are, from left to right, (first row) Paul Doucette, Thomas Ellis, Edward Gadbois, Leland Partridge, William O'Brien, Richard Nickerson, Francis Rose, Edward Bennet, Richard Walker, Robert Smith, George Morris, and Gilman Chipman; (second row) David Whellen, Arthur Sullivan, Richard Crowe, Robert Savage, Richard Cleary, Wilfred Dewey, and Wilson Smith; (third row) Richard Horrigan, Joseph Kennedy, Richard Surette, and Francis O'Brien.

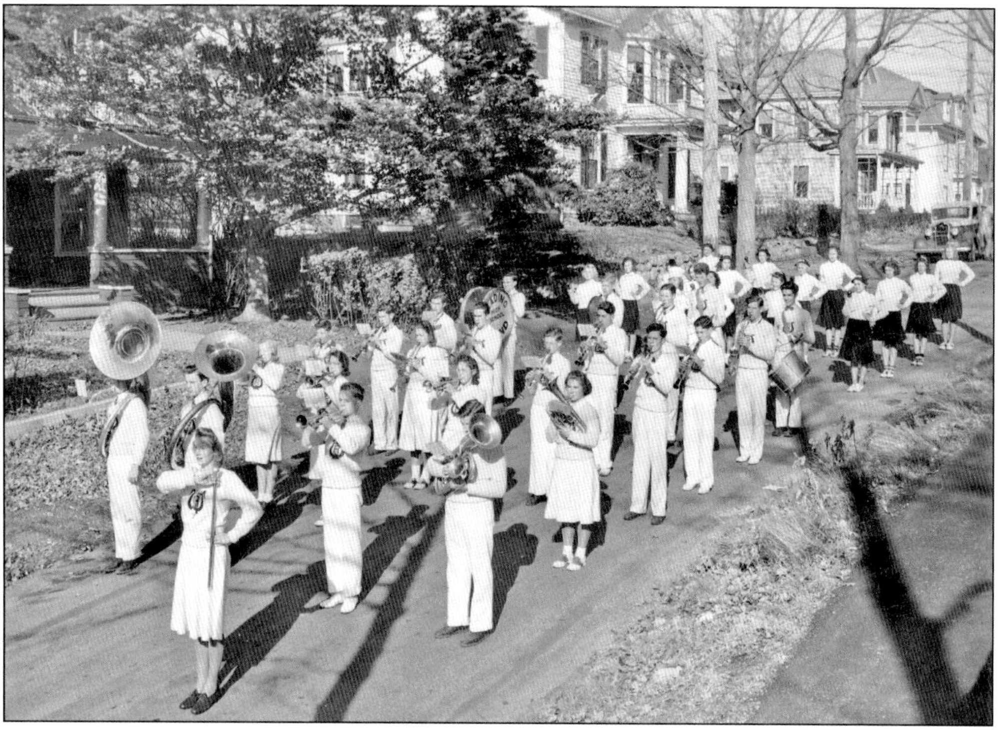

The Reading High School band is ready to perform. Even without the date on the back of the photograph (1933–1934), the uniforms and saddle shoes help to determine the period. This photograph shows the band on Linden Street not far from the high school, which at the time was on Sanborn Street. The four houses on the left are, from left to right, 58, 62, 68, and 72 Linden Street.

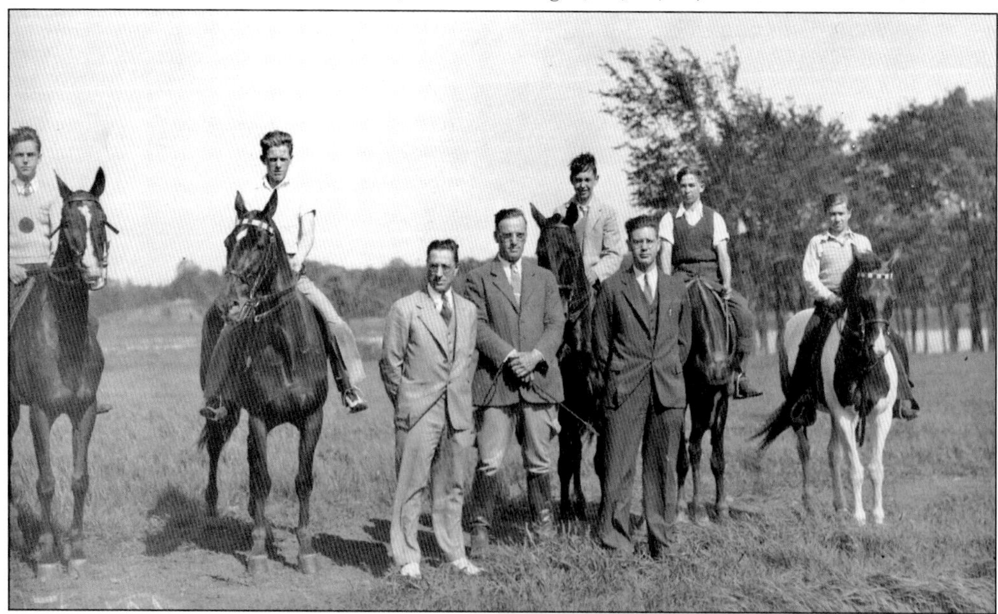

Most folks probably do not recall that at one time Reading High School had a riding club, but with Reading's history of farms and plenty of open land, it should not be too much of a surprise. This photograph shows the members of the club and their coaches for the school year 1933–1934.

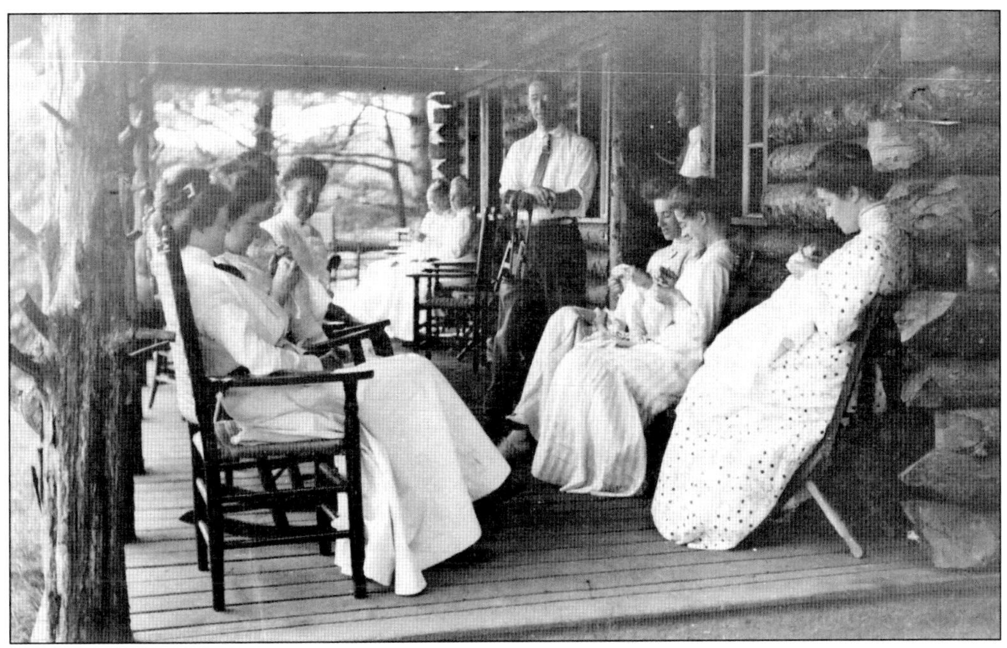

Meadowbrook Golf Club was organized in the spring of 1898 and held its first tournament that fall. The first clubhouse was a log cabin set on a rise to the east side of Grove Street. The photograph above shows a golfer with his bag of clubs and ladies working on their hand work on the porch of the log cabin. That building burned down in 1928. The photograph below, taken in the spring of 1934, shows the Reading High golf team and their coach standing on the front steps of Reading High School, then located on Sanborn Street.

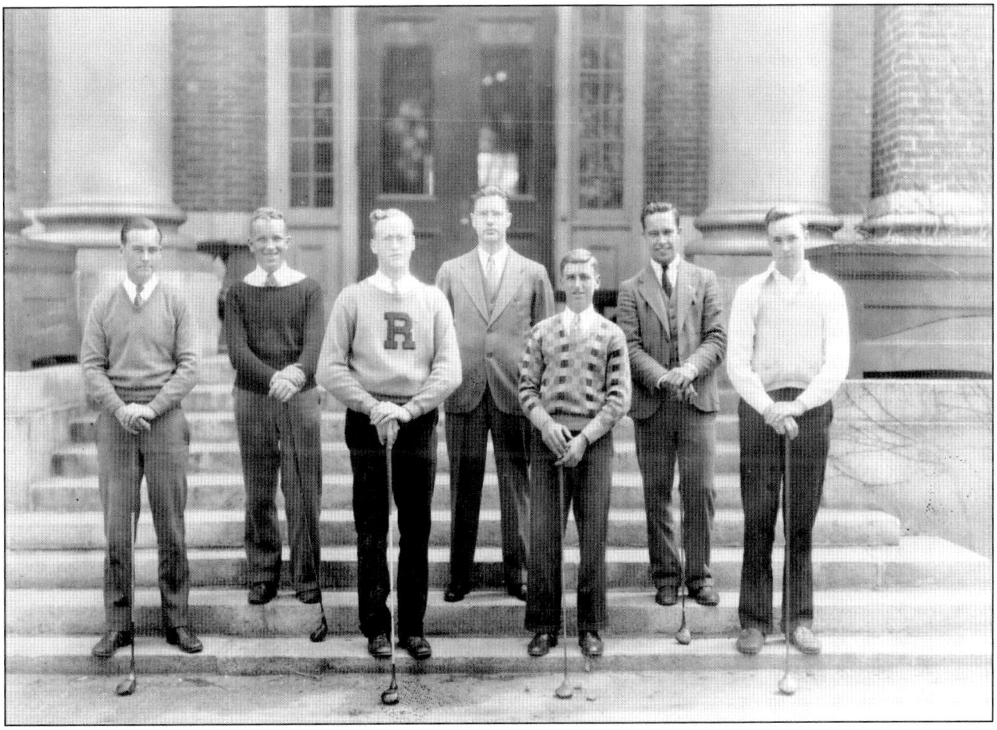

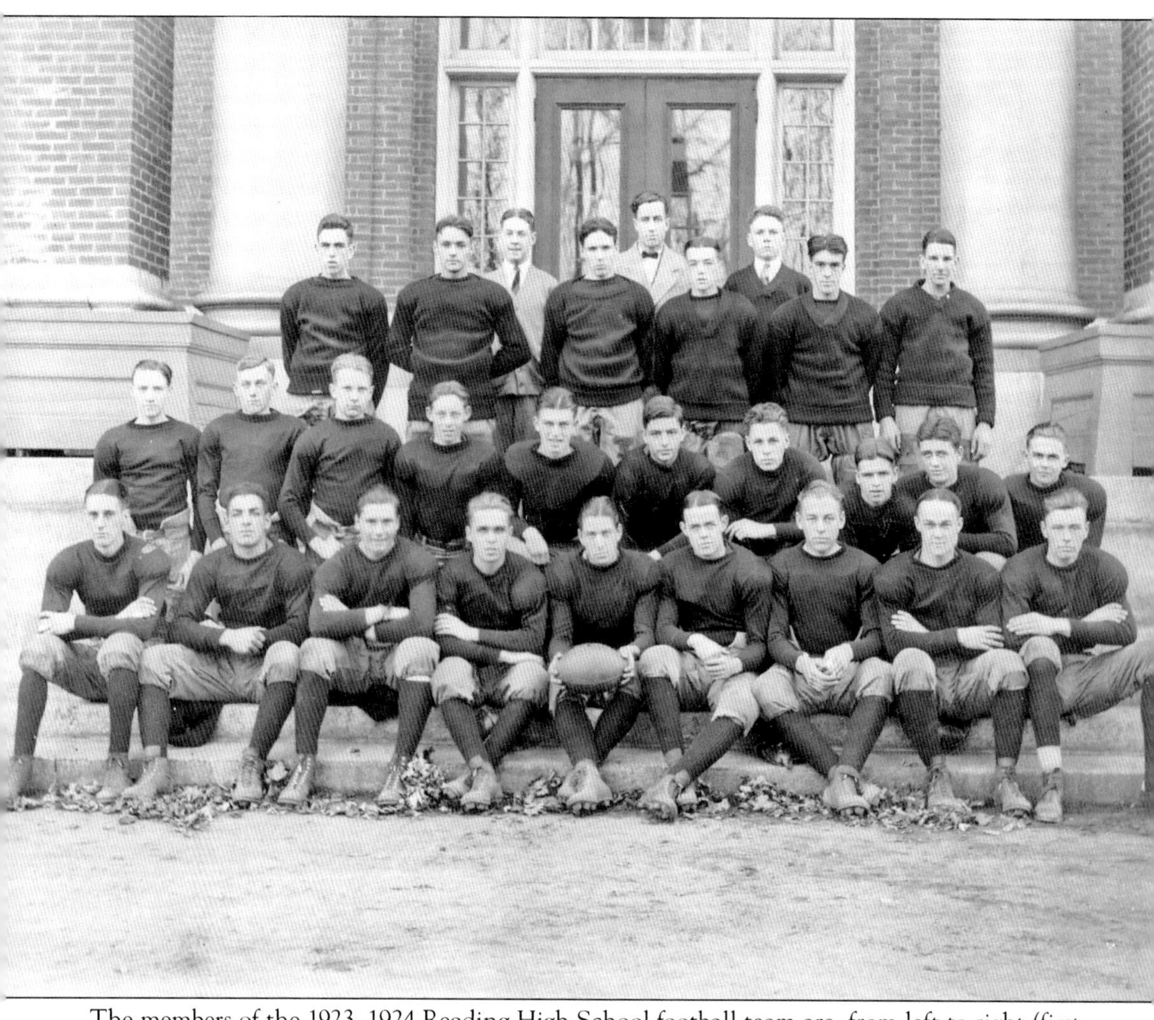

The members of the 1923–1924 Reading High School football team are, from left to right (first row) Norman MacInnis, Edward Eisenhaure, ? Davis, Richard Elwell, Henry Milton (captain), Guy Crosby, Charles Eeles, Donald Davis, and Norman McClintock; (second row) Donald Lyons, Norman Gratton, Inglis VanBuskirk, Stanley Promfret, Randall Weeks, Solomon Horwitz, unidentified, Charles McKenney, Edwin Doherty, and Howard Farwell; (third row) ? Doherty, Brooks White, George Bruce, Niles Pierpont, Robert Merritt, and Robert Rooney; (fourth row) Ralph Sias (assistant manager), Russell Taylor (coach), and Robert Barclay (manager). This photograph was taken at the high school on Sanborn Street. Since Parker Junior High School was not built until 1927, football teams played at Washington Park.

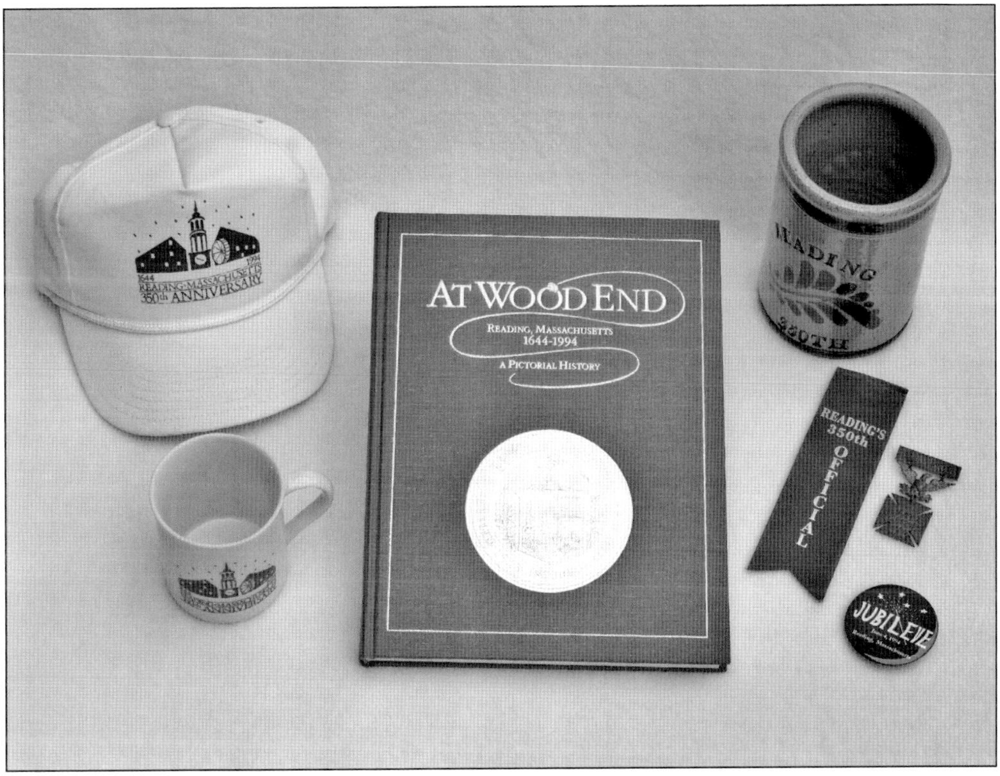

Shown above are some of the memorabilia of past Reading celebrations. The small medal at far right is a memento of the celebration in 1894. Above the eagle is the word "Souvenir," and below it is "250th Anniversary, May 28 & 29 Wakefield and Reading," as well as the dates 1644 and 1894 on the left and right. One hundred years later, in 1994, Reading celebrated its 350th anniversary with a 10-day celebration that included a parade, grand ball, field day, Jubileve, the publication of *At Wood End*, and many other events. Now, 25 years later, Reading will celebrate its 375th anniversary. The new logo for that event is shown at right. The authors would like to encourage everyone to continue to work to keep Reading's history alive for future generations. Enjoy Reading 375!

Bibliography

Baldwin, Thomas W. *Vital Records of Reading, Massachusetts to the year 1850*. Boston, MA: Wright & Potter Printing Company, 1912.

Bishop, C. Nelson and Eleanor C. *Reading's Colonial Rooftrees Built Before 1800*. Reading, MA: DelCotreau Offset Printing Service, 1978.

Eaton, Chester W., Warren E. Eaton, and Will Everett Eaton. *Proceedings of the 250th Anniversary of the Ancient Town of Reading Once Including the Territory Now Comprising the Towns of Reading, Wakefield, and North Reading with Historical Chapters*. Reading, MA: Loring & Twombly, Publishers, 1896.

Eaton, Hon. Lilley. *Genealogical History of the Town of Reading, Mass. Including the Present Towns of Wakefield, Reading and North Reading with Chronological and Historical Sketches, from 1639 to 1874*. Boston, MA: Alfred Mudge & Son, Printers, 1874.

Morang, Bruce N. *A Town That Went to War*. Reading, MA: *Reading Chronicle*, 1975.

Reading 350th Book Committee. *At Wood End: Reading, Massachusetts 1644–1994 A Pictorial History*. Wakefield, MA: Wakefield Press, Wakefield Item Company, 1994.

Town of Reading. *Annual Report of Receipts and Expenditures for the Financial Year*. Boston, MA: C.M. Barrows & Co., Printers, 1883–1896.

———. *Annual Report of Receipts and Expenditures for the Financial Year*. Reading, MA: W.E. Twombly & Sons, Printers, 1896–1915.

———. *List of the Polls and Estates in the Town of Reading*. Reading, MA: Town of Reading, 1880, 1890, 1900, 1910, and 1916.

———. *Street and Alphabetical List of Residents 20 years of age and over*. Reading, MA: Town of Reading, 1907 and 1909–2017.

INDEX